70.

The Effect
of the Infant
on Its Caregiver

The Origins of Behavior

Michael Lewis and
Leonard A. Rosenblum, Editors

Volume 1
The Effect of the Infant on Its Caregiver

Michael Lewis and
Leonard A. Rosenblum, Editors

The Effect
of the Infant
on Its Caregiver

Edited by

Michael Lewis
Educational Testing Service

and

Leonard A. Rosenblum
State University of New York
Downstate Medical Center

A Wiley-Interscience Publication
JOHN WILEY & SONS
New York • London • Sydney • Toronto

Chapter I, "Contributions of Human Infants to Caregiving and Social Interaction" by Richard Q. Bell is exempt from the general copyright for this title. This paper was prepared under U.S. Government auspices, and is, therefore, in the public domain.

Library of Congress Cataloging in Publication Data:

Lewis, Michael, Jan. 10, 1937-   comp.
  The effect of the infant on its caregiver.

  (The Origins of behavior, v. 1)
  "A Wiley-Interscience publication."
  Outgrowth of a conference sponsored by Educational Testing Service, Princeton, N.J.
  Includes bibliographies.
  1. Infants—Congresses. 2. Mother and Child—Congresses. I. Rosenblum, Leonard A., joint comp. II. Educational Testing Service. III. Title. IV. Series. [DNLM: 1. Child behavior—Congresses 2. Ethology—Congresses. 3. Maternal behavior—Congresses. 4. Mother-Child relations—Congresses. W1 OR687 v. 1 1973 / WS105 E27 1972]

HQ774.L45   155.4'22   73-12804

ISBN 0-471-53202-9

Printed in the United States of America

10 9 8 7 6 5 4 3

Contributors

Richard Q. Bell

Chief, Child Research Branch
National Institutes of Mental Health
Bethesda, Maryland

Gershon Berkson

Illinois State Pediatric Institute
Chicago, Illinois

T. Berry Brazelton

Clinical Assistant Professor
Harvard Medical School
Cambridge, Massachusetts

C. Dreyfus-Brisac

Centre de Recherches Biologiques
  Neonatales
Hopital Port-Royal
Universite de Paris
Paris, France

Selma Fraiberg

Director, Child Development Project
University of Michigan
Ann Arbor, Michigan

Anneliese F. Korner

Senior Scientist
Department of Psychiatry
Stanford University School of Medicine
Stanford, California

Barbara Koslowski

Center for Cognitive Studies
Harvard University
Cambridge, Massachusetts

Susan Lee-Painter

Educational Testing Service
Princeton, New Jersey

Michael Lewis

Director, The Infant Laboratory
Educational Testing Service
Princeton, New Jersey

Mary Main

Johns Hopkins University
Baltimore, Maryland

Leonard A. Rosenblum

Director, Primate Behavior Laboratory
State University of New York
Downstate Medical Center
Brooklyn, New York

Gerald P. Ruppenthal

Regional Primate Research Center
University of Washington
Seattle, Washington

Gene P. Sackett

Regional Primate Research Center
University of Washington
Seattle, Washington

Daniel N. Stern

Assistant Professor of Psychiatry and
Chief, Department of Developmental
    Physiology
New York State Psychiatric Institute
New York, New York

J. M. Tanner

Institute of Child Health
University of London
London, England

Kenneth P. Youngstein

State University of New York
Downstate Medical Center
Brooklyn, New York

Series Preface

*"The childhood shows the man,
as morning shows the day."*

Milton, Paradise Regained

None can doubt that the study of man begins in the study of childhood. Few would contend that the newborn lacks the challenge of his evolutionary heritage. This series addresses itself to the task of bringing together, on a continuing basis, that confluence of theory and data on ontogeny and phylogeny which will serve to illustrate *The Origins of Behavior.*

Whether our social, human, and professional concerns lie in the psychological disorders of childhood or adulthood or merely in the presumptively normal range of expression in development in different cultures, varied environments, or diverse family constellations, we can never hope to discern order and regularity from the mass of uncertain observation and groundless speculation if we fail to nurture the scientific study of development. Fortunately, the last two decades have seen an enormous burgeoning of effort toward this end, both at the human and nonhuman level. However, despite this growth of effort and interest, no single means of pooling our growing knowledge on development in children and animals and communicating that fusion of material to the broad scientific community now exists. This series seeks to fill the gap. It is our intention to have each volume deal with a specific theme that is either of social or of theoretical relevance to developmental issues. In keeping with the integrated perspective that we consider to be vital, and to provide a meaningful context within which these issues may be considered, each volume in the series will contain a broad range of material and will seek to encompass theoretical and sound empirical studies of the behavior of human infants as well as pertinent aspects of animal behavior with a particular emphasis on the primates. It is our view, furthermore, that not only is it necessary to focus our interest on both human infants and animals, but that the levels of analysis which will explicate the processes of development that are our concern must ultimately involve the study of behavior at all levels of discourse. Thus studies of developmental significance may be found in genetic, physiological, morphological, dyadic, and societal levels and an increased interdigitation of these separate disciplines is among the major goals of this series.

In light of the diversity of topics to be considered, the breadth of material to be covered, and the variety of orientations that will be included in these discourses on the origins of human behavior, we expect this series to serve the needs of the broad social science community, not merely of those interested in behavioral development alone. Just as the series itself will draw upon the knowledge and research of psychologists, ethologists, sociologists, psychiatrists, pediatricians, obstetricians, and devoted scientists and clinicians in a number of related disciplines, it is our hope that the material in this series will provide both stimulation and guidance to all among us who are concerned with man, his past, his present, and his future.

Michael Lewis
Leonard A. Rosenblum
Editors

June 1973

Preface

The theme of this volume centers in the effect that the infant may have on its caregiver. For many years workers in child development have neglected the significance of the interaction between mother and infant, and in a sense the subtle contributions that each makes to the other in shaping their ongoing dyadic behavior. There have been few voices stressing the necessity of observing both partners in this dyadic bond. It is important that we now focus attention on the impact of the infant as *a source of* the formation, regulation and indeed even the malevolent distortion of the caregiver's behavior. As the original chapters included in the current volume admirably attest, this serious gap in our early studies of child development has begun to be filled. As a result we have begun to see in quite explicit terms that the infant even at birth is no mere passive recipient of stimulation from those around him, ready to be molded like clay on the potters wheel. As a reading of the chapters will clearly indicate, whether we seek to account for the mother or caregiver as the essential force in shaping the child through her interaction with it, we have closed our eyes to half the picture. It is noteworthy that in keeping with the major tenet of this series, the current volume encompasses the effect of infant defects on caregivers from a variety of viewpoints, using both humans and monkeys as subjects, while also examining in normal infants data drawn from many levels of discourse including morphology, physiology, and behavior. Thus, as we expect of the series as a whole, the material contained should prove of interest to workers in a wide array of disciplines, from anthropoligists to zoologists, as well as the diverse array of workers in psychology, psychiatry, and pediatrics.

This first volume grows out of a conference sponsored by Educational Testing Service, Princeton, New Jersey. The papers presented here represent both the original views of the authors as well as the effects of three days of discussion between the contributors themselves and several invited discussants. In this regard the editors and contributors would like to express their appreciation to the following participants: Dr. Beverly Birns, Dr. Howard A. Moss, Dr. Harriet L. Rheingold, and Dr. Leon J. Yarrow. In addition to the incorporation of the ideas and criticisms emerging from the discussions found in the contributions themselves, the introductory chapter of this book represents an effort to integrate the most salient features of this material. Each of the subsequent volumes in this series will contain similar overviews of the issues under consideration distilled by the editors from the papers and discussions held at these meetings; thus we hope, each volume will be a more coherent arena of discourse.

Michael Lewis
Leonard A. Rosenblum

Princeton, New Jersey
Brooklyn, New York

July 1973

Contents

Introduction

MICHAEL LEWIS
Educational Testing Service

LEONARD A. ROSENBLUM
Downstate Medical Center

We have chosen the effect of the infant on the caregiver[1] as the theme of the first volume of this series because we wish to underscore a very important point, often paid lip service in the past but too frequently neglected in actual research and theory: Not only is the infant or child influenced by its social, political, economic, and biological world, but in fact the child itself influences its world in turn.

Historically, it is true that most emphasis has been placed on the effect of the social and physical environment on the development of the infant and child. For example, the literature is replete with examples of how certain maternal behaviors affect specific infant functions. This emphasis needs to be corrected, lest we conclude that the infant is a passive organism constantly being affected but having no effect, constantly being altered but producing no change itself. Such a model of the developing child in fact is not only false but is on its face illogical. Even the mere size of a child in terms of its height and weight,

---

[1]We use the term caregiver to refer to the person responsible for giving care to an infant. The neuter quality of this term pays heed to the fact that males may well be just as capable of giving care as females, and fail to do so, in humans at least, only because of societal pressures. In any event it has not been demonstrated that males are unequal to this task. While using a nongender term we recognize, however, that most of the work reported and all the chapters included in this volume look primarily at female caregivers. This immediately suggests that we have little information about male caregivers, their behavior, the patterns of their interactions, or infants' specific responses to them. Moreover, our understanding is further limited in that most of our information deals with *adult* females as caregivers rather than individuals of any other age categories. Clearly, our ultimate understanding of the nature and dynamics of caregiving must include more broadly representative age and sex classifications.

Finally, and somewhat arbitrarily, we have chosen to use the term "caregiver" rather than "caretaker," the former being the less ambiguous term. For us the person responsible for providing the care of the infant or young child is a caregiver, rather than one who takes upon himself the cares of the child. It seems to us that the term caregiver more directly reflects what in fact occurs, and as such we prefer to use this term.

immediately and with no other information, acts upon an approaching adult set upon engaging in social interaction.

Thus our task is not so much to convince the community that the organism affects and alters its caregivers, but rather to determine what might be the manner of this effect and how it might be measured. Hence one can quickly bypass the issue of whether the infant affects its caregiver and deal with how and perhaps even why it does so and with what specific effects. Several strategies are available and in fact many have been employed in the material included in this volume.

One such strategy suggests that we consider different aspects of the infant, vary these along some known and defined dimension, and observe the effect on caregiving. One way of doing this is to alter a particular attribute experimentally. Berkson, as described in this volume, produced lesions in the eyes of infant monkeys, greatly reducing their visual acuity, and observed the effect on the caregivers. Fraiberg similarly observed blind human infants, although congenitally blind from birth. Rosenblum, again studying monkeys, rendered the infant unconscious and immobile and in this way studied changes in caregiving behavior.

Still another way of approaching the problem is to look at some of the more biological dimensions that characterize the infant, variables such as sex, physical stature, state, or arousal level, and to consider their real and potential impact on the caregiver. In the present volume Tanner, Korner, and Dreyfus-Brisac turn their attention to these considerations. One may also look at a specific maternal behavior in terms of experimentally presented differences in infant characteristics. Sackett, for example, using several types of nonhuman primates, examined approach behavior as a function of a variety of attributes—the species or age of the infant for example. In this case the approach behavior of the adult is taken as the reflection of caregiving potential.

All these various strategies and dimensions have in common the somewhat bifurcated study of single elements in what is a dyadic system. While former research tended to stress the effect of the parent on the child, these studies stress in turn the effect of the child on the caregiver. Lewis, Brazelton, and Stern suggest that none of these methods really captures the dynamic elements of the developmental system. For them the phenomenon under study is dyadic in nature, and only through dyadic study can we come to assess the nature of each participant's contribution. For these three authors there is ongoing effectiveness, a chain which must be studied in terms of its integrity rather than through observation of its component elements. Stern and Brazelton observed the mother–infant interaction in a fixed situation, while Lewis observed a free-field interaction of the very young. All three offer a wide variety of measures, which it is hoped capture what they believe to be the interactive, dynamic, and changing phenomenon of a dyadic relationship.

Our comments suggest that the volume divides itself into several sections, although we have not formally divided it as such. The first portion, including articles by Bell, Lewis, and Brazelton, deals with general issues in the study of the effect of the infant on its caregiver, as well as various models and approaches to a dyadic study of mother–infant. Stern's chapter, which also deals with these issues, is primarily concerned with the visual response system and so is placed in the section dealing with this specific dimension. However, Stern offers some interesting and important measurement procedures for the study of dyadic relationships. Rosenblum, although dealing with a specific phenomenon, approaches the interaction issue by looking at the effects of a sudden and complete lack of responsiveness, brought about by induced unconsciousness, as it affects both the caregiver and infant on different occasions. In this sense he is sensitive to the position that it is necessary to study both components in order to generate an interactive model. In his discussion Rosenblum offers us such an interactive model. Whether or not dyadic relationships can be studied in pieces by looking at the elements one at a time still needs to be explored. However, it offers us a clear example of how such research might be undertaken.

The second portion of the volume, which comprises the work of Tanner, Korner, Dreyfus-Brisac, and Sackett, deals with a wide variety of subject variables including state, sex, prematurity and sleep, age, and species. Each of these is an important dimension of the infant, which should affect the caregiver. Clearly, a sleeping infant affects its caregiver's behavior differently than one who is awake and alert. A responsive infant is more likely to produce continuing interaction than a nonresponsive one. Implicit in these studies is the assumption that there exist relatively stable dispositions or characteristics of the infant. For an interactionalist these assumptions may be questioned, especially in the opening of life, when individual stability is hard if not impossible to demonstrate and variables such as temperament are virtually impossible to define to everyone's satisfaction. Some variables, such as sex or age, for example, on the surface at least appear not to be quite so subject to this problem; but even here the caregiver's interpretation of the meaning of an infant's sex or age may well be critical in the determination of the caregiver's response.

The final chapters, those of Fraiberg, Stern, and Berkson, deal mostly with the visual system—Stern from a dyadic point of view, Fraiberg by considering language systems alternative to the visual, and Berkson in terms of the adaptations of free-ranging primates to visually debilitated young in their midst. The reader may find more salient divisions of the articles present here. The structure suggested above is an attempt to suggest some lines of interrelatedness of the chapters and is not intended to impose constraints upon a further possibility for more diverse interpretations.

While one can never hope to capture and summarize all the issues raised by the articles included in this volume, we attempt to present four major problem areas which emerge repeatedly in various forms and contexts. To be sure, most often questions and issues are raised rather than answered. The following discussion underlines this uncertain state of our knowledge. The four issues considered are: (1) biological and cultural (or experiential determinants in development), (2) the primacy of particular sense modalities in influencing interactive processes, (3) the characteristics of the stimuli exchanged in the dyadic interaction, and (4) the interactive process itself.

BIOLOGICAL AND CULTURAL ISSUES

There is never a discussion of any topic in psychology that does not sooner or later arrive at a nature-nurture or biology-culture discussion. The major forms in which the issue arises regarding the effect of infant on caregiver are two: the specific characteristics of individual infants and the differences among infants, and how and why infants and caregivers behave as they do. Let us first consider individual characteristics.

One method for considering the effect of the infant on its caregiver(s) is to try to describe with precision the observable characteristics of each. This approach implies that, by knowing the detailed features of each partner, one is capable of describing what will transpire when they are placed together. It is assumed furthermore that there are stable and measurable characteristics of both members. These characteristics can be the product of either experience or genetics. Such characteristics as height and weight produce little discussion or heat. It is assumed that early in life, at least, they are primarily biologically determined (although we also know they are subject to diet, etc.) and that they affect the caregivers' behavior in numerous ways. Such differences as gender, however, raise considerably more contention. Does the designated sex of the child produce differences in the caregiver primarily due to cultural bias, or do male and female infants act innately different and therefore produce differential behavior in the caregiver, which in turn is responded to in a differential fashion by the infant? These questions and their corollaries have not yet been answered, but data do exist indicating that as early as one can demonstrate sex differences in infant behavior, or even explicit gender designation, one can also demonstrate differences in some aspects of the caregiver's behavior.

Other characteristics of both infants and caregivers, such as arousal level, species characteristics, and so on, are also discussed in this volume. Clearly, however, we do not at present have enough information on any of the various dimensions along which individual characteristics may be considered. Undoubtedly, of even more importance than these obvious physical characteristics are the "mental" or personality characteristics of the caregiver and developing infant. It is through the mediation of these elements that each organism comes to interpret the action of the other. An "optimistic" mother may interpret the withdrawal of infant gaze as an interest in something else, whereas another mother might interpret this to mean that the infant is tired of looking at her.

However, the larger theoretical issue remains: Can one understand the dyadic relationship by studying these elements in isolation? If this is to be our strategy, we must be confident that the characteristics being measured have at least some significant degree of stability, at least across some determinable temporal internal or repeatable circumstances. On this score we must admit some pessimism. The infancy data to date do not strongly suggest many such stable constructs.

This strategy of looking at elements unilaterally may be useful if we are able ultimately to incorporate these characteristics within an interactional framework. Thus it appears that if particular characteristics of individuals may be fit into a model of characteristic level, situational content, and outcome possibilities, measurement of such features might be useful after all. This is, however, a considerably larger task than the simple description of individual characteristics, however detailed and precise they might be.

The second problem raised under the nature-nurture banner is the question how and why organisms behave the way they do to each other. This is a most important issue, given only passing notice in the chapters. There is a variety of models which can be evoked to account for the occurrence of behavior, and we examine three of them—ethology, learning in an instrumental/classical conditioning sense, and ideology.

The ethological position argues for a predominantly biological basis for the occurrence of the infant's responses, including facial expressions, bodily positions, vocal production, and so on. Moreover, this view suggests that many of the caregiver's responses are in some sense prewired and are "released" at the appearance of a particular infant behavior, or vice versa. For example, it might be argued that a human infant's cry is innately aversive to other humans. This aversive quality is independent of any cultural factors and produces behavior in the caregiver "designed" to "turn it off." Within this model we must also consider that some responses of the caregiver are better than others in producing normal growth and adaptive potential. For example, while a flashing light may serve to reinforce an infant's vocalization, it may be that a caregiver's responsive vocalization is the best stimulus to provide, best here being defined in terms of subsequent use of vocalization (language and communication).

This ethological position has increasing appeal and requires considerable naturalistic observation of the type, for example, incorporated in Brazelton's, Stern's and Lewis' material. The actual degree to which this is possible in view of the fact that the caregiver is observed and therefore not entirely "natural" is a question that must be dealt with in future work.

The learning of behavior is so well established that little new may be said for or against its unquestionable significance. While the ability of very young infants to be classically conditioned is in some doubt, there is no question that instrumental learning can be demonstrated very early. This being the case, it is clear that the infant can learn to modify its behavior in terms of environmental demands. Of interest is the learning of the caregiver's behavior. Can they easily learn to alter their behavior in light of the infant's responses? The interaction data collected and reported in several of these chapters indicate that mothers are able to alter their behavior in terms of what their infants do. However, although there are conditioning studies of infants, there are no comparable ones for adults. What are the learning processes through which caregivers go, and what factors control them? Can caregivers' smiles be conditioned? What are the minimum cues? These may be important questions to explore.

The final consideration is ideology, by which we mean the cognitions involved in plans and strategies. These ideologies are often what is considered when we talk of social class or culture. The term ideology is intended to mean the plans and strategies (including intentions) that exist for both the infant and its caregivers. This approach evokes the concept of deliberate acts and seeks to explore the strategies used to produce specific outcomes. For example, some mothers respond to an infant's cry with vocalization, holding, and rocking; others by just looking at their infant. We know little about the behavior unless we understand the ideological constraints that may underlie it. For example, we might talk about one mother as more "responsive." In one sense at least this might not be true, in that both behave in some fashion toward their infants. Investigation of their ideologies, however, reveals that one wants to teach the infant that it cannot have what it wants all the time—"let him cry it out"—while the other seeks to protect it from a "cold" world for as long as possible. Both parents seek to teach their infants, and both are responsive, but their ideologies result in different behaviors. What might be the consequence of similar maternal behavior derived from different ideologies? This, of course, we do not know. Nor do we know about the plans, strategies, and cognitions of the infant. What might these be? And how do they develop and change? Thus while our information on adult ideology and behavior is very limited, even a conceptualization of infant ideology is totally lacking.

To summarize, we must conclude that we understand little of why or how the behaviors of the infant and its caregiver come about. At this point we must be satisfied with actual description (this must include more than what we have done—situation variation, for example), while considering further the ultimate integration of the material provided by each of these overlapping approaches.

SENSE MODALITIES ISSUES

Most investigators have centered their interest on the visual mode, and it is recognized that vision, both the infant's and caregiver's, is indeed a most important mode. However, it is logical that we consider more explicitly the issue of the use of a variety of sensory systems in the human organism's interaction with its world. In thinking about the role of the several sensory modalities, it is useful to consider the division between distal and proximal sensory input. Distal refers to stimulation or stimuli at a distance, which are experienced primarily through the visual, auditory, and olfactory modalities (the last-mentioned may operate, in some instances, only proximally, but has the potential for distal stimulation). Proximal stimuli are experienced through the tactile, kinesthetic, and gustatory modalities. This division, of course, does not imply that visual and auditory stimuli may not be provided while infant and caregiver are in close proximity or contact, but rather that only these sensory inputs, and to some degree olfactory stimuli as well, may be provided while the members of the dyad are physically apart. Unfortunately, there has been very little work on the diverse means of experiencing the social and physical environment during development, most of the theoretical burden having been placed on the visual and auditory systems. This is a particularly striking deficit, in that for the human (and other primate) infant (unlike the adult) so much of its contact with its environment is experienced through touch, taste, and movement.

It is clear that more information must be gathered to observe the use of the other modalities. Fraiberg, by studying blind infants, allows us to explore alternative "languages" of communication, and it becomes clear that the use of alternative modalities quickly can become available to both parent and child if they learn their signs and use. This material suggests, however, that unless intervention (learning) is instigated, most caregivers do not automatically become sensitized to the use of body movement instead of facial expression. Berkson's data also suggest that primate infants in the wild are able to survive (presumably by using alternative systems) with minimal sight when the environment is not overly harsh. However, these examples are extreme, and we need to explore the use and organization of the various modalities as they occur in "normal" development. Lewis, after looking at a wide variety of responses and their interactions between infant and mother, discusses the relationship between a tactile contact and a visual regard. Just this type of multisensory data is important. Study of the different modalities separately may fail to provide a complete hence accurate picture, although detailed studies within a modality may well be the necessary prelude to the study of the entire multisensory system. For example, Stern gives us an excellent description of the visual regard system but omits potentially relevant behaviors impinging upon other than visual sense receptors. One may anticipate that as the function of each such intramodality system is defined we will be able to consider the whole array of multisensory exchange in the dyad. An infant not only looks at what it sees, but looks toward what it hears.

Still another point that was not brought up in these chapters concerns the use of various sensory modalities. It must also be kept in mind that different modalities may be used to experience the world in different manners, and that the integration of these experiences results in a much higher level of organization.

No information is available as to how this organization develops. We cannot even answer questions concerning the relationship of object permanence over different modalities.

We strongly suggest therefore that modalities other than the visual mode be explored further, and that exploration of these modalities consider the interaction and complementarity of the various systems.

STIMULUS MEANING ISSUES

We have discussed stimulus issues in much of what we have already said. The conceptualization of elements versus interaction is in some sense a discussion of what the infant and caregiver respond to. What we now consider are two or three issues relating to the general topic of stimulus meaning.

The first issue concerns stimuli as they relate to situation. It is widely held that a stimulus event, for example, a touch or vocalization or some combination, is often treated as if it carries the same meaning regardless of context. We maintain that this is not necessarily true, and that it is necessary to study the contextual or situational setting as well as behavioral events themselves. Thus a stimulus event may change its meaning for both infant and caregiver, depending on the situation. A simple example may suffice. The infant cries—in one case it has just been fed, in the other it is feeding time. The caregiver through contextual cues realizes that in the former case the infant is in need of a burp, while in the latter the infant is hungry. The behavior of the infant is the same, but the meaning of the behavior is quite different. Interestingly, comparable examples of a caregiver's behavior are not as easily found. For example, a caregiver may pick up an infant because she thinks the infant wants to be held, whereas another time the caregiver picks up the infant because she wants to hold it. At issue then is the meaning of behavior. One way this can be explored is to observe given behaviors in different contextual situations. Parenthetically, it might be mentioned that context may be very important for a developing organism. The infant may utilize behavior-context situations to learn meaning.

Another stimulus issue involving the relationship between stimuli has been mentioned before. It seems quite plausible to us that some stimuli may have more salience in eliciting or affecting behavior than others. For example, as suggested in a prior section, for language development a vocalization–vocalization interaction may be more important than a vocalization–other. That there already exists cerebral hemisphere selectivity for human sounds suggests that such a relationship may well hold. Lewis and Stern believe that there may be more of these types of adaptive pairings. This of course suggests that some interactive events are more biologically adaptive. One might account for this in at least two ways. The first explanation is an ethological one which argues that a particular infant/caregiver behavior sets off a corresponding behavior in the other member's response repertoire. To hold this view one would need to show this to be invariant over situation (it becomes difficult to maintain the releaser view when the relationship holds only in select situations) and to demonstrate that it is invariant over the human species. The second view holds that the pairing relationship is a learned one, in that only specific behaviors produce desired outcomes, or that these occur only under certain specifiable conditions. These possibilities must remain conjectural in that neither has been explored.

The final point we wish to attend to deals in a broad way with the general nature of the stimuli we refer to when we talk of the infant and its caregiver. It must not escape our notice that generally we are talking about human beings, and putting aside for the moment other aspects, specifically considering the face of the human. We think it safe to assume that while other aspects of the human form impart meaning, the human face is by far the most outstanding source of information. Stern makes this point, and we think it well taken that the human face is a rather unique complex of stimuli, at once variable and constant. What a remarkable characteristic that the face can change so much and yet remain the same. That it can express such a wide range of feeling and still be the same face must be of crucial importance for the young infant. With this in mind we suggest that careful studies be made of faces, the infant's as well, in order to better understand a major source of stimulus change and constancy.

INTERACTION MEASUREMENT ISSUES

Most of the chapters in this volume show some concern at least with the continuous, ongoing nature of the interaction of the infant and caregiver. As suggested earlier, the authors are concerned with a model that argues that behavior elements of either caregiver or child studied alone are insufficient for understanding what transpires between them. Lewis, Brazelton, Stern, and Rosenblum each have directly tried to approach the study of this interaction. In the reading of their chapters, it becomes obvious that, if the often subtly woven fabric of interaction is to be understood, we must think about whole new types of measurement systems. Rather than consider only the frequency of single behaviors shown by both caregiver and infant, these authors suggest various other techniques which utilize such processes as sequential analyses, conditional probabilities, and simultaneous occurrences or critical intervention in its ongoing relationship, to mention a few. One overriding impression is that we have just begun to consider these kinds of measurement and as yet know very little of their promise and limitation. Clearly, the task of demarcating *what* ought to be studied, and *how*, is still before us. We must not lose sight of the fact, however, that measurement problems are *always* related to theoretical issues and must be viewed as such.

Of particular interest in the study of interaction is the issue of point of entry.

This is a most difficult question, for if we do not believe in elements per se but rather in the continuity of interaction, then there is no logical point of entry. That is, each observed behavior within the dyad is taken to be a function of the interconnected chain of behaviors that preceded it in time (or for that matter, it may be related to cognitions about future events). How then can we know where to enter this chain of events? We can offer no concrete solution but suggest that we consider context as a potentially important intervening variable in our understanding of the interaction. By looking at the beginnings of the interactive flow in a wide variety of circumscribed contextual settings, such as the play situation (see Stern and Brazelton), or during feeding or changing, we may better be able to understand the nature of the chain of interaction.

At the same time it becomes important to consider longitudinal studies so that some questions regarding presumptive "first causes" may be answered. If, for example, we are interested in nursing behavior, that is, why some mothers nurse their infants and others do not, would it not be wise to consider questioning the pregnant mother on her nursing views and then watching the interaction between mother and infant to see how the initial step in the mother's nursing contacts with the infant is set by a combination of her prior attitudes and her actual experience with the infant?

We also might look directly at the earliest contacts between caregiver and infant. It is interesting that at this time there are few detailed interaction studies concerning the first contact between a mother (or father) and her (or his) infant. In any event these approaches should facilitate meaningful expansion of our knowledge. Whether they can actually solve the problem concerning point of entry, however, is not as certain.

CHAPTER I

Contributions of Human Infants to Caregiving and Social Interaction

RICHARD Q. BELL
National Institute of Mental Health

There are several indications that we need a way of thinking about how the young affect parent behavior. In the last decade there has been increasing advocacy of greater attention to this area (Bell, 1971); it has been pointed out that the behavior of the young represents its own integrations and patterning, and exerts a very important effect on parents in one period, even if it has developed out of interactions with parents in a prior period. New findings are emerging from a variety of research strategies which make it possible to isolate child and parent effects (Berberich, 1971; Hilton, 1967; Osofsky & O'Connell, 1972; Siegel, 1963). While in the past the effect of the young on parents has even been underestimated in research literature on other mammals, Harper (1970) has now drawn our attention to the fact that the young of many species affect parents to the extent of determining patterns of utilizing food resources and territory.

It has been contended that it is no more parsimonious to interpret a correlation found between parent and child characteristics at a single point in time as due to the effects of parents on children, than it is to offer the opposite interpretation (Bell, 1968). Recent reviews of research on the effect of parent practices or techniques (Mussen, 1970) now uniformly recommend caution in interpreting correlations between parent and child characteristics in a unidirectional fashion, and some even go further, offering substantive interpretations of the correlations in terms of the effects of children on parents. Clearly, some steps toward the development of a theory of the effects of the young on their parents and caregivers is in order, and the present chapter undertakes the first step toward such a theory. The present chapter is one-sided in treating only the effects of the young, but this is necessary to work toward a balance in our perspectives. It is hardly likely that another imbalance will be created, considering that such an occurrence would necessitate offsetting over three decades of socialization research committed almost entirely to studying the effects of parents on their children.

This is a review of the many ways in which it appears likely that the effects of

1

the young may be shown in early development, particularly with reference to physical caregiving and social interaction. The chapter is frankly speculative. While interest in this area is rising, there is not sufficient research at present to provide an empirical basis for a theoretical structure. The conceptual elements have been drawn together in more of an expositional than a theoretical structure. The next logical step is to introduce general propositions which will align and organize the elements. Only a start is made in this direction.

In drawing together these guidelines toward a theory, it is clearly appreciated that meaningful and useful application of the guidelines must be found in the minute-to-minute and day-to-day ongoing interactions of parents and children. The concepts are of value only if they draw our attention to aspects of these interactions that might otherwise be overlooked, or help us focus on the task of teasing apart determinants of these interactions.

CONTRIBUTION OF THE YOUNG TO PARENT LIFE-SUPPORT AND PROTECTION ACTIVITIES

For purposes of discussion the effects of the young are detailed in terms of two very different aspects of the parent-child interaction. One aspect concerns the provision of life support and protection. In this case the parent primarily behaves so as to avoid undesirable immediate or long-range outcomes. From the parent standpoint this is an aversive system. At the other extreme is a kind of interaction which involves mutual, reciprocal, social interactions. This may be referred to as an appetitive system, in that both parent and offspring behave so as to produce or maintain the behavior of the other. There are many other kinds of interactions which this chapter does not attempt to treat, since the strategy is to develop guidelines out of a contrast between different systems, rather than to provide a comprehensive review of all kinds of parent-child exchanges.

Launching Parental Behavior

First, we present some speculations on how pregnancy and the neonate's characteristics set in motion the support and protection activities of the parent, which are subsumed under the term caregiving for brevity in most discussions for the remainder of the chapter. Harper (1972) has pointed out that pregnancy itself, with its physiological effects, and the signaling of a new role for the mother, lays the groundwork for these parental activities, which are then set in motion by the delivery of the infant. The behavior of the newborn further stimulates parental behavior. The thrashing and uncoordinated limb movements create an appearance of helplessness. The human infant's appearance alone could also have some effect on parental responsiveness in this early period, since the shape of the head (a short face relative to a large forehead and protruding cheeks) shows characteristics in line with several other species (Tinbergen, 1951). It is well known in comparative studies that the distinctive appearance of the young produces differential response from the members of a colony. Brooks and Hochberg (1960) have reported data more specifically applicable at the human level, namely, that variations in line abstractions of the human infant's face are responded to discriminatively and positively by adults—the concavity of the face, the height of the eyes, and other characteristics.

Postpartum hormonal effects could be operating at the human level, since we know from Rosenblatt's (1969) studies of rats that maternal behavior is enhanced by a pregnancy termination effect involving hormone changes. It is well to keep in mind that the human mother is not static physiologically but is maturing physiologically in the course of the process set in motion by the pregnancy.

The arrival of the infant is also capable of altering role relationships in the marriage. Ryder (1973) has reported that there is a decline in marital satisfaction reported by wives in young couples after having their first baby, in contrast to comparable couples without a baby. The decline in marital satisfaction seems to be due to less attention from the husband.

Sensory-Motor Matching · It is evident in cross-fostering animals that the sensory and motor system of the young is set up so that it matches that of the parent and not that of other species. An amusing example is described by Hersher, Richmond, and Moore (1963). When lambs and kids were cross-fostered, they retained their species-typical tendencies to follow (in the case of the lambs), or to leave the mother and lie down when sated (in the case of the kids) during the first few days postpartum. This resulted in the ewes rearing kids becoming highly disturbed, since they were constantly required to leave the flock to locate their foster charges, while the goats rearing lambs were incessantly "shadowed."

It is easy to overlook the importance of sensory-motor matching at the human level, because there are few opportunities to see the effects of cross-fostering. A mother rearing a chimpanzee infant commented on the oppressive effect of the infant's clinging (Hayes, 1951). There are other kinds of data that are suggestive. Eisenberg (1970) reports that human tonal patterns and speechlike signals are remarkably effective with newborns. Richards (1971) has remarked on the fact that an endogenous patterning of neonatal sucking has an effect on the feeding interaction. There are short and long intervals between the bursts of sucking. The mother moves between short bursts, and talks to and smiles at the infant during the long intervals between bursts.

Launching the Caregiving Bout

To bring the discussion down to the level of actual interaction, it is helpful to think about how the infant initiates bouts of interaction (meaning in this context simply that both mother and infant are interacting following a period during which they were not). During the first few weeks, many bouts are started by the fussing or crying of the infant. The young mother is recovering from the birth process, and is in most cases quite willing to let the infant sleep and rest as much as possible.

The cry brings the caregiver to a position where the visual, olfactory, and tactile stimuli provided by the infant can be effective. Later in the first year, the type of cry produced by the infant will have communication functions, but it is sufficient at first that it simply brings the caregiver into the vicinity.

As a predictable pattern of infant behavior develops, the mother's response to the early items in a sequence averts a later item. For example, Wolff (1966, p. 86) has described how infants move from quiescence to highly aroused crying. First, a soft whispering was detected, then gentle movements, rhythmic kicking, uncoordinated thrashing, and then fussing or spasmodic crying. If the thrashing is overheard, it may provide discriminative stimuli for maternal behavior which averts the rest of the sequence.

After the infant can recognize and discriminate the mother, and has developed some minimal time concepts, one other way of starting bouts can be seen. Anticipatory protests occur when behaviors are shown by the mother that have been associated in the past with separation.

In placing emphasis on the contribution of the infant's cry, I nonetheless recognize that its role should not be overestimated. Bernal (1972) has reported diary data indicating that few mothers respond to what they feel is the nature of the cry as such during first 10 days of life. Their knowledge of how long it has been since the last feeding, and how adequate the feeding was, are important determinants of their response. In other words, the infant's cry is important, but mothers are in no sense puppets on a string, responding without a second thought, and cued in only by the cry qualities.

In short, it seems a reasonable proposition that the pregnancy, the infant's appearance, and the infant's behavior all interact with the mother's role proscription to create the mother-infant subsystem of the family. It might be well to add that these infant characteristics at times only interact with the mother's existence as an adult. She may simply be trying to maintain her life, without any intention of socializing anyone.

Maintaining the Caregiving System

Maintaining Behavior within Tolerance Limits of the Parent · Here again the cry is used for illustrative purposes, simply because we have so much data on infant crying. During the first year, according to Bell and Ainsworth (1972), the duration of crying drops from 7.7 minutes/hour (range, 21 minutes/hour to none) in the first 3 months, to 4.4 minutes/hour in the last 3 months. Parmelee's (1972) data indicate a substantial reduction in crying between 1½ and 4 months.

The tolerance of parents probably shows a great range, but we do not have any quantitative data at present. However, from three different studies there are indications that parent tolerances are exceeded. Occasionally, crying is so excessive that it reaches the level of threatening and even breaking down the caregiving system. Robson and Moss (1970) traced changes in subjective feelings of attachment from retrospective interviews conducted with mothers in the third postnatal month. They concluded that attachment decreases in some mothers after the first month if crying, fussing, and other demands for physiological caregiving do not decrease as they do in most infants. In one case from their study, the mother was enthusiastic during pregnancy, but her positive feelings ebbed during the first month. Her infant fussed a great deal, was not responsive to holding, and was late in exhibiting smiling and eye-to-eye contact. The mother reacted violently, wanting nothing to do with the infant. She felt estranged and unloved. The infant was later found to have suffered relatively serious brain damage.

From the normative studies of crying I have discussed, we have some idea that in the first month or so there is a period during which the mother is in essence at the mercy of the crying of her infant. Whether or not her efforts are the determining factor, by the third month crying is well within what seems to be the tolerance limits of most parents. However, the question of the effectiveness of the mother, and of the baby's testing her limits, is not settled by the third month for all cases, according to Bell and Ainsworth's (1972) analysis of sequential relations between infant crying and maternal ignoring of crying eqisodes in the four quarters of the first year. These investigators interpret the correlations between quarters as indicating that infants in their sample cried more in any given quarter that was preceded by a 3-month period during which their mothers ignored their crying. However, there was an increasing tendency, toward the last half of the year, indicating that the more the infant cried in any given quarter, the more the mother ignored the cry in the subsequent quarter. Of course, correlational data of this kind cannot identify causal factors, but if these interpretations are correct, for some pairs there was evidence of a breakdown in the caregiving system as such, and something of a vicious cycle developed. Apparently, some infants exceeded their mother's limits. The mother's efforts to cope with the crying were inadequate. The infant responded by crying even more, and the mother withdrew even more.

Gil (1970) has summarized several clinical and epidemiological studies of "battered children." From the early clinical studies of parents who battered their children, it was concluded that the attack on the child was an outlet for frustrations. Parents, however, saw the *child* as the cause of the problem. Many of the parents thought they were being abused by the child. This could readily be dismissed as a parental defense mechanism, except that it is quite typical to find that other children in the family of an abused child are not abused. This fact raises questions about the stimulus qualities of the child. Constant fussing, strange and highly irritating crying, or other exasperating behaviors, were often reported for the one child subject to abuse in the family. Some children were abused in successive foster homes in which they were placed after the initial abuse. No other child had been abused previously in these foster homes. Gil's survey indicated that deviance in the child was at least as substantial a factor in explaining the incidents as was deviance in the parent, and the stressful circumstances under which they lived. Obviously, the stimulus characteristics of the child do not operate by themselves to induce mistreatment.

Most of the examples I have given involve testing the upper limits of parents. It is less obvious that extreme lethargy in infants can impair the caregiving relation. At first the young mother may feel relieved that she has a quiet baby. After the first month or two, however, she may become uneasy. She then stimulates her baby in various ways. She seeks the advice of friends or professional help if such measures, carried out over a long enough period of time, do not arouse the infant sufficiently.

Infants Define Their Own Limits · In the neonatal period the infant defines what it will or will not incorporate by swallowing or spitting out what is given to it. It turns its head away from aversive odors. Some infants reject solids and force their mothers to return to bottle or breast feedings. Others fall asleep during rigidly scheduled feedings, and this effectively limits the mother's behavior.

But what about the great volume of caregiving that is not in response to specific stimuli? Here the infant may make an unseen contribution. Startles or sustained distress reactions have sufficient impact on a mother that she is likely thereafter to prevent exposure of her baby to sudden noises, to too much noise, or to play that goes on overly long. If the mother has formed some concept of fragility and helplessness from the smallness and the thrashing, uncoordinated behavior of her newborn, she is quite likely to have this concept strengthened in later instances by the infant's startles or distress reactions. These reactions inform the parent when sensory and fatigue limits have been exceeded.

Readability of the Infant · There is a possibility that an empirical approach may be opened up to throw light on the problem of what it is that makes it difficult or easy to take care of some infants. Korner, in another chapter in this volume, has raised the possibility that the "readability" of an infant may be a function of the clarity of cues to its state. In studies of observer agreement, all of us who have studied very young infants have encountered those whose states are unclear. Mothers must have the same problem. This possibility is readily accessible to research.

Inducing a Singular Caregiving Relationship · A sequence of developmental changes in the infant contributes to the mother's concept that she has a singular and essential role to carry out. The sequence starts with discrimination of human from inanimate forms, discrimination of the mother from others, reactions to strangers, and, finally, protest at separation. Considered as a whole, these infant behaviors indicate to the mother that she has been selected for an intense one-to-one relationship, even if there were no cultural sanctions or role proscriptions to convey the same message. Of course a singular relationship is not always possible, as in some institutional settings, and yet caregiving goes on. The point here is that, where a singular relation is possible, the infant's behavior can be counted on to promote its emergence.

CONTRIBUTION OF THE YOUNG TO THE SOCIAL INTERACTION SYSTEM

In a social interaction system, the responses of each participant serve as stimuli for the other. Kohlberg (1969) amplifies this definition in the context of socialization:

"In general, even simple social play and games have the character of either complementarity, reciprocity, (I do this, then you do that, then I do this), or of imitation (I do this, you do this too). In either case there is a shared pattern of behavior, since reciprocal play is a sort of reciprocal imitation (you follow me, then I follow you) [p. 463]."

Watson (1966) has offered an explanation of how "contingency games" involving complementarity and reciprocity may develop between parent and infant increasingly after the first 3 months. Applying his line of thinking in the present context, responses of the infant that follow quickly parent behaviors could by that contingency acquire reward value, just as those of the parent could for the infant, leading to a social interchange system in which the responses of each are rewarding for the other—an appetitive system, in contrast to the aversive system in operation relative to provision of life support and protection.

In placing emphasis on the infant's contribution to noncaregiving interactions, I am assuming, as do Walters and Parke (1965), that socialization does not develop exclusively out of primary drive reduction. In the same vein, Escalona (1968) has challenged the classical psychoanalytic formulation that psychological development occurs in states of displeasure incident to delay of gratification. She feels that development from interaction is best favored by moderate levels of arousal. However, caregiving may lead to a state from which the infant starts the type of social interaction in which we expect socialization to be maximized. For example, the infant may quiet down after a diaper has been changed, or smile, and thus launch a social interaction.

Initiating the Social Interaction

Reduction in Demand for Caregiving · It is possible for social interaction to develop gradually out of early caregiving as the infant shows a decrease in the duration of crying and fussing and an increase in the time it is awake and attentive. Thus the infant provides an increased opportunity for noncaregiving activities to occur. It can be readily understood that a mother is less likely to start a playful interaction with her infant if she is stressed by inconsolable crying, or by her infant's short periods of sleep that do not come at a time permitting her to rest. When the caregiving demand has been reduced by changes that occur in normal development, the infant's changing condition can release one of the most powerful parental contributions to early social interaction—spontaneous play. Possibly even before, certainly increasingly after the third month, the mother's effort to reduce unpleasant excitation has reduced sufficiently, and the occasions on which positive affective responses have been elicited have increased, to an extent that we could say that the social interaction system is well on its way.

Manipulability of States in the Infant · The ability of infants to show alterations in state in response to the efforts of parents is a more active contribution to the initiation of the social interaction system than the conditions just mentioned. Escalona (1968) has described how a mother stimulates a drowsy infant to bring it back to a state in which they can interact. Then the mother may have to calm the infant down and soothe it as it becomes too agitated. During visual attention the mother adjusts the level of stimulation to the infant's interest and arousal. The infant behavior that supports these parental efforts is state manipulability. Bridger and Birns (1963) have reported quantitative data indicating that infants vary greatly in response to identical efforts to manipulate states.

Approximately 18% of infants have what is termed "colic," a condition in which there is nearly a complete breakdown in state manipulability. Colic maximizes caregiving interactions and minimizes social interactions. Turning to conditions still farther from the normal range, Brazelton (1962) has described in detail a case in which an infant's inflexibility of states, as well as limited range, had a severe effect on the mother.

Responsive Behavior · The mere fact that an infant does something, literally anything other than fussing or crying, as a response to a mother's stimulation, is another and still more active contributor to the launching of the social interaction. A mass movement or a babble are responses, and again the mother learns that what she does matters. Watson (1966) was impressed with the excitement he saw developing in his infant as a response to contingency games.

Initiating Social Interactions at the Level of Bouts

Jones and Moss in our laboratory (1971) have reported that infants in the awake-active state tend to babble much more when they are by themselves than when the mother is present. The mother who hears these episodes of noncrying vocalizations, even though busy, often cannot resist the appeal, and comes to the infant to enter into the game. The infant's babbling thus may come to serve as a discriminative stimulus for a reciprocal "game." In such instances the infant often discontinues the babbling and shifts into a reciprocal relation in which the mother vocalizes or touches, and the infant responds by smiling and vocalizing.

Often, a sitting infant gurgles and smiles when a mother passes on her way to do a household chore, thus inveigling her into interaction. One of the infants in our studies could emit a special noncrying vocalization which was quite effective in bringing the mother in from the kitchen to start an interaction. One other way in which bouts of interaction are started during these early months is by the infant remaining quiet for a longer time than the mother would ordinarily expect, after awakening. The infant may simply be quiet and attentive, and not even moving. This brings the mother, and the interaction bout ensues.

Maintaining the Social Interaction System

The Role of Attachment · Both the difficulties and the advantages of attempting a distinction between caregiving and social interaction are illustrated by application of Bowlby's (1969) theory of attachment in the present context. The signal aspects of the infant's repertoire (crying, smiling, babbling, and vocalization) and the executive aspects of behavior (clinging, approach, and following) create and maintain the proximity that is essential to caregiving. Also, without proximity, one cannot have a social interaction system. The shortcoming of the theory of attachment that Bowlby has developed is that it does not speak sufficiently to the social interaction that is the key to socialization. Proximity is necessary but not sufficient.

Smiling and vocalization are not only signals for promoting and maintaining attachment but are also responses that maintain mothers in the social interaction. In that they are partial equivalents of what the mother herself is doing, they are precursors of what will prove to be very engaging for the mother in later development—observational learning. The young child reproduces parts of what the model is doing, and then puts the components together in fascinating new combinations. The young are able to play with these components, as Bruner (1972) has pointed out. The mother can be maintained in the social interaction by watching this play, as well as by being played with.

Bruner (1972) also adds that a special quality in the responsiveness of the young is a positive reaction to novelty when in a secure setting. This facilitates the mother's play. She can try very ridiculous things and is often rewarded with a laugh or smile.

If we follow Cairns' (1967) position, behavior that has saliency (and the infant's behavior certainly seems to have saliency for parents) can maintain social interaction systems. Gewirtz (1961) has made room in his theories for the possibility that maternal behaviors may be unlearned reinforcers. By the same token, some infant behaviors could be reasonably considered unlearned reinforcers for maternal behavior.

Successive Production of Novel Responses · Each of the infant's responses may have an inherent value in triggering specific parental behavior. Cutting across all this specificity is the feature of novelty. The infant continually shows new behaviors which excite and interest the parent, as Gewirtz (1961) pointed out long ago. If the mother is attentive to the infant during the first 3 weeks, she may notice a strange little smile appearing in some phases of sleep and she may see that some noises she makes while the infant is asleep produce this smile. Later this smile appears when the infant is open-eyed, immediately after a feeding period. Toward the end of the third week, the smile may appear in response to her voice more than to the other sounds. During this same 3-week period, she sees changes in attentive behavior. She sees that the infant quiets and looks bright-eyed when attending. She sees an increase in general activity and thrashing about in connection with attentive behavior.

In the fourth and fifth weeks she is treated to a continuing kaleidoscope of novelty. She is suddenly aware that her baby focuses on her face, that they have eye-to-eye contact, that her face is beginning to register more than some other stimuli, and that some smiles appear when she moves her head. Between the fifth and seventh weeks, she sees fewer mouth and head movements, sees much more smiling, and is delighted to hear soft cooing vocalizations accompanying the infant's periods of attention. The rapid succession of these novel behaviors makes more than a contribution to attachment. The novelty could very well contribute to the positive quality of the interaction and thus play a role in maintaining a social system.

Changes during the first few weeks have been described in detail. It is easy to imagine the impact of many other changes manifested by the infant, such as the beginning of capability for manipulating objects, the replacement of indiscriminate reaching with reaching toward the most salient object, sitting up, inhibition of reaching toward unfamiliar objects, crawling, and then standing. The toddler finally moves beyond a "stilt" walk, and then begins to emit words. The early preschooler utters sentences.

Again we need not be concerned in the present context about the earliest origins of these behaviors. The important point is that at certain points in time new behaviors emerge, and these have an impact, however maturational processes may interact with the mother's caregiving and stimulation. The average mother cannot help but be affected by these changes. The mother who essentially maintains a caregiving system may not know much about the infant, and what has been shown during the last week or so, when one asks her to report. The mother who functions both as a caregiver and as a partner in social interaction is likely to be more aware of the novel behaviors showing up in each period.

Behaviors Showing Developmental Progress · That novelty itself is not enough can be clearly seen in the fact that periods of reorganization and regression in young children are very disturbing to parents. To understand why temporary setbacks are upsetting to parents, it is well to keep in mind that most of the novel changes that have been mentioned above are changes in the direction of increasingly adultlike behavior. There are oddities along the way, but generally the infant or young child continually moves in the general direction of being more like the adult and less like the strange and enigmatic physiological being with whom the parents were first confronted in the neonatal period.

Behaviors Showing Modifiability · It seems likely that the kaleidoscopic movement toward more and more adultlike behaviors would in itself have a considerable supportive function, even if there were no indication that the infant's behavior is responsive to maternal behavior. However, it is clear that the infant has some basic ways of telling the mother that what she does matters. It has been mentioned earlier that responsiveness itself has a supportive role to play in the interaction. Then there is the next level of modifiability—learning. To achieve a satisfactory criterion of conditioning, Papousek (1967 a, b) found it necessary to use 177 trials when conditioning was started within the newborn period, but used only 42 when starting in the third month and 28 when starting in the fifth month. Thus if a mother behaved in such a way as to incorporate the basic elements of Papousek's procedure, she might feel by the fourth month that she could have some effect on the infant beyond mere responsiveness or distraction. If the mother persisted as long as scientists who have conditioned social responses (Brackbill, 1958; Rheingold, Gewirtz, & Ross, 1959; Weisberg, 1963), she might see that the infant's smiling or vocalization was coming under her control. In the months and early years to follow, she would see observational learning in motor behavior, and then reproduction of partial speech forms. Finally, she would see a stage when her own verbal description of consequences could alter a child's behavior so that a trial and error process was not necessary for the child. All in all, under this heading the infant's contribution to maintaining the social interaction lies in the fact that responsiveness and modifiability are shown.

Altering the Basis for Social Interaction · Birch and Lefford (1967, p. 110) have described the shift from response to tactile stimuli to visual stimuli in the first year. Studies of evoked potential on both human infants and lower animals (Ellingson, 1964) have shown that cortical response to tactile stimuli is relatively mature in earliest infancy, whereas response to auditory and visual stimuli becomes mature in form sometime later. During this same developmental period, several investigators who attended primarily to the nature of the mother-infant interaction (Lewis & Ban, 1971; Lusk & Lewis, 1972; Moss, 1967) noted a proximal-distal shift in infant behaviors, and recorded differences in maternal behavior that paralleled this shift. For both sexes, touching, a proximal behavior, decreases over age, and looking, the most distal behavior, increases. There are some sex differences which make this more complicated, but for the present purpose it is enough to note that the proximal-distal shift, whatever the origins, changes the basis for the social interaction process. In a sense the change in the infant's behavior places the relationship more on an adult basis. Interactions can occur at close range as well as at a distance.

The young child's behavior often makes a contribution to some further changes in development. To quote Maccoby and Masters (1970):

"The scraps of information that we do have point to a decline in proximity seeking, with attention seeking and approval seeking maintained at a constant level or increasing. There appears to be a shift in target from the mother and other adults to age-mates. With respect to these changes one is struck by the parallel with human primates, in whom infant play and other social contacts with age-mates take more and more of the infant's time, while occasions where the infant flees to the mother for comfort and protection decline in frequency, and the amount of time simply spent staying near the mother becomes progressively less [p. 145]."

Terminating Social Interaction Bouts

The supine and sitting infant can terminate a bout by fussing, becoming irritable, and turning its head away, or by simply falling asleep. In Papousek's studies (1967a,b) which have already been mentioned, infants subject to the conditioning procedure before the third month often showed distress. This distress was sufficiently effective to even terminate an experimental procedure (let alone a mother-infant interaction). The crawling infant can show any of the termination behaviors of the younger infants, as well as crawling away from the parent. The toddler and preschooler can also show any of the preceding but, in addition, has still more effective motor behaviors for terminating the interactions.

GENERAL PRINCIPLES

Emergent Child Behavior · It is necessary to realize that each period of interaction is capable of altering the status of a child, so that during the subsequent period of interaction the child stimulates the parent in a different fashion, or reacts differently to parent behavior. This principle may be operative in the findings of Hartup (1958) and Baer (1962) that withholding positive reinforcement only increased dependency in children who were already highly dependent. Whatever conditions led to high dependency prior to the child's participation in the study altered the responsivity of the child to withdrawal of positive reinforcement. To pursue the implications of this principle, we should study parent-child interactions during one period, assess child behavior at some point when it appears stable toward the end of this phase, and then, during the next period, assess the effects on the parent of the child's way of functioning. I have not found any examples of research that have done this.

Homeostatic Model · One very general principle about the behavior of the young is that they contribute too much or too little in the way of some behaviors, or show some behaviors too early or too late in terms of parent expectations (Bell, 1971). Briefly, it is assumed that each participant in a social or caregiving interaction has upper and lower limits relative to the intensity, frequency, or situational appropriateness of behavior shown by the other. When the upper limit for one participant is reached, that participant is likely to react in such a way as to redirect or reduce the excessive or inappropriate behavior (upper-limit control reaction). When the lower limit is reached, the reaction is to stimulate, prime, or in other ways to increase the insufficient or nonexistent behavior (lower-limit control reaction).

This homeostatic concept needs implementing propositions before it can lead to testable hypotheses. However, it has proved helpful in thinking about findings that have already been uncovered. For example, one of Beckwith's (1971) findings, from an observational study of mother-infant interaction in 7-month-old adopted infants, becomes meaningful when looked at from the homeostatic standpoint. Verbal discouragement was correlated .49 with infant Gesell scores, the only significant correlation found between measures of maternal speech and the Gesell. The explanation offered was that infants showing more locomotion and reaching out for objects, and thus scoring high on the Gesell, were more difficult to manage in a property-conscious home. Verbal discouragement was presumably one of the mother's upper-limit control techniques.

Maccoby and Masters (1970) have used a homeostatic concept in explaining data from Emmerich's (1964) longitudinal study in which it was found that an interesting developmental transformation occurred over a 2-year time in the preschool period. Previously interpersonally negative children became poised, while their previously interpersonally positive counterparts manifested social insecurity. The explanation offered by Maccoby and Masters (1970) was

"Perhaps in anticipation of the child's entry into the more formal kindergarten setting, socializing agents at this time were putting pressure on the outgoing child to modulate his aggressiveness, while a simultaneous attempt is being made to influence a self-contained child to become more outgoing [p. 99]."

The Nature of Control · It is evident that one of the individuals in the parent-child socialization system is much more mature than the other, and more closely approximates the adult patterns of the culture. This feature of course led to the first oversimplification of socialization research, namely, the model of an agent of socialization acting upon a malleable and unformed infant. In counteracting this earlier simplification in the history of our research, it is easy to become attracted to another simplification, that the infant and young child socialize the parents. The controls involved are far too complicated to make it likely that this other oversimplification will lead to any better understanding of the interaction system.

First of all, what are the implications of the inequality of maturity for control exerted by the infant or child on the parent? The inequality does not preclude the existence of a reciprocal relation. As Skinner (1971) has pointed out, there is even a reciprocal relation between the physicist and the subatomic particles whose behavior the experiment is designed to control. The experimenter's behavior is shaped and controlled by the nature of the particles.

. It should also be considered that an individual who starts an interaction by that very fact is exercising control over the other. The other has to react on the initiator's behavioral "home ground," so to speak. Thus, when we realize that an infant or young child starts approximately 50% of the interactions (Bell, 1971), we must consider that a substantial degree of control is exerted thereby over the parent, even if it is not exerted in any other way. In this respect there is a type of balance in the relationship, which fits neither the notion of the parents socializing the young in a unidirectional fashion, or the opposite, that the young socialize adults so that they become parents.

There is also a type of balance in control due to the fact that the infant selectively reinforces parent behavior, thus modifying socialization efforts. Also, the fact that the infant or young child is more competent in one sense than the young, inexperienced parent, offsets the greater maturity of parent. The neonate is very competent in bringing the parent to the general area, and in producing desired behavior. It has a set of behaviors which are highly effective in bringing about support, protection, and maintenance of optimal states. In other words, competence in controlling the behavior of another so as to produce a certain outcome is different from maturity, which is the stage of movement toward adult forms of behavior in a culture.

At first, Skinner (1971) notes that the infant controls the parent without adjusting its own behavior to achieve certain consequences. Initially, only the parent's behavior is intentional. The parent acts so as to achieve certain consequences. (In many instances, however, as I have mentioned, the parent is simply functioning as an adult). Parents in the socialization role are presumably guided by the norms and values of the culture in which they were reared, including the subculture defined by their own families. Even though there is increasing evidence of intentional behavior in the child by the second year of life, it is obvious that the intentional behavior of the parent covers a much longer span of time and involves much more general objectives.

In summary, then, the parent-child system is a reciprocal relation involving two or more individuals who differ greatly in maturity although not in competence, in terms of ability to affect each other. The relationship involves much more and longer-range intention on the part of one participant than on the part of the other. There is a certain balance of controls, in that the greater intentional behavior of the parent is offset by two features of the offspring's behavior: (1) the active short-range initiation of interactions, and (2) the organization of the behavior so that it is compelling and selectively reinforcing. Much of the modification of child behavior toward cultural norms occurs in the context of parental adjustments and accommodations to the initiations of the young.

Summary

Pregnancy, the infant's physical appearance, the helpless thrashing movements, as well as the fact that the infant's sensory and motor system matches that of the mother, all contribute to launching caregiving, defined as the provision of life support and protection. As the behavior of the infant becomes increasingly organized, early items in a sequence become discriminative stimuli for maternal avoidance behavior, so that much of caregiving consists of preventing undesirable and unpleasant outcomes (an aversive system). Caregiving is maintained in part because infants provide interpretable cues to their conditions, define their own sensory and fatigue limits, and maintain their protest behavior within the limits of a caregiver's tolerance. Their progressively discriminating attention to the caregiver, and their proximity-maintaining behaviors, tend to induce a singular, one-to-one relationship with the caregiver, where this is possible.

Social interactions between the young and the parents involve the reciprocal exchange of behaviors with positive value, so that the contribution of the young lies not in providing signals to parents of aversive consequences that may develop. Infant behavior in this case generates appetitive parental behavior. The young contribute to social interactions by reducing the demand for caregiving (by being in states that favor mutual exchange), by being susceptible to manipulations of states, by being responsive in a very general sense, and by actively initiating social interactions.

Although the signal and executive behaviors of the young that maintain proximity are important to both caregiving and social interaction, they are not sufficient to maintain the latter. The infant's responses that have positive values for the parent, rather than those that are cues to avoid unpleasant outcomes, are the contribution of the young to social interaction. Examples are smiling and vocalization, partial reproduction of adult behaviors, playing at combinations and recombinations of these partials, successive and kaleidoscopic production of novel responses, showing developmental progress, and general modifiability of behavior. While playing their part in maintaining social interaction, the young also alter its basis, as seen in the shift from response to proximal versus distal stimuli in the first year. Increasing activity, and behaviors directed to the production of variety in stimulation, also alter the basis for social interaction. Peers can provide more activity and variety in stimulation than parents, as the young child's motor and communication capabilities make peer interaction possible.

Three general principles emerge from a consideration of the above contributions made by the young. In both caregiving and social interaction, the young change the general status of their behavior in one period of development, so that their effects on parents in a subsequent period are different. Research strategies are needed that can detect these changing effects of emergent behavior. The origins of the emergent behavior are no more important than the changing effects. Another very general principle is that the behavior of the young falls between the extremes of quantitative excess or deficiency, or inappropriate timing relative to parent expectations. Excessive or premature behavior induces what is termed upper-limit parent controls that are intended to redirect or reduce behavior. Lower-limit parent controls occur in response to insufficient or delayed onset of behavior in the young. Extensions of this homeostatic model have proved helpful in explaining findings in the literature on socialization. Finally, reflection on the nature of controls exerted over parent behavior by the young leads to the thought that there may be a balance in controls due to the fact that the greater maturity and long-term intentional behavior of parents is offset by the sheer volume of interactions started by the young, by the compelling nature of these behaviors, and by the way they selectively reinforce parental behavior.

References

Baer, D. M. A technique of social reinforcement for the study of child behavior: Behavior avoiding reinforcement withdrawal. *Child Development,* 1962, **33,** 847–858.

Beckwith, L. Relationships between attributes of mothers and their infants' I.Q. scores. *Child Development,* 1971, **42,** 1083–1097.

Bell, R. Q. A reinterpretation of the direction of effects in studies of socialization. *Psychological Review,* 1968, **75,** 81–95.

Bell, R. Q. Stimulus control of parent or caretaker behavior by offspring. *Developmental Psychology,* 1971, **4,** 63–72.

Bell, S. M, & Ainsworth, M. D. Infant crying and maternal responsiveness. *Child Development*, 1972, **43**, 1171–1190.

Bernal, J. Crying during the first ten days of life, and maternal responses. *Developmental Medicine and Child Neurology*, 1972, **14**, 362–372.

Berberich, J. P. Do the child's responses shape the teaching behavior of adults? *Journal of Experimental Research in Personality*, 1971, **5**, 92–97.

Birch, H. E., & Lefford, A. Visual differentiation, intersensory integration, and voluntary motor control. *Monographs of the Society for Research in Child Development*, 1967, **32** (2, Serial No. 110).

Bowlby, J. *Attachment and loss*. Vol. 1. New York: Basic Books, 1969.

Brackbill, Y. Extinction of the smiling response in infants as a function of reinforcement schedule. *Child Development*, 1958, **29**, 115–124.

Brazelton, T. Observations of the neonate. *Journal of the American Academy of Child Psychiatry*, 1962, **1**, 38–58.

Bridger, W., & Birns, B. Neonates' behavior and autonomic responses to stress during soothing. *Recent Advances in Biological Psychiatry*, 1963, **5**, 1–6.

Brooks, V., & Hochberg, J. A psychophysical study of "cuteness." *Perceptual and Motor Skills*, 1960, **11**, 205.

Bruner, J. S. Nature and uses of immaturity. *American Psychologist*, 1972, **27**, 687–708.

Cairns, R. B. The attachment behavior of mammals. *Psychological Review*, 1967, **73**, 406–426.

Eisenberg, R. B. The development of hearing in man: An assessment of current status. *Asha*, 1970, **12** (3), 119–123.

Ellingson, R. J. Cerebral electrical responses to auditory and visual stimuli in the infant (human and subhuman studies). In P. Kellaway and I. Petersen (Eds.), *Neurological and electroencephalographic correlative studies in infancy*. New York: Grune and Stratton, 1964. Pp. 78–116.

Emmerich, W. Continuity and stability in early social development. *Child Development*, 1964, **35**, 311–332.

Escalona, S. *The roots of individuality*. Chicago: Aldine, 1968.

Gewirtz, J. L. A learning analysis of the effects of normal stimulation, privation and deprivation on the acquisition of social motivation and attachment. In B. M. Foss (Ed.), *Determinants of infant behavior*. New York: Wiley, 1961. Pp. 213–290.

Gil, D. G. *Violence against children*. Cambridge, Mass.: Harvard University Press, 1970.

Harper, L. V. Ontogenetic and phylogenetic functions of the parent-offspring relationship in mammals. *Advances in the Study of Behavior*, 1970, **3**, 75–117.

Harper, L. V. Effects of the parent-offspring relationship upon the parent. Unpublished manuscript, 1972, Department of Applied Behavioral Sciences, University of California, Davis.

Hartup, W. W. Nurturance and nurturance-withdrawal in relation to the dependency behavior of preschool children. *Child Development*, 1958, **29**, 191–201.

Hayes, C. *The ape in our house*. New York: Harper, 1951.

Hersher, L., Richmond, J. B., & Moore, A. U. Modifiability of the critical period for the development of maternal behavior in sheep and goats. *Behaviour*, Leiden, 1963, **20**, 311–320.

Hilton, I. Differences in the behavior of mothers toward first- and later-born children. *Journal of Personality and Social Psychology*, 1967, **7** (3), 282–290.

Jones, S. J., & Moss, H. A. Age, state, and maternal behavior associated with infant vocalizations. *Child Development*, 1971, **42**, 1039–1051.

Kohlberg, L. Stage and sequence: The cognitive-developmental approach to socialization. In D. A. Goslin (Ed.), *Handbook of socialization theory and research.* Chicago: Rand McNally, 1969. Pp. 347–480.

Lewis, M., & Ban, P. Stability of attachment behavior: A transformational analysis. Paper presented at the meeting of the Society for Research in Child Development, Minneapolis, Minnesota, 1971.

Lusk, D., & Lewis, M. Mother-infant interaction and infant development among the Wolof of Senegal. *Human Development*, 1972, **15**, 58–69.

Maccoby, E., & Masters, J. C. Attachment and dependency. In P. H. Mussen (Ed.), *Carmichael's manual of child psychology.* (3rd ed.) New York: Wiley, 1970. Pp. 73–158.

Moss, H. A. Sex, age, and state as determinants of mother-infant interaction. *Merrill-Palmer Quarterly*, 1967, **13**, 19–36.

Mussen, P. H. (Ed.) *Carmichael's manual of child psychology.* (3rd ed.) New York: Wiley, 1970.

Osofsky, J. D., & O'Connell, E. J. Parent-child interaction: Daughters' effects upon mothers' and fathers' behaviors. *Developmental Psychology*, 1972, **7**, 157–168.

Papousek, H. Experimental studies of appetitional behavior in human newborns and infants. In H. W. Stevenson, E. H. Hess, & H. L. Rheingold (Eds.), *Early behavior: Comparative and developmental approaches*. New York: Wiley, 1967. (a)

Papousek, H. Conditioning during early postnatal development. In Y. Brackbill & G. G. Thompson (Eds.), *Behavior in infancy and early childhood.* New York: Free Press, 1967, Pp. 259–274. (b)

Parmelee, A. H. Jr. Development of states in infants. In C. Clemente, D. Purpura, & F. Mayer (Eds.), *Maturation of brain mechanisms related to sleep behavior.* New York: Academic Press, 1972, Pp. 199–228.

Rheingold, H. L., Gewirtz, J. L., & Ross, H. W. Social conditioning of vocalizations in the infant. *Journal of Comparative and Physiological Psychology*, 1959, **52**, 68–73.

Richards, M. P. Social interaction in the first weeks of human life. *Psychiatria, Neurologia, Neurochirurgia*, 1971, **74**, 35–42.

Robson, K. S. & Moss, H. A. Patterns and determinants of maternal attachment. *Journal of Pediatrics*, 1970, **77**, 976–985.

Rosenblatt, J. S. The development of maternal responsiveness in the rat. *American Journal of Orthopsychiatry*, 1969, **39**, 36–56.

Ryder, R. G. The relationship between having a child and changes in reported "marriage satisfaction." *Journal of Marriage and the Family*, 1973, in press.

Siegel, G. M. Adult verbal behavior with retarded children labeled as "high" or "low" in verbal ability. *American Journal of Mental Deficiency*, 1963, **68** (3), 417–424.

Skinner, B. F. *Beyond freedom and dignity.* New York: Knopf, 1971.

Tinbergen, N. *The study of instinct.* London: Oxford, 1951.

Walters, R. H., & Parke, R. D. *The role of the distance receptors in the development of social responsiveness.* In L. P. Lipsitt and C. C. Spiker (Eds.), *Advances in Child Development and Behavior*, Vol. 2. New York: Academic Press, 1965. Pp. 59–96.

Watson, J. S. The development and generalization of "contingency awareness" in early infancy: Some hypotheses. *Merrill-Palmer Quarterly of Behavior and Development*, 1966, **12**, 123–135.

Weisberg, P. Social and nonsocial conditioning of infant vocalizations. *Child Development*, 1963, **34**, 377–388.

Wolff, P. H. *The causes, controls, and organization of behavior in the neonate.* New York: International Universities Press, 1966.

CHAPTER 2

An Interactional Approach
to the Mother-Infant Dyad[1]

MICHAEL LEWIS and **SUSAN LEE-PAINTER**
Educational Testing Service

Psychology, of all the sciences, may be the most interactive; the study of elements per se the least fruitful. Slowly the models for studying human behavior have begun to reflect this. Models for the acquisition of knowledge (Piaget being the most representative of this class), the development of interpersonal relationships (for example, Lewis, 1972) reflect the realization that only through interaction can we study, without distortion, human behavior. This interactionalist point of view is in general still foreign to psychology and is resisted. This is due primarily to the prevailing reductionist philosophy. That this is the case is rather strange. While the study of physics has surrendered its reliance upon the nineteenth century model of science, psychology still clings to this view.

In this chapter we take a rather extreme interactionalist position in order to present a strong counterposition to the prevailing view. We begin our discussion with various models of the caregiver-infant[2] relationship. In this regard it is important to note that the nature of the model of the caregiver-infant relationship is often implicitly given in the observation and measurement techniques of the study. Although the researcher may claim to have no underlying model of the relationship, his observation and measurement procedures belie this fact.

After presentation of the models, we discuss the measurement procedures that form a part of the models. To do this we take data obtained in an empirical study. Finally, we consider the interactionalist approach to the environment-organism dyad.

MODELS OF INTERACTION

The first model, and that most widely held today, might be aptly called the element model (see Figure 1). In this model there are two elements, and one

[1]This research was supported by the Spencer Foundation.

[2]We prefer the term caregiver rather than caretaker since we interpret the adult as giving care rather than taking the cares of the infant away. Note that even our language reflects the interactive nature of the relationship.

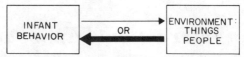

FIGURE 1. Simple element model indicating relatively little interaction.

simply asks what one of these elements does. In most cases we study what the mother does—the thicker arrow reflects this. For our consideration one of the elements is the infant, the other the environment. More specifically, the infant element is a set of infant behaviors which vary as a function of age of the child. The environmental element can either be things, such as toys (adult-defined) or objects. Alternatively, it could be people. The arrows in this model represent the direction of study. This model reflects studies that ask the basic question how much of what kind of behavior occurs. If we ask it of the infant, we ask specifically, for example, how much smiling or vocalization does an infant produce in an hour or two of observation. For the environment we usually refer to people. In some sense this reveals the illogic of this model. No one is interested in how many times the cradle rocks in 2 hours, for we realize, although we never state explicitly, that the study of that element in the model makes little sense unless we study it in interaction with another element, namely, the infant. Thus on the environment side we study only people. The question we usually ask, for example, is, How much does the mother talk to or look at the infant?

This model implicitly can become interactive when we start to look at either individual differences or developmental consequences. When we begin to ask about differences between the sexes or among social classes in terms of either the infant's or caregiver's behavior, we may be implying that the middle-class infant does something more than the working-class infant because the caregiver does something different. Interestingly, caregiver differences are usually not considered to be caused by infant differences.

We recognize that instead of an interactional approach some investigators prefer to talk about basic biological differences. Thus one infant cries more or less than another not because of any interaction, but because of some "basic" biological difference between them. Again, however, caregiver differences are not usually relegated to a biological cause. Because of this, individual differences not considered a function of an interaction are asymmetrical with respect to the model, biologically caused for the infant, learning caused for the caregiver. Only the interactional position is symmetrical to both elements.

Besides individual differences there are developmental differences. In this model, seen in Figure 2, we observe what is usually studied. In this case there is infant behavior at times $I1$ and $I2$ and environmental behavior at times $E1$ and $E2$.

In this model there is also asymmetry. What is usually studied here is the caregiver's behavior at time $E1$ and the infant's behavior at time $I2$, for example,

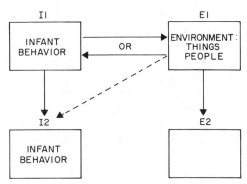

FIGURE 2. Element model used to describe the relationship of present to subsequent behavior.

the amount of the mother's vocalization when the child is 3 months old *(E1)* and the infant's language ability at 2 years *(I2)*. This use of the model by correlating these two events clearly is interactional in nature. Observe, however, that neither infant behavior at *I1* or environment at *E2* is studied, nor for that matter is *I1* correlated with *E2*—thus the asymmetry. In general, the asymmetry of this kind of model centers on the failure to compare the infant's effect on the caregiver; however, even these comparisons would not render the model interactive.

The second type of model, seen in Figure 3, has more of an interactionalist approach. Here again we have two elements—the child's behavior and the environment—but here we see that the various arrows connecting these elements are more interrelated. What we chose to call these connections is explicit in our theoretical orientation. For example, the same infant behavior emitted under the same circumstances and responded to in the same manner could be called an elicitor or initiator; likewise, a behavior could be called a response or a reinforcer. What we choose to call these connections depends on many things. For example, if we feel that the infant has intention, then his behavior is an elicitor, whereas without this assumption we might refer to it as simply an

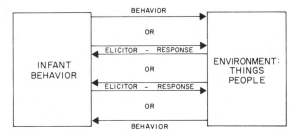

FIGURE 3. Simple interaction model.

initiator. Some investigators might not wish to give any interactive quality to the events and therefore label them "first behavior–second behavior." This type of categorization avoids interaction.

Whatever we wish to call these connections, this type of model is concerned with the behavior of the elements in interaction with one another. In this figure we can see more symmetry between the elements; the infant's behavior interacts with the environment either to cause something to happen or to respond to something that is happening. Likewise, the environment acts both to cause or to respond to something that is happening. Interestingly, and in order to account for all behavior, there are two connections which we have called "behavior" for which we cannot determine whether they constitute cause or response. The inclusion of this type of category of behavior allows for the admission of behavior that may not be interactive, or for which we can find no interaction. It is extremely hard for us to imagine noninteractive behavior—a point we return to later—however, empirically it would allow us to consider emitted behavior for which no interaction can be observed.

The present model reflects the fact that behaviors occur in interaction, and that an infant's behavior can be in response to or can initiate a maternal behavior. Even so, it does not quite reflect the type of interactive model we imagine. Rather than a static representation, we feel a flow diagram is more apt to express what we have in mind. The model in Figure 4 approaches this. In this flow chart we can see that a proportion of both infant and environment (maternal) behavior cannot be specified as to interaction both as initiated or response behavior. That is, we assume that all behavior is interactive, but we cannot observe the nature or direction of the interaction (MX or IX). What is of more concern is the circled portion of the flow model. Consider a specified infant initiation; this can lead to an unspecified maternal response (MR). This then terminates the series. Alternatively, the specified infant initiation can lead to a specified maternal response which then acts as a specified maternal initiation. This has two alternatives, leading either to an unspecified infant response (IR) and termination of the interaction, or to a specified infant response. This specified infant response in turn becomes a specified infant initiation which then has two alternatives. Thus the flow can continue to cycle as long as infant and maternal behavior remain specified (i.e., remains directed toward and effective on one another). As soon as this ceases, we are led into either a MR or IR and termination of the sequence. As expected, the response of either member of the pair also becomes the stimulus initiator for the other (response = initiator, in the flow diagram).

Using this type of flow model, we become aware of at least two difficulties in interactive models. The first involves point of entry into this flow. Our point of entry may mislead us into thinking that a particular behavior is an initiator of a series, when in fact it is only a part (in response) of a larger interaction. For example, consider the looking relationship between child and caregiver. Let us

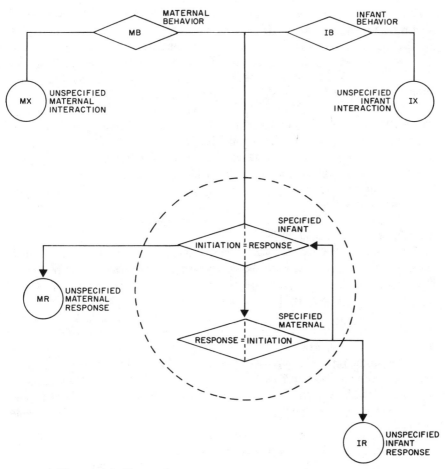

FIGURE 4. Flow model of interaction.

say that the series is mother vocalizes toward infant, infant looks at mother, mother looks at infant. If we enter at infant looks at mother, mother looks at infant, we might be misled into believing that it was the infant who initiated the sequence, when in fact it was the mother, through her vocalization, who initiated the interaction. Point of entry is a very important issue and must be dealt with in some manner.

The second issue concerns the nature of the sequences described by the model. Implicit in this model is that the last behavior of one member of a pair is responsible for the next behavior of the other member. This type of sequence is Markovian in nature, since it assumes that it is only the last event that affects the next. There is no reason to believe that this must be the case, and somehow it is necessary to introduce a composite or some set of the previous behavior into the flow model. We do not wish to imply that it is only the last event of one member that is solely responsible for the other member's behavior. Moreover, since both dyadic members are capable of mental operations, such as memory, we must consider that memory can be used in responding to past events which are not necessarily those of the *most* immediate past. This suggests that the Markovian model assumptions become less valuable the older the infant in the dyad.

Examples of the kind of interactional analysis presented by the flow model are relatively rare in the literature. In a series of articles (Lewis, 1972; Lewis & Wilson, 1972), we have touched upon this interaction analysis wherein behavior in the context of other behavior takes place. For example, in one group of very young infants, we found that 44% of the behaviors that occurred during 2 hours of observation were in interaction (Lewis, 1972). This varied both as a function of the infant-mother relation and the nature of the interaction. For example, smiling nearly always occurs during a specified interaction, while vocalization only on half the occasions.

The form of the models we have discussed has been extremely broad. Specifically, we have discussed the general category of behavior on the part of both elements. However, we have learned that specific behaviors do not all have the same consequences, and it is necessary to make use of this in any model.

In Figure 5 we have broken into the flow of interaction to illustrate this consideration. Observe that there are two infant behaviors, *IA* and *IB*, and two maternal behaviors, *MX* and *MY*. Infant behavior *A* elicits maternal behavior *MX* 20% of the time and *MY* 40% of the time; whereas infant behavior *B* elicits maternal behaviors *X* and *Y* each 40% of the time. Thus in this case one infant behavior is as likely to elicit the same amount of two different maternal behaviors (*B*), whereas another infant behavior is twice as likely to elicit one of the same

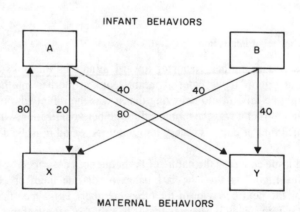

FIGURE 5. Section of flow model relating the infant and maternal initiation and respond interaction.

two maternal behaviors (A). To complicate the model further, while infant behavior A leads to 20% MX and 40% MY, both MX and MY are equally likely to lead to infant behavior A. If one wishes, it is possible to generate from these specific behavior patterns an almost unlimited interactive model.

This complexity is not conjecture, and examples are readily available. For example, an infant look can elicit more maternal vocalization than touch; however, both maternal touch and vocalization elicit equal infant vocalization. Still another consideration in any interactional model is individual differences. In some of our previous work, we have found extremely large individual variance in the complex interactions we have described. Interestingly, these individual differences do not appear when more simple models are used. Thus, for example, there are often no individual or group differences when we consider frequency of a response measure of the kind we have suggested in the simplest model (see Figure 1), while clear differences emerge when we consider a more interactional approach. These individual or group differences take many forms, and by looking at the complex interaction between different response probabilities (such as those described in Figure 5), we often see their nature. Thus, for example, we showed (Lewis & Wilson, 1972) that while there were no differences in the frequency of vocalization in the presence of their infants between mothers from a middle-class background and mothers from a working-class background, there was a difference in the interactional use of their vocalizations. Middle-class mothers were more likely to *respond* to their infants' vocalization with a vocalization than were working-class mothers (78 and 43%). Note that vocalization as a response per se (i.e., in the most general interaction) did not show these differences; rather they were present only in the specific interaction of vocalization–vocalization.

Social class is not the only dimension in which individual or group differences in interaction have been found. Differences as a function of sex have been found by Moss (1967) and Moss and Robson (1968) as early as 3 weeks, and we have found similar differences by 3 months. Moreover, in some of the more interactive analyses, we have found individual differences in the likelihood of the infant's response to the maternal behavior. Thus, for example, girl infants are more likely to respond to a maternal behavior with a vocalization than are boys, although again there is no total amount of vocalization difference between the sexes (Lewis, 1972). Some of the work of Korner and Thoman (1970) also supports early differences in the interaction between environment and infant, and Thoman, Leiderman, and Olson (1972) find these differences as a function of the sex and birth order.

Before turning to our attempts to study the interactive process, one further dimension needs some attention, for it undoubtedly plays a role in the interactive relationship. This dimension is best called context. We wish to convey our belief that much of what we have already spoken about varies as a function of the situation or context. Indeed, we have argued rather forcefully that context probably is instrumental in the development of meaning, and that this takes place through the differential interactive process varying as a function of context/meaning.

To quote from a recent paper by Lewis and Freedle (1972),

"Meaning may initially rely upon the perceptual isolation and recognition of featural or *relational differences* in the external world, such as noticing the direction of approach versus withdrawal, who does what to whom, which is a subject-object distinction, etc. One can deduce that the organism probably perceives such differences by noticing a significant shift in its behavioral patterns that occur in situations which distinguish, for example, whether the infant is or is not the object of the mother's vocalization [p. 5]."

In effect, what we are trying to say is that the nature of the interaction may undergo significant changes as a function of the context in which it occurs, and as such imparts differential meaning. The mother is not as likely to respond to a child's behavior with a rocking behavior when it is playing with a toy as when it is crying. Thus crying and the events that give rise to crying are more associated with rocking than is playing and the events that give rise to this behavior. Is this the basis for the meaning of comfort? On a more molar level the interactions between feeding in the kitchen and diaper changing and washing in the bathroom may give rise to the infant's ability to differentiate its physical world. This is a function of the differential nature of the interaction.

METHOD

To obtain interaction data each infant-caregiver was seen when the infant was 3 months old (± 1 week). In all, 55 infants' data have been analyzed and are presented here. Twenty-eight infants were female and twenty-seven male. In all cases the primary caregiver was the mother. Thus in this discussion we always refer to the infant-mother interaction. In general, there are relatively few data on the father's relationship with the young child—in fact we know of only two studies looking at this dyad within the infant's first year of life (Ban & Lewis, 1971; Rebelsky & Hanks, 1971). This lack represents a serious deficiency in the infancy literature which needs to be filled. We strongly suspect that the nature of the interaction differs not only as a function of the sex of the infant but of the sex of the parent as well. In the Ban and Lewis study (1971), it was found that, while both girl and boy infants touched their mothers twice as much as their fathers, they were as likely or more likely to look at their fathers as their mothers. Thus different modes of interaction at 1 year probably have their beginnings in the earliest interaction between parents and their children.

Unlike almost all studies of infants, these 55 children are distributed equally across the Hollingshead Social Class Scale so that they represent a true cross section of the population at large. This should allow us to generalize our findings further than if we had selected the professional middle-class sample that is used most of the time. We have shown several class differences in interaction (Lewis & Wilson, 1972), and should thus be alerted to the bias of a select sample. Contact with the mothers was made in a variety of ways: through the mother's initiative, through selection of a mother-infant by looking through birth announcements in the newspaper, and through a variety of groups which contained people of lower socioeconomic backgrounds—for example, churches in poorer neighborhoods.

The mother-infant dyad was seen in the home. No restriction on the everyday activity of the family was imposed. This meant that both mother and infant were able to move freely from situation to situation—for example, from feeding to changing—and from location to location—from room to room. This enabled us to collect data from a wide variety of situations and, as we have recently shown (Lewis & Freedle, 1972), much of the interactive quality of the dyad was dependent on the nature of the situation. In fact, we found consistent and stable patterns of responses which were dependent on the context in which they occurred.

The observer instructed the mother that she was interested in observing the infant during 2 hours of a normal routine. The mother was told to try to ignore the presence of the observer and to conduct herself in as normal a fashion as possible. For her part the observer stayed close to the infant and was able to observe the child while not being seen by it. The observer was always in the presence of the infant, so that if the mother left the infant the observer remained behind. Two observers were used in data collection, and observer reliabilities varied from .40 to .60, depending on the nature and occurrence of the behaviors observed. These also varied widely depending on the infant. Observation of children with low behavior output resulted in higher reliability scores than observation of infants who continually produced behaviors. Thus while more interactive dyads produced less interobserver reliability, the introduction of filming or television taping was thought to elicit less realistic behavior on the mother's part. The whole issue of behavior reliability, across observers as well as across observation, or its lack, has been raised before (Lewis & Lee-Painter, 1972) and awaits considerably more empirical study before we can decide what observational procedures produce what effects.

Two full hours of infant awake time were recorded. If the infant closed its eyes for more than 30 seconds, the observer stopped recording and waited to determine the "state" of the infant. When the infant was asleep or drowsy, no observations were made. This meant that for many infants several different observation periods were necessary in order to obtain two full hours of awake time.

Methods of Data Collection

Mother-infant interaction data were collected using a checklist sheet with a fixed time base. Each sheet represented 60 seconds, divided into six 10-second columns. Infant behaviors were listed in the upper portion of the sheet, while adult behaviors were in the lower portion. When any behavior that was not listed on the sheet occurred, the observers wrote it in. The infant behaviors scored were vocalization, extra movement (all gross physical movements such as limb movement or rolling of the body), fret/cry, feeding, quiet play (this consisted of the child watching a toy move, playing with his fingers, etc.), noise/nonvocalization (similar to extra movement except that noise accompanied the behavior—for example, kicking feet against the crib), smiling, and looking at mother. While these behaviors are not totally exclusive, the observers were in general able to differentiate between them.

Maternal behaviors consisted of touching, holding, vocalization, looking, smiling, playing with, caregiving (such as washing and changing of diapers), feeding, rocking, reading or watching television, and vocalization to others. These behaviors are not mutually exclusive categories. For example, if during a "hold" the mother also touched the child, both categories were scored. The categories of reading/television and vocalizing to others were used to indicate that the mother was involved in activities *not* directed toward the child.

Each 10 seconds the observer checked off the occurrence of both infant and mother behaviors, also recording, when possible, their interaction. Thus when an infant vocalized and this was followed by the mother vocalizing back to the infant, the observer checked a "1" on the infant vocalization line and a "2" on the mother's vocalization line. If both vocalized in the same 10-second period but the observer could not determine the nature of the interaction, both maternal and infant vocalization were scored in the same column. [A more explicit discussion of data collection is given in Lewis (1972) for the reader who wishes a more exact description of the technique.]

LEVELS OF DATA ANALYSIS

The various levels of analysis follow from our theoretical discussion of interactional models. The application of these various models to data analysis becomes more obvious as we proceed.

Frequency Distribution

In this analysis all that is obtained is the amount of infant or maternal behavior that has occurred. For example, how much vocalization, smiling, touching, or fret/cry has occurred. These types of data are those most reported in mother-infant studies, for they are the easiest to obtain and score. They are considered interactional, since they were obtained while the infant and mother were together, and thus are assumed to be causal. The manner of the causality and their true interactive quality, however, is highly limited. For example, while we might know that girl infants do more of something and boy infants less, and we know how much they each do, we still *cannot* answer the question what causes this behavior and what is the consequence of this behavior. Frequency data reflect for the most part the implicit assumptions of the simple element model in Figure 1.

Simultaneous Behavior

As we shall see, it is not always possible to describe the exact flow of an interaction, and as an approximation to this it is possible to record simultaneously occurring maternal and infant behaviors. By using a 10-second observational interval, it was possible to obtain this type of interaction data. One level of this type of analysis involves obtaining the number of 10-second periods in which there was simultaneous behavior for infant and mother. This provides some idea of the amount of general mother-infant interaction and, by looking at the ratio of total frequency of behavior to simultaneous behaviors, a general environment responsivity score can be obtained. Likewise, a similar analysis can be applied to each infant-maternal behavior, so that a matrix of maternal and infant behaviors can be obtained. These data are considerably more interactional in nature and are represented in the model shown in Figure 3. In this model behavior occurs in relationship to other behaviors. Although the flow of the interaction cannot be specified, the time-locked quality of the behavior insures a more interactional position.

There are some difficulties in this type of analysis. For example, the time period selected for such an analysis markedly affects the interaction results. Too short a time base and very few behaviors would be classified as interactive, while too long a time base would include all behaviors in one long interaction wherein specific behavior categories would become blurred. Ten seconds was selected, for it seemed to represent a time period that was a compromise between these two problems, as well as being a comfortable time period for an observer both to obtain and to record data. There are, however, two problems in this procedure which must be considered. First, of course, is the consideration that simultaneous behavior does not indicate any sort of causality (i.e., interaction). While this is true, the collection of a great deal of data should result in the low frequency of occurrence of random simultaneous events. The second problem involves the cutting of chains of events that would be longer than the 10-second base. The observers were instructed to cross the 10-second periods if they could observe chains that exceeded the 10 seconds. This they did. While long chains of events are not to be expected at this age (Lusk & Lewis, 1972), this procedure may raise some difficulties in this regard at older ages. In our discussion of sequential analysis we deal with this problem directly. However, the whole approach at older ages should be reconsidered, since the behavioral basis of observation should give way to more elaborate behavior categories.

Directional Interactive Analyses

In this type of analysis, we look only at directional interactive behavior. That is, by utilizing our coding system of "1" and "2," it is possible to determine not only that a maternal-infant behavior occurred in interaction, but also the flow of that interaction. For example, an infant fret is followed by a maternal look and vocalization, or a maternal vocalization is followed by an infant smile. This type of analysis is described by the models in Figure 4 and, if we try to examine the feedback from a particular two-chain behavior, that of the model in Figure 5. For example, we obtain all the two-chain infant initiations or infant responses. This tells us about the interaction and flow of two single behaviors (maternal and infant); however, we know little about what happens as a feedback to this set. For example, an infant vocalizes; this elicits a maternal vocalization. Now by adding the effects of maternal vocalization, we can describe this particular behavior chain cycle. It must be kept in mind that behaviors other than vocalization elicit maternal and infant vocalizations. This must be added (as in Figure 5) to the model. This problem becomes clearer when we apply it to our data.

While this type of interactional data is most useful in discussing the mother-infant dyad, it is also the most difficult type of data to obtain. The observation of flow or directional data is relatively infrequent, so that only a small proportion of the data can be so scored. Moreover, there is great variability in the amount of directional interaction of specific behaviors, which is probably a function of their differential occurrence rather than ease of observation.

Sequential Analyses

There is a variety of issues in looking at sequential analyses. Certainly, when we examine actor chains, we can look at *length of chain, initiator of chain, terminator of chain,* and finally *the nature of the chain.* The length of the actor chain involves the number of actor changes. Mother vocalize, infant vocalize; and mother vocalize, infant vocalize–infant smile are both two chain lengths. Lusk and Lewis (1972) found that this dimension increased with the age of the infant within the first year of life. Initiator and terminator of chain are also important chain parameters, and relatively little has been done with this dimension. Finally, the nature of the chain has received some attention, and we turn our attention to it.

One type of sequential analysis dealing with the nature of the chaining is to construct a matrix of transitional probabilities (Freedle & Lewis, 1971). In order to do this, it is necessary to assume that each 10-second period is a discrete trial. The same type of problems previously discussed can be raised about using 10 seconds as a time base for this analysis. Since the data were collected for two full hours, 720 successive 10-second periods exist for each dyad. Each infant behavior and maternal behavior, as well as each combination, can be categorized into a set of states. It is clear that with the present set of maternal, infant, and combination maternal-infant behavior the set of states is quite large and that this type of analysis is impossible. Thus it is necessary to take some smaller subset of behaviors, or else to combine behaviors into larger sets. For the sake of explication, we consider only the vocalization states of the infant and mother. These include: neither mother nor infant vocalize (0); infant vocalizes alone (1); mother vocalizes alone to some other person, not her infant (2i); mother and infant both vocalize (3); mother vocalizes to another person and the infant vocalizes (3i). We recognize that the consideration of just these six states grossly distorts the vocalization sequence of both members of the dyad since, as we will show, vocalization can be elicited by or be a response to behaviors other than vocalization. Even so, this example can provide the rationale and technique for larger more inclusive sets of data.

Given these states of infant, mother, and infant-mother interaction, and the 10-second time unit, we use the transitional matrix values as a measuring instrument in order to ascertain individual as well as state differences in infant vocalizations.

The transitional or conditional probabilities can be estimated as follows. Consider the following succession of states obtained from coding the successive 10-second periods for a particular mother-infant pair: 3, 0, 1, 3, 1, 2, ... Set up a matrix with six rows and six columns labeled 0, 1, 2i, 2, 3i, and 3, reading from the top down for the rows and similarly labeled reading from left to right across the columns. Using the above sequence, note that the first pair of states is 3, 0. Enter a tally in the rows labeled 3 and the column marked 0. The second and third states form the next pair of states, which is 0, 1. Enter another tally in the row labeled 0 and the column labeled 1. The next pair of states is 1, 3, so enter a tally in Row 1 and Column 3 and so on until all successive pairs of states have been tallied. When this is done, sum up the tallies for each row, and divide the frequency in each row cell by the sum for that row. The proportions that result in each row are then used as estimates for the conditional probabilities of the transition matrix. For the data under consideration here, there were 719 tallied entries for each mother-infant pair studied. This type of sequential analysis has been called Markovian, since it assumes that *only* what occurs on trial n can be used to estimate the occurrence of state on trial $n + 1$. To be more specific, this Markovian assumption asserts that it is irrelevant to the adequacy of our predictions if we also know the state that has occurred on any of the previous trials (10-second periods), such as trial $n - 1$, $n - 2$, and so on.

There are several ways such a modeling can be of value in the study of interaction. Observation of the transitional probability matrix (for each mother-infant pair) reveals the ways in which a current state of the mother-infant system influences the conditional probability of the next state. By examining the magnitude of the diagonal probabilities, one can obtain an immediate estimate of the degree to which the infant or mother or both will persist in a particular state.

RESULTS

In the following results we will move through each of the various data models and their analysis in order to demonstrate the various results that are possible, as well as to try to construct some picture of what in general transpires between a mother and her 12-week-old infant. Individual differences are presented to refine this normative description.

The frequency data for all infants are presented in Table 1. The frequency data are in mean numbers of 10-second periods in which an activity occurred. Since more than one activity could occur in a 10-second period, there is no reason to expect all the values to sum to 720 10-second periods (2 hours).

Observation of infant behavior indicated there were large individual differences. On the average infants vocalized in 162 10-second periods or 23% of the time, and varied from 4 to 62% of the time. There were only 74 10-second periods of fret/cry, or 10%—relatively little for this age group—with a range of 0 to 36%. Smiling occurred only 6% of the time, with individual differences varying from 0 to 22%. As expected, quiet play was the most engaged in activity accounting for, on the average, 31% of the time. Individual variability was again great—0 to 76% of the time.

In general, mother holding child was the highest activity (42%, ranging from 3 to 90% of the time). There were, on the average, 108 10-second periods during which the mother touched her child. This was 15% of the time and ranged from 3 to 44%. Vocalization was the next highest activity for mothers—34% of the time, with an individual range of 10 to 71%. Looking was engaged in 27% of the time, with a range of 2 to 92%. Smiling was engaged in only 6% of the time, with a range of 1 to 40% of the time. Finally, rocking was engaged in 2% of the time with a range of 0 to 17% of the time.

The frequency data indicate wide individual differences for both infant and maternal behaviors. Analysis of these individual differences indicates that some of the individual variability can be accounted for by the sex of the child (see Lewis, 1972). However, much of it is due to the nature of the interrelationship between these members of the dyad. As we shall see shortly, this type of analysis only taps one aspect of the relationship and does not allow us to really understand the dynamics of the interaction between the two participants.

The second column in Table 1 presents the overall interaction data, in this case the percent of the total frequency of behavior engaged in during an observable interaction. Note two points. First, this is not the number of simultaneous 10-second periods, but rather the percent of initiated or responded-to behavior.

TABLE 1   Mean Frequencies and Percent of Interactional Behavior of Infant and Maternal Behavior

	Total ($N = 55$), Mean	% of Total Interaction, Mean	% Interaction, Infant Initiation, Mean	% Interaction, Infant Response, Mean
Infant				
Vocalize	162.16	57.98	26.22	31.76
Movement	179.55	27.06	17.03	10.04
Fret/cry	73.61	56.13	51.46	4.67
Smile	42.26	109.89	15.68	94.28
Quiet play	226.67	3.56	2.04	1.52

	Total ($N = 55$), Mean	% of Total Interaction, Mean	% Interaction, Mother Initiation, Mean	% Interaction, Mother Response, Mean
Maternal				
Touch	108.16	23.36	15.93	9.32
Hold	304.81	2.93	1.37	1.00
Vocalize	248.05	51.71	20.41	31.31
Look	190.90	12.83	6.85	5.97
Smile	40.04	57.25	31.52	26.00
Play	70.01	29.85	24.04	5.81
Rock	13.24	13.69	3.21	10.83
Give toy/ pacifier	3.16	51.74	13.80	20.26
Vocalize/ other	109.13	2.75	1.42	1.34

Second, it is possible for the percentage to be larger than 100 since an infant behavior can evoke more than one maternal response. In this case each of the maternal behaviors is scored as a response to the same infant behavior, which is scored as having occurred in interaction more than once. The use of this procedure also suggests that some behaviors have a higher density of response around them (either initiating or responding to them). The density measure is a useful interaction construct since it implies, for example, that some infant behaviors cause the mother to respond with many *different* behaviors as well as to respond frequently. A baby's cry elicits frequent as well as many different behaviors. Likewise, an infant smile is elicited by many different simultaneous maternal behaviors.

Observation of infant behaviors indicates that smiling occurs most in interaction—over 109% with a range of 0 to 282%. The next highest interaction is vocalization, with a range from 0 to 120% and fret/cry with a range of 0 to 160%. Physical movement that can be associated with either upset or quiet play occurs only 4% of the time, with a range of 0 to 108%. As expected, since it is not an interactive behavior, quiet play has the least amount of interactive occurrence—1% on the average, with a range of 0 to 77% of the time.

Maternal behavior also indicates the most interaction for smiling behavior (57%, with a range of 0 to 131%). The next highest maternal interactive behavior is gives toy to infant (52%); however, since it occurs with such low frequency, it is difficult to know whether it is a true interactive behavior. Vocalization in interaction is equally as high as toy giving (52% on the average, with a range of 15 to 135%). Playing with the child is the next highest interactive behavior (on the average 30%, range of 0 to 100%). Touching, looking, and rocking follow as interactive behaviors, and except for touching occur in interaction less than 15% of the time. Interestingly, maternal looking is not a highly interactive behavior in this type of free field or unrestricted situation and probably reflects the mother's checking on the child's condition. Thus it is quite unlike what might be expected if the mother-infant were only seen in a face-to-face play situation (see Chapter 9).

These interaction data, regardless of the flow, offer additional information to that of the overall frequency analysis. It seems clear that whether or not a behavior occurs in an observed interaction may provide important information in understanding the dyadic phenomenon, as well as in understanding the effects on subsequent cognitive and social development in the infant. We often see reversals between how much in terms of frequency a behavior is produced and how much of it occurs in interaction. For example, one infant's mother may vocalize overall more than a second infant's; however, the second infant's mother vocalizes mostly in *interaction* with her infant. This same analysis between different measures can be applied to infant behavior as well. In our data we find, for example, that overall boy infants tend to vocalize more than girls; however, girls vocalize more in interaction. Perhaps a vocalization has a different meaning if it occurs spontaneously than if it occurs in response to another behavior. In the former case it could be related to movement, while in the latter to a communication system. Clearly, the communication function is of more value in studying language than is the movement function.

Table 1 also presents directional interaction data and lists percentages of the amount of time a particular behavior was a response to or initiator of the other member's behavior. As can be seen, the sum of initiation and response should add to the total interaction column. Infant vocalization presents some interesting results. First, infant interactive vocalization is somewhat more likely to be a response than an initiator of a maternal behavior, although vocalization is used in both fashions (sign test, $z = 1.08$). Of even more interest is that, for both initiation and response, it is in infants' use of vocalization as a response to maternal behavior that the largest individual difference appears; 0 to 83%, for example, as compared to 5 to 49% for initiation. As expected, infant fret/cry is primarily an initiator of behavior rather than a response (range of 0 to 160% for initiation, 0 to 33% for response; $z=7.00$; $p < .001$). However, smiling is predominantly a response (range of 0 to 58% for initiation, 0 to 380% for response; $z = 6.59$; $p < .001$). Movement and quiet play are both somewhat more initiators than responses ($z = 4.18$ and 1.28, respectively).

Individual differences are considerable. Consider, for example, vocalization. One infant uses vocalization 23% for initiation and 24% for response, while another uses vocalization 15% for initiation and 82% for response. These types of individual differences can be demonstrated for each of the infant behaviors.

Maternal interaction patterns indicate that maternal touch ($z = 3.57$; $p < .001$) and play ($z = 5.25$; $p < .001$) are initiations more than responses to infant behavior, while maternal vocalization ($z = 4.40$; $p < .001$) and rocking ($z = 2.91$; $p < .01$) are maternal responses to infant initiations. Maternal look, hold, smile, give toy, and vocalization to others were used equally as often as initiators as responses.

Like the infant behaviors several maternal behaviors also show interesting individual differences in the direction of interactions. For some infants maternal smiling behavior is more an initiation than a response, while for others the reverse is true. This same type of individual difference can be demonstrated for each of the maternal behaviors.

It was of interest to determine whether, for infants and mothers, the uses of a particular behavior were correlated; for example, whether or not high vocalization responders were also high vocalization initiators. For infant behaviors vocalization was significantly related. This means that infants who vocalized a great deal in response to a maternal behavior were also those infants who used vocalization as an initiation ($\rho = .36$; $p < .01$). For maternal behaviors this held for touch ($\rho = .64$; $p < .001$) and for play ($\rho = .35$; $p < .01$). Thus mothers who touched a great deal in response to their infants' behaviors were also those who touched a great deal as an initiation.

The direction of interaction data has some logical basis in that it seems reasonable to assume that an infant fret/cry initiates maternal behavior rather than responds to it. The results for the other behaviors, both maternal and infant, are not that clear. Maternal rocking can be either an initiator or a response, as can play with infant; however, the former is in general used as a response, and the latter generally as an initiator. This type of analysis gives us information as to the direction of the interaction between infant and mother. Moreover, these interactional results do not always agree with the frequency data. For example, while one infant is vocalized to more than another, the mother of the first infant might initiate vocalization to her child more than the second. However, while there are no individual differences in frequency of both infants' vocalizations, one is more likely to respond to maternal behavior with a vocalization than the other. The results are confusing to follow, but the level of complexity needs to be considered. What does it mean that the overall behavior is greater for one than for another while the amount of interaction is not? If we can demonstrate differential consequences, it may be possible, for example, for us to argue that behavior not in interaction has relatively less effect than behavior in interaction. Pure vocalization independent of its directional interaction may have less meaning than when it occurs in interaction. Recall that it is our belief that the interaction is the context in which behaviors gain meaning. Likewise, meaning is acquired by selective behaviors in a context. It therefore follows that interactional behavior should produce differential results. Also, consider how the behavior is used. What is the difference between one child who uses vocalization as a response more than as an initiator and another who uses vocalization more as an initiator?

The final type of analysis is outlined in Figure 5 and has been suggested in some of the previous analyses. This analysis looks at the relationship of each infant behavior as a response or initiator to *each* maternal behavior. Likewise, each maternal behavior is viewed as an initiator or response to each infant behavior. In this way it is hoped that the detailed infant-mother behavior matrix can be examined. Table 2 presents three infant behaviors—vocalization, fret/cry, and smiling—in terms of their occurrence (both as an initiator and as a response) with maternal behaviors. For example, we can see that infant vocalization is responded to by the following maternal behaviors: touch, 1% of the time; vocalize, 18%; look, 2%; smile, 3%; play, 1%; and vocalize to other, 1%. Likewise, infant vocalization is a response to a mother initiator for: touch, 4%; hold, 2%; vocalization, 15%; look and smile, 3%; play, 4%; and vocalize to others, 1%. This is schematized at the top of Figure 6. This figure shows in percentage the amount of infant vocalization in relationship to six different maternal behaviors. For all infants and mothers, the percentage of interaction between maternal behaviors and infant vocalization (either as response or initiator) reveals that the vocalization-vocalization bond is the strongest, accounting for 18 and 15% of all directed infant and maternal vocalizations. Maternal touch and play were the next most effective in eliciting infant vocalization, while infant smile was the most effective in eliciting a maternal vocalization.

The bottom of Figure 6 presents the data for two subject pairs and shows how variable individual differences in the dyadic relationship can be. The data are the number of 10-second periods that a particular interaction occurred. Observe that for infant A almost all of its directed vocalization occurred in vocalization-vocalization interaction, whereas only 41% of infant B's directed vocalizations occurred in vocalization-vocalization interaction. Infant B was likely to vocalize

TABLE 2 Matrix of Infant Behaviors and Their Relationship to Maternal Behaviors

	Vocalize, Total[a]		Fret/cry, Total[a]		Smile, Total[a]	
	$\overline{X}$	%	$\overline{X}$	%	$\overline{X}$	%
Maternal Response	*Infant Initiates*					
Touch	1.53	0.009	4.69	0.064	0.33	0.008
Hold	0.45	0.003	2.07	0.028	0.04	0.001
Vocalize	29.31	0.181	20.93	0.284	3.09	0.073
Look	3.20	0.020	3.33	0.045	0.93	0.022
Smile	4.09	0.025	0.51	0.007	0.38	0.009
Play	0.98	0.006	1.89	0.026	0.18	0.004
Change	0.22	0.001	0.04	0.001	0.00	0.000
Feed	0.24	0.001	0.91	0.012	0.02	0.001
Rock	0.07	0.0004	1.25	0.017	0.00	0.000
Give toy/ pacifier	0.04	0.0002	0.67	0.009	0.02	0.001
Vocalize/ other	0.98	0.006	0.17	0.002	0.09	0.002
Maternal Initiation	*Infant Responds*					
Touch	5.98	0.037	1.09	0.015	0.31	0.007
Hold	3.35	0.021	0.15	0.002	0.11	0.003
Vocalize	24.11	0.148	1.40	0.019	1.64	0.040
Look	5.25	0.032	0.07	0.001	0.27	0.006
Smile	5.05	0.031	0.00	0.000	0.04	0.001
Play	6.89	0.042	0.11	0.001	0.71	0.017
Change	0.36	0.002	0.15	0.002	0.00	0.000
Feed	0.60	0.004	0.27	0.004	0.11	0.003
Rock	0.18	0.001	0.00	0.000	0.04	0.001
Give toy/ pacifier	0.20	0.0004	0.00	0.000	0.11	0.003
Vocalize/ other	0.78	0.005	0.04	.001	0.07	0.002

[a]$\overline{X}$ = Mean number of 10-second periods; % = percentage of total frequency of behavior (vocalize, fret/cry, smile).

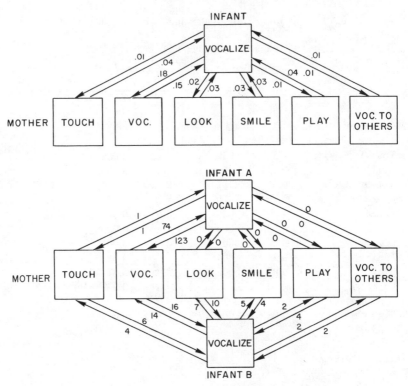

FIGURE 6. Top figure represents the mean percent of infant vocalization as it acts as an elicitor or response to a variety of maternal behaviors. Bottom figure represents the same data for two subjects.

to and be responded to by a variety of maternal behaviors, which was not the case for infant A. However, not only does the distribution of interactive vocalization differ between these two children. Examination of infant A and its mother indicates that in total frequency the infant vocalized in 240 and its mother in 485 10-second periods. Infant B vocalized in only 174 and its mother in 193 10-second periods. Thus they differ in frequency of vocalization as well as in distribution.

The dyadic pattern between these two infants is clearly different. If we wish to hypothesize that language is facilitated by a vocalization-vocalization relationship, then infant A appears to have an advantage. Infant A also has an advantage if we hypothesize that sharpened behavior, that is, very specific or discrete behavior, facilitates development. Here again only the vocalization-vocalization relationship (rather than others) appears. However, if variety of response-elicitation is indicative of development facilitation, then infant B has an advantage.

Obviously, the results await the children's ability to speak a formal language. Preliminary results (Lewis & Freedle, 1972) do indicate that some of the 3-month infant-mother interaction data are related to formal linguistic abilities in the 2-year-old.

Table 3 lists the comparable maternal data which are presented without comment so that one can obtain an idea of the relationship from the maternal point of view.

Having both pieces of the interaction data now allow us to construct a more flow type of analysis. When we add maternal and infant behaviors, we begin to consider the remainder of the various connections. For example, we can look at the maternal vocalization and other infant behaviors. In this manner, for example, we can determine the relationship of the infant's vocalization to other maternal behaviors and the influence of maternal vocalization on other infant behaviors. Finally, we can consider all the other infant behaviors as related to all the other maternal behaviors. In this way we complete the interactive circle. Let us look at an example in order to see how this works. To simplify we use only two infant behaviors, vocalization and smile, and two maternal behaviors, vocalization and touch.

Figure 7 presents the mean number of 10-second periods for all infants in which these directed interactions occurred. By using Tables 2 and 3 we can construct this flow for all behaviors. Observe that an infant vocalization is more likely to produce a maternal vocalization than a maternal touch. Likewise, a maternal vocalization is more likely to produce an infant vocalization than an infant smile. For example, an infant vocalization can produce ♦ a maternal touch which can produce ♦ an infant smile which in turn can produce a maternal vocalization ♦ and then an infant vocalization. However, the mean data suggest that an infant vocalization is more likely to produce a maternal vocalization. Thus there is little likelihood at this age for the flow to move to other behaviors. If, however, we start with an infant smile, we predict that it will lead first to maternal vocalization rather than touch, and then to infant vocalization. In like fashion it is possible to examine all the various patterns and predict from them the likelihood of sequential events. While we have chosen to use other analyses to look at our sequential data, a model developed in this fashion might be more predictive. It is important to note that this kind of model should be most influenced by the context in which it occurs. Observation of individual differences reveals that at this level there are highly individualistic patterns across dyads. This can be seen in the sequential analysis we present next.

The previous discussion has made us consider sequential analysis, and the remainder of this section is devoted to this issue. As we stated earlier in discussing Markovian sequential analyses, a transitional probability matrix can be generated for each dyadic pair for any set of behaviors. For the sake of exposition, we talk only about the vocalization data and the six states: no infant

TABLE 3 Matrix of Maternal Behaviors and Their Relationship to Infant Behaviors

	Touch, Total[a]		Vocalize, Total[a]		Look, Total[a]		Smile, Total[a]		Play, Total[a]		Rock, Total[a]	
	$\overline{X}$	%	$\overline{X}$	%	$\overline{X}$	%	$\overline{X}$	%	$\overline{X}$	%	$\overline{X}$	%
Infant Response					*Mother Initiates*							
Vocalize	5.98	0.056	24.11	0.097	5.25	0.028	5.05	0.126	6.89	0.098	0.18	0.014
Movement	4.25	0.039	7.95	0.032	1.38	0.007	1.36	0.034	2.64	0.038	0.05	0.004
Fret/cry	1.09	0.010	1.40	0.006	0.07	0.0003	0.00	0.000	0.11	0.002	0.00	0.000
Play	5.24	0.048	13.62	0.055	4.96	0.026	6.05	0.151	6.62	0.095	0.11	0.008
Smile	0.31	0.003	1.64	0.066	0.27	0.001	0.04	0.001	0.71	0.010	0.04	0.003
Infant Initiation					*Mother Responds*							
Vocalize	1.53	0.016	29.31	0.118	3.20	0.017	4.09	0.102	0.98	0.014	0.07	0.005
Movement	3.25	0.034	19.05	0.076	3.16	0.017	2.95	0.074	0.76	0.011	0.25	0.019
Fret/cry	4.69	0.049	20.93	0.084	3.33	0.017	0.51	0.013	1.89	0.027	1.25	0.094
Play	0.29	0.003	3.29	0.013	0.20	0.001	2.49	0.062	0.24	0.003	0.02	0.002
Smile	0.33	0.003	3.09	0.012	0.93	0.005	0.38	0.009	0.18	0.003	0.00	0.000

[a] $\overline{X}$ = Mean number of 10-second periods; % = percentage of total frequency of behaviors (touch, vocalize, look, smile, play, rock).

INFANT

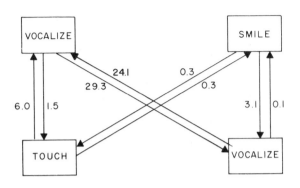

MOTHER

FIGURE 7. A flow model for studying sequential behavior.

or maternal vocalization (0); infant vocalize alone (1); mother vocalize alone to infant (2); mother vocalize to another (2i); infant and mother both vocalize (3); and infant vocalize, mother vocalize to another (3i). The transitional probability matrix for two subjects is presented in Tables 4 and 5.

In general, the largest conditional probabilities in each row are along the diagonal of the matrix. This indicates that if a vocalization state tends to persist in State 1, one can obtain an estimate of the degree to which the mother and infant together will persist in State 3, and so on.

For the first infant the largest conditional probability in each row is generally along the main diagonal of the matrix (see Table 4). This indicates that state tends to persist over time—that is, this subject tends to have many long runs of the same state. The second infant's data indicate, however, that most states

TABLE 4   The Markov Transition Matrix and Initial Probability Vector for Six Vocalization States

		State on Trial n					
		0	1	2i	2	3i	3
	0	.42	.09	.13	.22	.02	.12
	1	.22	.46	.00	.08	.02	.22
State	2i	.18	.04	.51	.12	.05	.10
on	2	.05	.01	.05	.71	.01	.17
Trial	3i	.27	.13	.20	.07	.07	.26
$n-1$	3	.05	.06	.01	.33	.02	.53

TABLE 5   The Markov Transition Matrix and Initial Probability Vector for Six Vocalization States

		State on Trial n					
		0	1	2i	2	3i	3
	0	.77	.05	.07	.08	.01	.02
	1	.71	.12	.07	.05	.00	.05
State	2i	.43	.05	.42	.06	.03	.01
on	2	.57	.06	.01	.28	.01	.07
Trial	3i	.56	.11	.11	.11	.00	.11
$n-1$	3	.41	.11	.07	.15	.00	.26

usually revert back to the State-0 category. This reflects the differences between these two infants in the amount of vocalization both they and their mothers exhibit.

Consider other individual differences. Let us take each row of the transition matrix that applies to the first infant and compare it with the entries for the same row in the matrix for the second infant. For the first infant we see that if the previous state of the vocalization system was State 0 the state of the system in the next time interval will again be State 0 (probability .42). The next most frequent state following State 0 is State 2 which occurs with probability .22. For the second infant there is again a large probability that if the vocalization system was in State 0 in the previous time interval it will persist in this state for the next time interval (probability .77). The next most frequent state is State 2; however, this occurs with a very low probability of .08. Hence for this first row both the first and second infant transition matrices are similar in the sense that the most probable event following State 0 is the persistence of the same State 0, while the second most probable event following State 0 is State 2. The first and second transition matrices differ, though, in the magnitude of these entries.

For the first infant the most likely state following State 1 is a persistence of the same state (probability .46); the second most likely event following State 1 is a tie between moving to State 0 and moving to State 3. The second infant shows a different pattern. The most likely event following State 1 is State 0 (probability .71), and the second most likely event following State 1 is to persist in that state (probability .12). One can continue in this way comparing the similarities and differences that occur for each subsequent row.

Special attention should be drawn to one additional pattern that emerges in comparing the remaining rows. For the first infant (Rows 2 and 3), we note that the most likely outcome following State 2 is a persistence of this state, while the second most likely outcome is the occurrence of State 3. For Row 3 the most likely outcome is a persistence of the same State 3, and next most often is a return to State 2. What this indicates is that a frequent change of vocalization events for this infant and its mother is for them to vocalize together, followed by mother vocalizing alone, followed by infant vocalizing along with mother, and so on. The table allows us to identify what can be called a frequent "subcycle" of two events (State 2 and State 3) which tend to alternate with each other. A somewhat different subcycle emerges when we examine the second infant and its mother for States 2 and 3. This same pattern holds for the second infant only if we ignore the largest entries in Rows 2 and 3 and observe the second and third largest. This suggests that for the first infant and mother this subcycle tends not to be interrupted, while for the second it tends to be interrupted by State 0.

It is clear that this type of analysis allows us to investigate the sequential aspects of the interaction and approximates the kind of flow analysis we have stressed. Lewis and Freedle (1972) have recently used this type of analysis to investigate sex and social class differences in the vocalization interaction of 12-week-olds. The procedure appears to offer an excellent method for investigating the flow of interaction.

DISCUSSION

For the most part the bulk of this discussion has been concerned with the various types of measurement that are possible in discussing the dyadic relationship between child and environment. As is most apparent, the number and type of analyses are almost unlimited. Moreover, it is clear that they do not all result in similar results. Quite to the contrary, the data suggest that the type of results obtained are highly specific to the type of measurement. Thus frequency of occurrence and directed interaction can give quite contrary results. Thus there may be no difference in frequency, but significant difference in directed interaction [see Lewis & Wilson (1972) for just such differences as a function of social class].

Moreover, whether the behavior is an initiator or a response also may lead to different conclusions and results, for example, in sex differences, which we have already reported (Lewis, 1972).

The data are highly complex. It is clear that in order to understand individual differences and their consequences it is necessary to consider the total pattern of behavior, taking into account each of the analyses. Frequency of occurrence, interaction direction density, and sequence must all be incorporated for us to understand truly the dynamics of the interaction. Unfortunately, this may be an extremely complex task. The consequence of ignoring this may be in our using just one (possibly more) measurement and making our conclusions from this. In this regard it is important to recall that we have suggested that the type of measurement used implicitly reflects the type of model the investigator has developed about the interaction itself.

This is not to imply that one measure is better than another. Quite to the contrary. It is basic to our discussion that each type of measurement *in concert* is needed to understand fully the dyadic relationship.

We have argued for an interactionalist approach. It is our belief that the analysis of elements rather than their interaction is a mistake. Elements never exist outside the interaction. For example, consider an element, condition, of the infant. At any given time (t) the infant is in interaction with his environment. The condition of a subject at time t equals the biology of the subject at time t and the environment at time t.

$$C_t = f(B_t, E_t)$$

However, B_t is always a function of B_{t-1} and E_{t-1}, so that $B_t = f(B_{t-1}, E_{t-1})$. Thus there is a regression with the limit at the time of conception. We choose conception rather than birth, since it is obvious that gestation itself is an interaction between fetus and environment. Our interactive analysis of regression suggests a limit, namely, genotypic structure. It must be remembered, however, that even basic genetic material is placed in an environment which is quite capable of affecting and altering that structure. Young, Groy, and Phoenix's (1964) work in altering the sex of monkeys is an example of how environment—in this case hormonal—can affect genetic structure.

Recently, Van den Daele (1972) has suggested that even within the genetic influence on the unfolding of structure it is necessary to introduce an uncertain principle or "indeterminance" variance. One might argue that genetically determined event A can occur only if B has preceded it, and so on. Thus even within the genetic unfolding there is an interaction between the predetermined event and its environment.

If this type of theorizing has any validity, it should argue against observing elements without trying to determine the environment in which they occur. Such a search reminds me of those who search for a pure response (behavioral or physiological) unaffected by the environment. What does this mean for the theme of this volume? It suggests that it is as mistaken to observe only the effects of the infant on the caregiver as it is to study only the effects of the caregiver. Any study—regardless of direction—that fails to consider the dyadic relationship cannot accurately describe the elements. Once we consider the dyad we must at once conclude that *both* actors actively and significantly influence each other.

In all the models we have presented, there have been "elements," however interrelated. This reflects the limits of our ability to theorize. What we need to develop are models dealing with interaction—perhaps like sequential analysis (Lewis & Freedle, 1972)—or with the interaction independent of the elements. This is by no means an easy task. Although many investigators have attempted to do this [for example, see Riegel's (1973) attempt to deal with language development by relational constructs], the elements rather than the relationship constantly reappear. This relational position not only requires that we deal with elements in interaction but also requires that we not consider the static quality of these interactions. Rather, it is necessary to study their flow with time. While proponents of static theories argue that their models can approximate flow through a series of still photographs, it is not at all obvious that such a technique is valid and does not seriously distort that which is being studied. Thus relationship and flow[3] must somehow find a way into our models independent of the elements. Exactly how this might be done is not at all clear. It may be necessary to consider a more metaphysical model, a circle in which there are neither elements nor beginnings/ends.

References

Ban, P., & Lewis, M. Mothers and fathers, girls and boys: Attachment behavior in the one-year-old. Paper presented at the meeting of the Eastern Psychological Association, New York, April 1971.

Freedle, R., & Lewis, M. Application of Markov processes to vocalization states. Paper presented at the meeting of the Psychometric Society, Princeton, March 1972.

Korner, A. F., & Thoman, E. B. Visual alterness in neonates as evoked by maternal care. *Journal of Experimental Child Psychology*, 1970, **10**, 67–78.

Lewis, M. State as an infant-environment interaction: An analysis of mother-infant behavior as a function of sex. *Merrill-Palmer Quarterly*, 1972, **18**, 95–121.

Lewis, M., & Freedle, R. Mother-infant dyad: The cradle of meaning. In P. Pliner, L. Krames, & T. Alloway (Eds.), *Communication and affect: Language and thought.* New York: Academic Press, in press, 1973.

Lewis, M., & Lee-Painter, S. An infant's interaction with its social world: The origin of meaning. Paper presented at the meeting of the Canadian Psychological Association, Symposium on Parent-Child Observation Studies and Their Problems, Montreal, June 1972.

Lewis, M., & Wilson, C. D. Infant development in lower class American families. *Human Development*, 1972, **15**(2), 112–127.

Moss, H. A. Sex, age and state as determinants of mother-infant interaction. *Merrill-Palmer Quarterly*, 1967, **13**, 19–36.

Moss, H. A., & Robson, K. S. Maternal influences in early social visual behavior. *Child Development*, 1968, **39**, 401–408.

Rebelsky, F., & Hanks, C. Fathers' verbal interaction with infants in the first three months of life. *Child Development*, 1971, **42**, 63–68.

Riegel, K. F. Language as labor: Semantic activities as the basis for language

---

[3] It is important to note that time flow implies a linear unidirection. This linear model has recently been questioned by Sachs (1972), and he suggests that we need to reevaluate our conception of time. The linear unidirection model, a product of our Western Newtonian viewpoint, may be an inadequate model.

development. In K. F. Riegel (Ed.), *Structure, transformation, interaction: Developmental and historical aspects.* Basel: Karger, 1973, in press.

Thoman, E. B., Leiderman, P. H., & Olson, J. P. Neonate-mother interaction during breast-feeding. *Developmental Psychology*, 1972, **6**(1), 110–118.

Van den Daele, L. D. Natal influences and twin differences. *Journal of Genetic Psychology*, 1973, in press.

CHAPTER 3

The Origins of Reciprocity: The Early Mother-Infant Interaction [1]

T. BERRY BRAZELTON
Harvard Medical School

BARBARA KOSLOWSKI
Harvard University

MARY MAIN
Johns Hopkins University

ETHOLOGICAL DESCRIPTION OF EARLY MOTHER-INFANT INTERACTION

Since the early mother-infant relationship forms the base for the child's future psychological growth, it seems fitting to analyze some of the earliest observable interactions between mothers and infants that make up this relationship. We attempted to analyze the behavior of the members of five "normal" mother-infant pairs from 2 to 20 weeks in a behavioral analysis of a short period of intense interaction between them.

In pediatric practice I had long been impressed with the rhythmic, cyclic quality of mother-infant interactional behavior. There appeared to be a kind of attention, nonattention, behavioral cycle—a rhythmic attention-withdrawal pattern present in differing degrees in each participant. Usually, the mother's pattern was synchronized with that of the baby. Occasionally, however, initial synchrony ended in dyssynchrony after a difficult or tense interaction.

We hoped on the basis of detailed film studies to be able to describe several of the significant behavioral components of mother-infant interaction, the patterns of behavior used by each member of the dyad, and the rhythms and cycles that underlie these patterns. The unit of choice became a cycle of looking and nonlooking, or attention and nonattention.

[1] This research was conducted at the Center for Cognitive Studies, Harvard University, and was supported by NIMH Grant No. 12623-02-03-04-05.

49

Method

Five white, middle-class mothers and their normal full-term infants from my Cambridge pediatric practice were seen weekly at the Harvard Center for Cognitive Studies. The mothers volunteered for the study just prior to their infants' births, and we ascertained that their pregnancies and deliveries were entirely normal. Apgars of the babies at delivery were all above 8-9-9, and my neonatal behavioral evaluation (Brazelton, 1972) and Prechtl's neurological examination (1964) were optimal in each case.

Before the first session each of the mothers was contacted by one of the experimenters who told her, in as much detail as possible, what we would be doing, what equipment we would be using, and what was expected of her—that is, each mother was told that we wanted to film and analyze the normal development of "interaction behavior" as it develops between a mother and her infant during the first 4 months of life. She was told that we were not judging her or her infant's behavior but wanted to see the development of his ability to respond to her. The initial contact with the mother was important in answering her questions and in establishing rapport with the subject before our first session. Each week she was given an opportunity to voice her concerns and to be reassured by the same person as to the child's development and her own role in mothering him. These prefilming sessions seemed very important in relieving some of the natural tension a mother feels about having her interaction with a child observed so intensively.

The study began with a home visit to each subject's house between the first and fourth week of the baby's life. These sessions were less controlled than the laboratory sessions that followed, but were important in becoming acquainted with the family. By the time each baby was 4 weeks old, his mother brought him to our laboratory once a week, at the same time each week.

One baby was not present for three consecutive weeks (11 to 13) because of a trip out of the country. Each of the other subjects missed from 1 to 3 weeks because of illness. None was absent for more than 3 weeks. For each subject we have a minimum of 13 films in the period of 4 to 20 weeks. Each session involved a standardized procedure. It began informally in the nursery at the Center, where mother and child took off their outer clothes and relaxed. The mother talked with the researchers before going to the laboratory. The infant was fed and diapers were changed when necessary. In the laboratory the mother placed her baby (with assistance from a researcher) in a custom-built, adjustable, reclining seat with a head rest for support designed by Colwyn Trevarthan. The baby reclines at a 30° angle, and the seat permits the limbs to move freely and the head to turn. The mother was seated in front of him, her face at a distance of about 18 in. She was free to lean forward, to touch him, or to hold onto him, as he sat securely strapped in his reclining chair. All efforts were made to relieve any distress the baby might feel, and he could be handled or rocked by his mother when his interest or cooperation lagged. (This experimental situation was likened to that at home when a baby is placed in the commonly used plastic form chair for infants, and the mother sits in front of him.)

Two mirrors were located in strategic positions around the mother and child, so that an image of each was registered simultaneously on the film. However, neither mother nor child was able to see either of the mirrors. A camera was concealed behind curtains in a corner of the room, out of sight. The room was white, free of patterns, distracting objects, or people. The actual filming was done in two segments. The first was of the mother and child; the second was of the child with an object, a small 3½ in. fuzzy monkey. Each segment was filmed for at least 5 minutes, and segments were separated by a 5-minute interval.[2]

In the segments of film with the baby and his mother, the camera began shooting after everyone had apparently become settled and was at ease. We filmed sequences when the infant was thought to be intently looking at the person opposite him. The camera then ran continuously for 90 seconds unless the baby became upset or appeared to lose interest in the person opposite him. The filming of the baby with the object began when object, suspended on a string, was brought toward him, from a distance, along his midline. The camera ran continuously as the object was brought into the baby's "reach space" (12 in. from his face), dangled there for a minute, and then slowly taken away along his midline.

Analysis of the filmed sequences resulted in two kinds of system analyses. (1) The object-infant sequence is being analyzed by Colwyn Trevarthan and Martin Richards, and their more detailed analysis will be presented elsewhere. Our grosser observations of the baby's interaction with objects are based on the comments we made as we became struck by the two very different systems we felt we were observing from the first 3 weeks of age. The senior author assumes responsibility for the present interpretations of the object-infant behavior. (2) One minute of intense interaction between mother and infant was selected for analysis of mother-infant interaction behavior. The cameraman was instructed to take the first sequence in which both mother and infant were observed to be relaxed and clearly attending to each other. When the minute was disrupted by an event that necessitated picking the infant up, or feeding him, we discontinued the filming and resumed it again after he was back in his chair. The initial segment of the next interaction was then added to the interrupted portion of the previous film to make a total of 60 seconds interaction for analysis. In effect, each minute was a sample of their interaction *while it was going well.*

---

[2] We had attempted to monitor vocalization in mother and infant by microphone attachments which transmitted impulses to flashing lights which were recorded on the film and could be analyzed. This method proved to be unreliable since (1) it recorded all noise from the environment, as well as the baby's movements and rustling of clothes, and (2) the lights and microphone distracted mother and infant.

TABLE 1 Coded Variables

Mother			Infant		
I	(1)	Vocalizing	I	(1)	Vocalizing
II	(2)	Smiling	II	(2)	Smiling
	(2A)	Laughing		(2A)	Laughing
III	(3)	Intent looking (LI)	III	(3)	Intent looking (LI)
	(4)	Dull looking (LD)		(4)	Dull looking (LD)
	(5)	Looking away (LA)		(5)	Looking away (LA)
				(6)	Eyes closed
IV	(6)	Reaching			
	(7)	Touching	IV	(7)	Reaching
	(8)	Holding		(8)	Touching
	(9)	Adjusting			
			V	(9)	Fussy, squirming
V	(10)	Moving into line of vision		(10)	Body cycling
	(11)	Bobbing and nodding		(11)	Jerky, excited movements
	(12)	Leaning forward		(12)	Leaning forward
	(13)	Leaning back		(13)	Leaning back
VI	(14)	Facial gestures	VI	(14)	Crying
	(15)	Hand gestures		(15)	Yawning
	(16)	Kiss		(16)	Spitting up
	(17)	Wiping face		(17)	Bowel movement
	(18)	Miscellaneous		(18)	Tonguing
				(19)	Miscellaneous

We analyzed our films according to several systems. We coded the occurrence of 18 behaviors for the mother and 19 for the infant (see Table 1). These behaviors were ones that we could define and code with an interscorer reliability of 85%. We prepared a descriptive manual for initial training and for reliability. Coding was done from stop-frame analysis of film by two observers simultaneously, and agreement was reached as we coded. Samples of film were analyzed by a third observer for interscorer reliability from time to time. Each behavior was clear-cut, and its onset and offset were unexpectedly easy to determine. Each frame was analyzed with a stop-frame projector, and behaviors were recorded on a running record sheet which allowed simultaneous recording of all the behavior for both parties. The record noted onset, continuation, and termination of each behavior. Mother and baby behaviors were recorded side by side on the same running record, which permitted visual comparisons of clusters of behavior.

Although this detailed analysis seemed complicated, we felt that this record of 37 coded variables did not adequately describe the interaction. For example, the quality and tempo of each behavior, the spatial relationships within the dyad, the descriptive form (contact was patting, stroking, or shaking), and the affective significance of the behavior within the incident could not be revisualized by this kind of analysis. Hence, in order to understand individual differences in dyads, as well as to make ethological descriptions of significant findings, it was also necessary to dictate a narrative account of the interactions.

OBSERVATIONS

Description of Behavior with Object

A furry monkey 3½ in. high was suspended by a wire and brought slowly along the midline into the baby's reach space (12 in. away from his face). The object was left there for a minute and then gradually moved out and away. This procedure was repeated each week while he sat in his infant chair, and was an attempt to contrast his responsive behavior to an object with that when his mother was seated in front of him. Marked differences in attention span, state behavior, buildup of excitement, and disruption of attention were noted as early as 3 weeks of age (cf. Bower, 1966). We felt that we could look at any segment of the infant's body and detect whether he was watching an object or interacting with his mother—so different was his attention, vocalizing, smiling, and motor behavior with the inanimate stimulus as opposed to the mother.

The infant stared fixedly at the object with wide eyes, fixating on it for as much as 2 minutes, by 6 weeks, without disruption of gaze or of attention. In this period, his face was fixed, the muscles of his face tense in a serious set, with eyes staring and mouth and lips protruding toward the object. This static, fixed look of attention was interspersed with little jerks of facial muscles. His tongue jerked out toward the object and then withdrew rapidly. Occasional short bursts of vocalizing toward the object occurred. During these long periods of attention, the eyes blinked occasionally in single, isolated blinks. The body was set in a tense, immobilized sitting position, with the object at his midline. When the object was moved to one side or the other, the infant tended to shift his body appropriately, so it was kept at his midline. His shoulders hunched as if he were about to "pounce." [This was observed as early as 4 weeks of age, long before a reach could be achieved, utilizing this antigravity posturing of the shoulders (Bruner, 1972).] Extremities were fixed, flexed at elbow and knee, and fingers and toes were aimed toward the object. Hands were semiflexed or tightly flexed, but fingers and toes repeatedly jerked out to point at the object. Jerky swipes of an arm or leg in the direction of the object occurred from time to time as the period of intense attention was maintained (White, 1964). In this period, his attention seemed "hooked" on the object, and all his motor behavior alternated between the long, fixed periods of tense absorption and short bursts of jerky, excited movement in the direction of the object. He seemed to hold down any interfering behavior which might break into this prolonged state of attention.

As the object was gradually brought into reach space, his entire state of attention and behavior changed. His eyes softened and lidded briefly but continued to scan it with the same prolonged attention. His mouth opened as if in anticipation of mouthing it. The tongue came out toward it and occasionally remained out for a period before it was withdrawn. His neck arched forward as his head strained toward the object. His shoulders were hunched, and his mouth protruded. Swipes of the arms and extensions of the legs at the knee increased in number. Hands alternately fisted and opened in jerky movements toward the object, as early as 6 weeks of age. Just before an extension of an arm toward the object, there was a very rapid flexor jerk of the extremity, as if extension were first preceded by an involuntary flexor jerk. This flexor jerk seemed to signify an intentional movement of extension in the 4-to-16-week period, at a time when mastery of the balance between flexor and extensor muscles is difficult (Twitchell, 1965, 1971). As he mastered extensor activity, by 16 weeks, this early signature of intention became lost. In an attempt to anchor one hand in order to reinforce the efforts of the other, he often grasped his chair, held onto a piece of his clothing or a part of himself, or put his thumb in his mouth. This seemed to free the other hand to reach unilaterally, at a time when bilateral arm and hand activity is still predominant (10 to 20 weeks), and was comparable to a kind of "place holding." Long before reaches could be completed successfully, these segments of such an intention were part of the prolonged states of attention toward the object.

This state of intense, rapt attention built up gradually to a peak which was disrupted suddenly by the infant's turning away from the object, becoming active, and flailing his extremities. He often cried out, breathed rapidly, and looked around the room as if to find relief by looking at something else. When he found another object, such as a door or a corner of the room, he latched onto it. He often looked down or closed his eyes in this interval, as if he were processing information about the object in this period of withdrawal. This flailing activity of body, arms, and legs was accompanied by facial activity, and he seemed to be "letting off steam." The period of disruption was followed by a turning back to the object and a resumption of the "hooked" state of attention.

Striking in all of this was the intent prolonged state of attention, during which tension gradually built up in all segments of his body until abrupt disruption seemed the inevitable and necessary relief for him. This behavior was most striking by 12 to 16 weeks. Habituation and more gradual turning away from the object seemed to start by 16 weeks and become an alternative to this "hooked" behavior (Brackbill, 1966). But before this, and as late as 20 weeks, each segment of his body reflected the "hooked," intense attention and disruption that seemed to be characteristic of his response to an object. This unit of cycling attention and disruption can be compared as a homeostatic model to the units of attention-withdrawal (A-W) described in the following mother-infant sequences (see Figure 1).

Description of Behavior with the Mother

The contrast of the infant's behavior and attention span when he interacted with his mother was striking as early as 4 weeks of age. We felt we could see brief episodes of these two contrasting modes of behavior as early as 2 to 3 weeks, but by 4 weeks we could predict correctly from watching parts of his body and observing his span and degree of attention whether he was responding to the object or to his mother.

Of course the expectancy engendered in an interaction with a static object, as opposed to a responsive person, must be very different (Piaget, 1953, 1955). But what surprised us was how early this expectancy seemed to be reflected in the infant's behavior and use of attention. When the infant was interacting with his mother, there seemed to be a constant cycle of attention (A), followed by withdrawal of attention (W)—the cycle being used by each partner as he approached and then withdrew and waited for a response from the other participant. In the mothers and infants we observed, this model of attention seemed to exist on several levels during an interaction sequence. If she responds in one way, their interactional energy builds up; if another, he may turn away. The same holds true of her response to his behavior. In order to predict and understand which behavioral cluster will produce an ongoing sequence of attention, one must understand the affective attention available in each member of the dyad. In other words, the strength of the dyadic interaction dominates the meaning of each member's behavior. The behavior of any one member becomes a part of a cluster of behaviors which interact with a cluster of behaviors from the other member of the dyad. No single behavior can be separated from the cluster

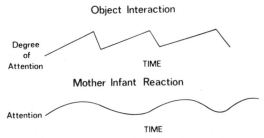

FIGURE 1. Alternating attention and nonattention with object and mother.

for analysis without losing its meaning in the sequence. The effect of clustering and of sequencing takes over in assessing the value of particular behaviors, and in the same way the dyadic nature of interaction supersedes the importance of an individual member's clusters and sequences. The power of the interaction in shaping behavior can be seen at many levels. Using looking and not looking at the mother as measures of attention-nonattention, in a minute's interaction there was an average of 4.4 cycles of such attention and apparent nonattention. Not only were the spans of attention and of looking away of shorter duration than they had been with objects, but they were observably smoother as the attention built up, reached its peak, and then diminished gradually with the mother. Both the buildup as well as the decrease in attention were gradual. A typical period might be described, in segments, as follows.

Initiation · The infant begins to look back at his mother with dull eyes, a relaxed face, and slowly moving extremities and body. The exception to this pattern occurs if the mother has turned away from the infant. He may then turn back abruptly. Although the infant may have been looking away from her, he often has kept her in his peripheral vision, so that when she turns away, he may quickly turn back to reestablish contact.

Orientation · As he looks toward her, his eyes and face brighten, his body orients so that it faces hers, and his extremities extend toward her. The same kind of pointing behavior of fingers and toes as is seen with objects may occur briefly at this time as well.

State of Attention · As she responds to his looking at her, the infant assumes a state of attention in which he alternately sends and receives cues. In this state his arms and legs may pedal slowly, his face alerts, and his eyes dull and then brighten, with fleeting smiles, grimaces, and vocalizations. Hands and feet open and close smoothly, and when his fingers or toes move, they move in slower and smoother movements than in the state of interaction with the object. Alternately reaching forward toward her and circling back into positions parallel to his own head, his extremities give him the attitude of alternately reaching out and waiting to receive from her. The constant waxing and waning of degree of tension in all parts of the body seems to parallel the degree of attention and expectancy present in his interaction with his mother.

Acceleration · As the looking sequence builds up, there are fewer oscilations of attention and inattention, and the jerky, lidded quality of the eyes drops out. *Vocalizing* may be preceded by body activity which builds up in intensity before he can make a vocalization. As he builds up to vocalizing, he seems to need to start with activity of his body. He may whirl his arms, twist his body, and strain forward, with face tense and arms stretched out as he builds up to a vocalization. His mother can cut short this vocal interchange by talking too much. Contingency scores support the observation that an infant vocalizes more when his mother quiets. *Smiling* is reinforced by her contingent smiling. As he begins with a tentative smile, she smiles back. He watches her intently and smiles for longer periods. His smiling may also involve cycling activity of his whole body, but it is smoother and less intense than the buildup in vocalizing. *Tonguing* and *spitting up* are seen as he accelerates toward the peak of interaction. *Cycling activity* of arms and legs involves wider and wider arcs. Occasional jerky reaches toward his mother are interspersed, but in general the body activity is smooth and rhythmic as he builds up.

Peak of Excitement · At the peak of excitement, his behavior may be very similar to that described with an object—jerky and intense. But there are observable differences. The duration of the intense state is shorter and interspersed with efforts to control the degree of excitement. He may bring his hand to his mouth to suck, suck on his tongue, yawn, or hold onto his hands or onto another part of his body in what appears to be an effort to decrease the building up tension. These efforts provide a more gradual buildup and a smoother plateau of excitement at the peak of their interaction.

On stop-frame analysis of filmed interaction, one can determine the subtle changes in intensity in behavior at this peak that differ from the linear intensity seen in interaction with an object. There is a background rhythm of subtle cyclical changes in attention and inattention, which monitor the degree of investment and provide a smoother appearance. The infant's *eyes* may appear to be intensely fixed on his mother's face. But saccadic movements can be noted, brief periods of dulling down of intensity, of lidding, and of blinks, which can be noted in a period of what appears to be intense looking. His *face* may be intent in smiling, vocalizing, or reacting to his mother's facial gestures. But there is constant slow movement and change in facial musculature as he reacts. His *vocalizing* may build up to a pitch of output, accompanied by intense activity. *Smiling* can be maintained for long periods at this intense peak, but laughing, spitting up, or even crying may be an end result. As his mother smiles back to him, he alternately dulls down as he watches and then responds with a wide, tense smile. His cycling activity gives way to more excited, high-pitched activity of his arms and legs. His neck may crane forward and then arch backward as he becomes excited, his body twisting from side to side. This intense activity alternates with more cyclic, smooth body behavior. Usually, in contrast to the object behavior, this peak is short-lived and ends in gradual deceleration.

Deceleration · Although this excitement may end in a disruption similar to that seen with objects, he usually ends a period of excitement by gradual rather than sudden deceleration of energy. His bright look dims, his eyes dull down and seem to lid over, his face assumes a duller, more relaxed attitude. His smiles fade, decreasing in number and intensity. Vocalizing either ceases or becomes decreased in pitch, intensity, and variability. He may even continue to vocalize, but with a dull, monotonous, "holding" quality. Tonguing and yawning may increase. Blinking increases in number and in duration of each blink. He leans backward into a more relaxed sitting position. Reaching out is replaced by holding onto parts of himself, the chair, or his clothes, thumb sucking, or fingering his hair or ears. His extremities may continue to cycle, but with smoother, more restricted activity. Hands may be loosely clenched or wide and flat. In this state he seems to be recovering. The outcome of this decelerated state may be toward another period of acceleration or toward a period of turning away from her.

Withdrawal or Turning Away · There are several ways a baby can be observed to withdraw from the looking and the interacting situation we have described. Since our major variable is the looking mode, looking away may represent an observed turning away, while the infant may actually continue to be in real contact with the mother. The fact that he turns back quickly when she turns her head, closes her eyes, or leans back in her chair demonstrates the extent to which he keeps her in peripheral vision.

An infant entering this portion of the attention-withdrawal cycle presents various patterns, represented by a glazed or dull expression, reduced activity, and face and eyes not oriented toward the mother. He can look down or away and find another person or object to fix upon. In this partial withdrawal his activity is reduced, and his body moves slightly or not at all. There is none of the fixed, intense attention directed toward a new object, which signals real competing involvement. Instead, the dull attitude toward a peripheral object or person is a signal that he is still basically in touch with the first object of attention—his mother. In fact, in this brief period of withdrawal, he may be processing information which he has received in the previous period of interaction (parallel to that with objects). He may lean back in his chair, suck on his fingers, finger his other hand, or turn his body halfway away from his mother. Other activities tend to reinforce his looking-away behavior; for examples, he may vocalize into the room, yawn or whimper halfheartedly and without focus, tongue his lips, suck on his tongue, play with his own clothing, finger his mother's hand absentmindedly, or smile into the distance. All these activities are without real investment, and seem to be in the service of maintaining his decrease in attention to his mother.

If he builds up to an intense looking-away state, he may begin to fix on an object in the room, orienting toward it, and behave as if he is now really interested in it. As he becomes more excited, he may begin to use real "object" attention and behavior to maintain his involvement with the newly found object. This state of interest is likely to be short-lived and ends in a smooth transition with decelerating interest, until he turns back toward his mother. He then shows he is ready for another period of interaction. This represents the cyclical withdrawal aspect of a synchronous interaction. In this the infant has responded to his own inner timing rather than to any new, noxious, or dyssynchronous aspect of his mother's stimulation.

These withdrawing techniques may be substituted for each other. They serve to initiate the negative part of a cyclical curve with the same smooth, cyclic transition from the positive curve which is represented when the infant is attending to his mother. Thus it appears that an infant withdraws and even invests energy in the negative part of the cycle—that of turning away and looking away—just as he does when he is attending to his mother. He then adds on behaviors—such as looking at the door, fingering his clothes, and coughing—in order to continue to look away. He can use the period of looking away as if he were attempting to reduce the intensity of the interaction, to recover from the excitement it engenders in him, and to digest what he has taken in during the interaction. These perhaps represent a necessary recovery phase in maintaining homeostasis at a time in infancy when constant stimulation without relief could overwhelm the baby's immature systems.

When the interaction is not going well, more intense withdrawal or active rejection of the other actor may occur. This may be the result of a specific, inappropriate stimulus, or after a series that overloads his capacity for responsiveness.

We have determined at least four clear strategies for dealing with an unpleasant, inappropriate stimulus:

1. Actively withdrawing from it—that is, increasing the physical distance between the stimulus and oneself by changing one's own position, for example, arching, turning, shrinking.

2. Rejecting it, that is, dealing with it by pushing it away with hands and feet while maintaining one's position.

3. Decreasing its power to disturb by maintaining a presently held position but decreasing sensitivity to the stimulus—looking dull, yawning, or withdrawing into a sleep state.

4. Signaling behavior, for example, fussing or crying, which has the initially unplanned effect of bringing adults or other caregivers to the infant to aid him in dealing with the unpleasant stimulus.

All these were observed in our infants in the first few weeks in responses that appeared to be individually characteristic in tempo and vigor.

CYCLICAL NATURE OF THE INTERACTION

The most important rule for maintaining an interaction seemed to be that a mother develop a sensitivity to her infant's capacity for attention and his need for withdrawal—partial or complete—after a period of attention to her. Short cycles of attention and nonattention seemed to underlie all periods of prolonged interaction. Although we thought we were observing continuous attention to her stimuli, on the part of the infant, stop-frame analysis uncovered the cyclical nature of the infant's looking–not–looking in our laboratory setting. Looking away behavior reflects the need of each infant to maintain some control over the amount of stimulation he can take in via the visual mode in such an intense period of interaction.

This approach-withdrawal model in infants was first described by Schnierla (1965), and the response was related to the qualities of the stimulus. Habituation and withdrawal from repeated stimulation have also been described (Brackbill, 1966; Gewirtz, 1969; Sharpless, 1959). Although the quality and quantity of stimulation must play important roles in determining the timing of the infant's withdrawal, there seemed to be a basic regulatory mechanism which was most evident in the early weeks but which persisted throughout our observations. Just as there is an oscillating regulatory mechanism that maintains homeostasis in physiological parameters such as temperature control, cardiovascular mechanisms, the curve of activation, discharge, and recovery seems to be necessary for attention in an ongoing interaction (Kimberly, 1970). The autonomic system is dominated by this kind of homeostatic mechanism. This homeostatic model, which underlies all the physiological reactions of the neonate, might also represent the immature organism's capacity to attend to messages in a communication system. In the visual system it was apparent that this model was pertinent. Unless she responded appropriately to these variations in his behavior it appeared to us that his span of attention did not increase, and the quality of his attention was less than optimal. For example, in the case of two similarly tense, overreactive infants, the mothers responded very differently. One mother responded with increased activity and stimulation to her baby's turning her off; another maintained a steady level of activity which gradually modulated her baby's overreactivity. The end result was powerfully in favor of the latter dyad. This latter baby was more responsive, and for longer periods, as our study progressed. Although this effect could have been based on baby variables we were not able to analyze, we felt that the quality of communication changed in this pair; however, the linear tenseness of the first dyad remained throughout the 20 weeks of observation. This baby has learned "rules" about managing his own needs in the face of an insensitive mother. He has learned to turn her off, to decrease his receptivity to information from her. This must be necessary for him in order to maintain physiological and psychological homeostasis. When this rule is learned, he can then tune in at times when he can tolerate cues from her. These two parallel cases demonstrate that a mother's behavior must not only be reinforcing and contingent upon the infant's behavior, but that it must meet more basic "needs" of the infant in being aware of his capacity to receive and utilize stimuli. This, then, becomes the first rule each must learn from the other. And, as our discussion indicates, we feel that the small infant's needs are greater and must shape the mother first, if she can be sensitive to him. When she is not able to be, communication must assume a different shape.

A striking way of illustrating the behaviors of the mother and the child, as well as the interaction of the two, is to present them in graphic form. To illustrate, figures 2 to 5 are graphs drawn from interaction periods. Time is measured along the horizontal axis, and the number of behaviors along the vertical axis. Curves drawn above the horizontal line indicate that the person whose behavior the curve represents was looking *at* his partner. Curves drawn below the line indicate that he was looking *away*. Solid lines represent the mother's behavior; broken lines, the baby's. Thus a deep, broken line below the horizontal line indicates that the baby was looking away while engaging in several behaviors.

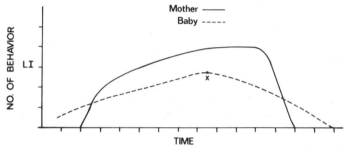

FIGURE 2. Number of behaviors added in period of 16-second looking interaction. Baby looking (LI, looking intent).

As reflected in Figure 2, the mother looks at the baby after he turns to her. As they look at each other, she adds behaviors, smiling, vocalizing, touching his hand, and holding his leg, to accelerate their interaction. He responds by increasing the number of his own behaviors (smiling, vocalizing, and cycling his arms and legs) until the peak at X. At this point he begins to decrease his behaviors and gradually cuts down on them toward the end of their interaction. She follows his lead by decreasing her behaviors more rapidly and ends her part of the cycle by looking away just before he does. Figure 3 shows a baby starting a cycle by looking at his mother. She follows by looking at him and adding four more behaviors in rapid succession—touching him, smiling, talking, and nodding her head. He watches her, vocalizes, smiles back, cycles briefly, and then begins to decrease his responses and turns away at *a* . She stops smiling as he begins to turn away but rapidly adds facial gestures to try to recapture his interest. She continues to talk, touch him, nod her head, and make facial gestures until *b*. At this point she stops the gestures but begins to pat him. At *c* she stops talking briefly and stops nodding at him. At *d* she makes hand gestures in addition to her facial grimaces but stops them both thereafter. At *e* she stops

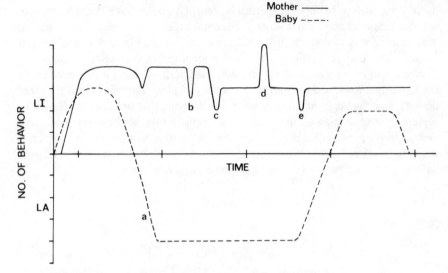

FIGURE 3. Number of behaviors added in a 5-second period of interaction.

vocalizing and he begins to return to look at her. He vocalizes briefly and then looks away again when her activity continues.

In Figure 4 the mother and infant are looking at each other; she is vocalizing, and he is smiling. As she increases her *a* activity by patting him, he turns away. She begins to nod at him at *a* , and he begins to look at the curtain across the room. She tries to quiet at *b* and again at *c* . After a period of less activity from

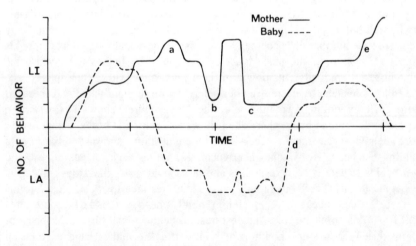

FIGURE 4. Number of behaviors added in a 4-second interaction.

her, he begins to turn to her at *d* . As he returns to look at her, she begins to build up by smiling, vocalizing, and eventually at *e* to pat him. At this he begins to turn away again.

In Figure 5 the mother and baby are looking at each other, smiling and vocalizing together. The baby begins to cycle and reach out to her. At *a* he begins to turn away from her. She responds by looking down at her hands and she stops her activity briefly. This brings him back to look at her at *c* . Her smiling, vocalizing, and leaning toward him bring a smiling response from him. In addition, his arms and legs cycle and he coos contentedly as he watches her. As he turns away she first adds another behavior and gestures. He, however, adds to his activities extraneous to her reminders and turns away from her. She gradually cuts out all her activity and by *e* she looks away from him. Immediately afterward he begins to look back to her, and the cycle of looking at each other begins again at *f*.

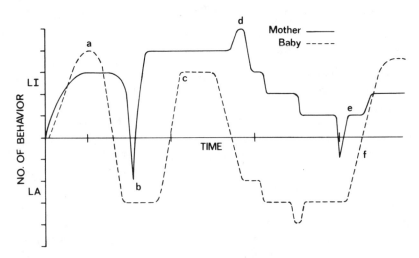

FIGURE 5. Number of behaviors added in a 5-second interaction.

The kind of sensitivity to each other's needs for attention and nonattention that a couple might exhibit is represented by these cycles. Examples *a* and *d* seem to represent real sensitivity. The kind of insensitivity of the mother to the baby's turning away represented by Figure 3 seems to prolong the period of looking away. In Figure 4 reducing her activity acts as a stimulus to bringing him back to respond to her after a long period of withdrawal. Figure 5 represents a more cyclical approach on the part of the mother, and an increasing number of cycles of attention from the baby.

MOTHER'S ROLE

A mother's response to her infant's rhythm changes in attention can fit into her infant's needs in one of three ways:

1. By adjusting her rhythm to his, following his cues for attention and withdrawal, and adding her cues when he demonstrates his receptiveness. This approach served to increase the amount of time during which the infant looks at her (see Figure 2).

2. By not responding to his rhythm or his withdrawal but continuing her steady bombardment. This serves to reinforce the time the infant spends looking away, and rapidly dulls down the amount of attention he pays to her cues when he looks at her (see Figure 3).

3. By attempting to establish her own rhythm to regulate his—in these instances a mother unconsciously increases and decreases her bombardment of stimuli, but out of phase with her infant, often resulting in short, unsatisfying periods of interaction between them (see Figure 4).

A mother's behavior in a period of interaction might be summarized by five kinds of experience which she offers an infant:

1. Reduction of interfering activity.

2. Setting the stage for a period of interaction by bringing him to a more alert, receptive state.

3. Creating an atmosphere of expectancy for further interaction by her behavior.

4. Acceleration of his attention to receive and send messages.

5. Allowing for reciprocity with sensitivity to his signals, giving him time to respond with his own behavior, as well as time to digest and recover from the activation her cues establish.

Each of these segments of her behavior is endowed with an intention on her part. The intention is signified by the quality of her behavior. Variations in each segment can be observed as follows:

1 Reduction of Interfering Activity

The most obvious examples of this are: (a) regulating and satiating needs, such as hunger, being wet or dirty, lack of sleep; (b) containing reflex startle behavior which interferes with the infant's ability to maintain attention; and (c) soothing him when he becomes upset or disintegrated. A mother soon learns the conditions for containing her infant—that she can use restraint by adjusting him in the chair or swaddling his arms or legs with her hands. She finds that she can also hold him with her face, her gestures, or her voice. One mother used smiling to "maintain" her baby's attention and thus reduce his random activity. A mother often interchanges one behavior for another in a particular stage of her infant's becoming upset, expecting the change of mode to maintain his attention a while longer. Thus a particular mother might initiate her interaction with a simple readjustment, and go on to hold his body or legs which startled as she adjusted him. She continues by stroking or patting his belly as she endeavors to keep him and his startling behavior under control. As this soothing, monotonous activity wears out its usefulness, a mother may begin to talk in a steady, monotonous voice, or to smile continuously. Another may begin to rock and bob her head—all these activities become the individualized background for the rest of their interaction.

When the infant demonstrates unexpected random behavior, such as the jerk of a leg or an arm, the mother responds by stroking or holding that extremity, or by making a directed use of that extremity to jog it gently up and down, thereby turning an interfering activity into one that serves their interaction. In these ways she might be seen to teach the infant how to suppress and channel his own behavior into a communication system.

2 Setting the Stage

As part of containing behavior, she might use a method that orients him toward her. She can adjust his body to the midline so that he faces her, pulling up his sagging torso so that he is in an alert position, reclining at a 30° angle, but alert rather than relaxed. She can move her head so that she is in his direct line of vision, bobbing or making facial gestures to attract his attention. One mother used kissing and another wiped her baby's face in what appeared to be efforts to alert the infants. (Instead, these two behaviors usually caused the baby to turn away.)

When she pats or strokes him, she does so with a rhythm and an intensity designed to alert as well as soothe (e.g., there was a two-per-second rhythm which most mothers used for soothing *and* alerting, and a slower rhythm for simple soothing). When he sags, her intensity and speed increase, or they decrease when he becomes overexcited. The part of his body that she touches also serves a double purpose—of soothing and alerting, for example, as he quiets to her stroking his legs or abdomen, she moves her hands up to his chest and finally to his cheek in order to arouse his attention and focus it on her.

3 Creating an Expectancy for Interaction

As she attempts to elicit a signal from the infant confirming that he is in touch with her, the mother uses any or all of the behaviors at her command. Characteristic of communication, her behaviors have certain features: (*a*) *Rhythm and intensity*—although they may start off explosively or slowly, they are quickly modulated to respond to the attention of the infant. Vocalizing, nodding, facial gestures, and patting, which starts off explosively *or* soothingly, are quickly geared to maintain the interaction. (*b*) *Amplitude* is meshed in the same way. Large facial or arm gestures might initiate the sequence but are rapidly decreased in amplitude as his attention is caught. (*c*) *Direction*. Since her effort is to orient him to her face as the central focus, all these movements are reduced in amplitude and from the periphery inward in a way that will bring his focus to her face, using her movement to activate and then to siphon his attention into a central focus on her eyes and mouth. (*d*) *Quality* is especially "appropriate" to an interaction with an infant. Speech is simplified in rhythm and pitched to gain and hold his attention; for example, baby talk was high pitched, vowel-like, and interspersed with alerting consonants such as b, d, h, and tch.

A mother's eyes and lips widen and close in rhythmic movements designed alternately to alert and soothe her baby. As he quiets, her vocalizations and facial movements become rhythmic and "holding," and then speed up with more staccato and a faster pace. Her eyes alternately narrow and widen; bright and dull in a measure appropriate to his state. When he overreacts, her eyes take on a soothing look, becoming wider and brighter, to attract and "hold" his attention.

4 Intensifying His Attention

Within the context of acceleration of attention, 15 of the 18 mother behaviors have the effect of intensifying their interaction. Only 3—looking dull, looking away, and leaning back, can be considered decelerative in function. The mother starts with a behavior which seems appropriate to the particular interaction, for example, a smile in response to her baby's smile, or vocalization if she hopes to bring him to vocalizing. Each behavior can be substituted for another in order to accelerate the interaction. Or, behaviors can be added in sequence and in clusters, to heighten their information value. For example, one mother held her baby's trunk with both hands. She added smiling to alert the infant further. As she received her alert look back, the mother bagan to vocalize, stopped smiling, and finally began to emphasize her speech rhythms with head bobbing toward the baby. These behaviors were all designed to heighten the information-giving aspect of this interaction sequence. As long as this mother was sensitive to her infant's increasing interest, these behaviors served their accelerative function. But at a certain point when her baby seemed to be tiring, she added a touch to her baby's face and the infant turned away from her. (A stimulus that might be accelerative at one point may serve to overload the infant and result in looking away on the part of the baby. Buildup of added behaviors had to be sensitively attuned to the point in the timing cycle of the infant's attention.)

5 Allowing for Reciprocity

When the mother can allow for the cyclic turning away from her, which seems to be necessary for the infant, she can be assured of longer periods of attention when he turns back to her. One of our mothers was particularly striking in her capacity to subside as he decreased his attention to her. She relaxed back in her chair smiling softly, reducing other activity such as vocalizing and moving, waiting for him to return. When he did look back, she began slowly to add behavior on behavior, as if she were feeling out how much he could master. She also sensed his need to reciprocate. She vocalized then waited for his response. When she smiled, she waited until he smiled before she began to build up her own smiling again. Her moving in close to him was paced sensitively to coincide with his body cycling, and if he became excited or jerky in his movement she subsided back into her chair.

We felt she was outstanding in her sensitivity to the importance of reciprocity in this interaction. Whether she felt the danger of overloading him and cutting short their communication, or whether she sensed that pacing her behaviors decreased habituation effects and increased the value to him of each behavior as a signal, she brought out clear evidence of a more intense communication system between them. She provided an atmosphere that led to longer periods of interaction. She seemed to teach him an expectancy of more than just stimuli from her in the guise of her sensitivity to his needs and his cues. As she allowed for these, she seemed to be teaching him how to expand his own ability to attend to stimulation, for "long-term intention" as well as "long-term interaction." Thus her role took on deeper significance as she established not only the climate for communication but gave him the experience in pacing himself in order to attend to the environment.

COMMUNICATION WITH NEONATAL INFANTS

There seemed to be special characteristics of the behavior of a mother with her new infant. When mothers were asked to communicate with infants of 1 week, they were essentially being asked to communicate with beings commonly thought "nonintentional." Our mothers were faced with the problem of communicating with infants who, if they were not crying or thrashing, were often hanging limply in the infant seat with closed or semiclosed eyes or, just as frequently, were "frozen" motionless in some strange and uninterpretable posture—staring at nothing. While infants in the first weeks did seem to look directly into the face of their mothers, the communicative aspects of eye-to-eye contact sometimes were dampened when the mothers moved their heads and found the infants still staring off in the original direction.

Their movements contained "startles"—fingers suddenly splayed out, feet and legs shot straight out or up—and seemed purposeless. Most of the time they adopted a peculiarly constricted posture with hands and arms brought up tight against the chest, arms tensely tucked under the neck, legs tense and toes pointing in, while the eyes were either semiclosed or staring into space. In the first week the most definite "interactive" activities we noted on the part of the infants were (1) withdrawal from a "noxious" stimulus such as contact in a sensitive area, (2) efforts to push away the noxious stimulation, (3) slight and quickly fading apparent effort to maintain eye-to-eye contact, (4) lulling to a caress or another stimulus from the mother, (5) brightening of the face and turning of the head to her voice or her face, and (6) responding to holding efforts from her by a gradual quieting and alerting to her.

Perhaps the most interesting response to the challenge of facing an unresponsive infant is this. The mother takes on facial expressions, motions, and postures indicative of emotion, as though the infant were behaving intentionally or as though she and he were communicating. Frequently, in response to a motionless infant, she suddenly acquires an expression of great admiration, moving back and forth in front of him with great enthusiasm; or, again in response to an unmoving infant, she takes on an expression of great surprise, moving backward in mock astonishment; or, in the most exaggerated manner, she greets the infant and, furthermore, carries on an animated extended greeting interchange, bobbing and nodding enthusiastically exactly as though her greeting were currently being reciprocated. It is interesting that surprise, greeting, and admiration seem to share the common elements we have mentioned earlier: raised brows, widely exaggerated eyes, and in two cases even a faintly pursed mouth. Less frequently, mothers mock-scolded an infant who was unresponsive.

Most mothers, in sum, are unwilling or unable to deal with neonatal behaviors as though they are meaningless or unintentional. Instead, they endow the smallest movements with highly personal meaning and react to them affectively. They insist on joining in and enlarging on even the least possible interactive behaviors, through imitation. And they perform *as if* highly significant interaction has taken place when there has been no action at all.

DISCUSSION

We had hoped that we would be able to identify synchrony and dyssynchrony in the mother-infant relationship by examining their interaction at a microscopic level. The need for guidelines in diagnosis of mother-infant harmony is great. Failures in mothering—such as is seen in infantile autism, failure to thrive, and child abuse—might be substantiated by such an analysis. We had hoped to identify such a diagnostic and research tool by using a kinesic model suggested by the work of Condon (1967) and Birdwhistell (1962). Condon demonstrated in psychotherapeutic interviews that the physical movements of the listener are parallel to transitions in the speech of the speaker. For example, gross bodily movements such as changes in posture coincide with the speaker's moving from one paragraph to another, whereas small movements of the listener's finger, for example, coincide with transitions between syllables. And to our point, he demonstrated that this parallel between speaker's speech and listener's body movements is greater when the listener is attracted to the speaker than when this attraction is absent.

Important to our point, Watslawick (1967) speaks of the rule of interaction in a setup such as ours—that it is impossible for two persons confronting each other *not* to interact, and that one might speak of positive or negative interaction between two persons, but never of *no* interaction. Our experimental design was constructed in such a way that we could visualize and analyze periods in which the *kind* of interaction could be assessed, in which interaction was obligatory. For analysis of the film sequences, we used Gesell's (1935) stop-frame cinemanalytic techniques of behaviors and had combined Kestenberg's (1965) qualitative assessment of movement patterns. But we quickly became aware of the bimodal quality of interaction behavior. No actor's behavior was *ever* independent of the expectancy of interaction. Each behavior then was either positive or negative in its "intent" within this expectancy. It became important to attach an intentional significance to each behavior and cluster of behaviors, based largely on the context within which it occurred and the result it achieved in the sequential shaping of the interaction. We wanted to avoid the classic event recording that had characterized mother-infant interaction behavior in the past. In other kinds of film studies, both event recording and narrative record tended to equate interactions that seemed importantly different.

The interaction we described in this study became delineated by the nature of our study. The mothers were "programmed" to seek *attention* from their infants. No amount of reassurance from the observers could counteract the set in each mother's mind that she was expected to bring her infant into a period of constant attention to her and her maneuvers. Hence the laboratory test situation became a period of heightened attention-getting behavior on the mother's part. The anxiety about performance and being observed seemed to be translated into behavior in different ways by each mother. Although we do not presume to think that this filmed behavior is representative of all interactional behavior for each mother, we can assume that it is an example of the behavior she used under certain kinds of stress to produce attention in her infant. In this way it may be a sample of behavior to which the infant must *learn* to react.

We felt that we saw evidences in the infants' responses that demonstrated their awareness of unusual conditions in the laboratory setting. For example, smiling and vocalizing were difficult to produce in the laboratory at a time when they were already responding at home. Our impression was that we were not seeing unusual behavior, but a distortion of each infant's behavior which was characteristic under tension-producing circumstances. A parallel study of filmed interaction at home without the tension-producing qualities of a laboratory would be helpful to establish this.

Our most striking observation was that there were two very different patterns of attentional behavior present early in each infant, which were called upon in response to an object versus a familiar person. These two patterns seemed to be governed by the different kinds of attention and expectancy present as early as we saw these babies. These two modes may be represented in the neonatal period, and their anlage can be seen in the neonate's differential alerting reactions to a human voice versus a similar but nonhuman sound, as well as a human face versus a representative of a human face. Even in a neonate, the intensity and duration of attention seem to be clinically different. Habituation studies, such as studies of attention using cardiac deceleration and other autonomic measures, should establish these differences in time.

At any rate, if there are two differentiated pathways set up in early infancy—with intrauterine preconditioning to human stimuli as fuel for shaping them—we might explain some of the evidence for reactions of the infant to mothering cues that set off complex reactions in the infant and might fit into a kind of readiness for "imprinting" behavior, as well as the reactions to violation of expectancy, which are seen as early as 4 weeks (Aaronson, 1970; Tronick, 1972). Certainly, the pathways for complex behavior, such as imprintinglike responses, habituation to novel and familiar objects, and expectancy of familiar patterns, may be inborn, and little else in the way of an explanation may be necessary. But if the cue value of a human response is received and treated differently by the infant because of his experience in the uterus, as opposed to the cues of a nonresponsive object, there may be earlier integration and expectancy of interaction cues than we have heretofore credited the infant with.

Evidence for a different degree and duration of attention, as well as disruption of attention with the mother and with the object was certainly observable in all our infants as early as 2 and 3 weeks. The physiological demands of such attention and recovery from the periods of attention appeared to be very different in the two modes of interaction. How they may reinforce each other as the infant "learns" to overcome interfering motor behavior in order to attend to his environment must be at the crux of any study that emphasizes the importance of a nurturing environment to an infant's capacity for cognitive acquisitions. They did not appear to be competing patterns in these infants. The mother tends to provide a "holding" framework for her own cues. That is, she holds the infant with her hands, with her eyes, with her voice and smile, and with changes from one modality to another as he habituates to one or another. All these holding experiences are opportunities for the infant to learn how to contain *himself*, how to control motor responses, and how to attend for longer and longer periods. They amount to a kind of learning about organization of behavior in order to attend. With more disruptive mothering or with none at all, one might expect this kind of learning about self-organization to be delayed. Not only in a disturbed environment would the experiences be sparse that contribute to learning in the sphere of social interaction, but the crossover to learning the organization necessary for cognitive acquisitions may not be provided, hence learning would be delayed in an infant who had to acquire this organization by maturation alone, without appropriate environmental experiences. We felt we saw some of the possible variations for such learning in these five infants. In the cases in which mothers were not as sensitive to the attentional organization of their infants, and regularly added more behavior of their own when the infant tried to withdraw his attention, we felt that the periods of attention did not increase over time in the same way they did for the infants of the more sensitive mothers. Our study did not provide evidence for assessing whether this made any real difference in cognitive development among these five babies. We did see evidence for the development of very different interactive styles. Although our focus was not on individual differences but on the regularities in an interaction system between mothers and infants, we were drawn into comparisons of styles and conjectures as to their significance for the infant's future development. A future study should be reserved to follow up the many questions raised in this all-too-brief follow-up.

Some of the questions about mothering styles might be answered by a more detailed analysis of individual differences. Contingency scores did not detect these differences, nor explain the effect on the infant's responsive behavior. The areas in which differences in mothers' behaviors seemed to produce a difference in outcome of infant responses are:

1. *Individual variations in use of specific behaviors.* The choice of behavior may depend on a mother's individual preference for a particular behavior, as well as the specificity in her mind as she uses it. In the first instance, one mother may use a caressing kind of contact in preference to holding which may be characteristic of another mother. The effect on the infant is likely to differ in quality of response over time if not in quantity. The specificity of her behavior at any time may be tuned to a learned expectation of the infant's response. For example, some mothers smile at their infants, not intending to evoke a response. No change in their facial expression is noted when their infant fails to smile, cr even cries. In others the intent to evoke a returning smile can be inferred from succeeding behaviors. If a mother smiles, receives no response, and then slowly leans back with a slight frown and a down-turned mouth, we may infer that she smiled with the intention of eliciting a smile in response.

Two mothers whose scores for percentage of time spent smiling, vocalizing, touching, and so on were equal might differ in their individual expectation for the behavior, one using it as a specific response to a specific type of situation, and the other using it nonspecifically. One of our mothers, for example, smiled with pleasure or amusement but not in response to specific infant behaviors; another smiled almost exclusively in response to specific performances, such as a first smile, a first vocalization, a first directed touch. Contingency scores did not differentiate these mothers. Under these conditions a high contingency of smiling with any particular infant behavior was not expected.

2. *The substitution of behaviors to gain a response.* Some mothers tried one

thing over and over in order to gain a response, while others substituted one behavior for another. Again, using our example of smiling, some mothers seemed to try smiling over and over to elicit smiling. Others vocalized, or touched in a playful way, or assumed exaggerated expressions. Some engaged in a series of differing behaviors to the end of producing one type of response in the infant.

3. *Qualities of specific behaviors that change its meaning.* (*a*) *Force.* For example, a series of light pats on the cheek differ radically from a series of heavy, forceful pats. Light pats bring out an alerting response, whereas infants attempt to withdraw from the latter. (*b*) *Tempo.* Quantitative changes in the tempo of the mother's physical contact seem to occasion qualitative shifts in the "meaning" of the communication to the infant. A slow movement on the part of the mother may fit into the infant's present rhythms. For instance, we have observed mothers moving an arm up and down in synchrony with an infant's kicking. As such it became a soothing form of communication. Movement made at the same speed might serve to alert an infant if he were not moving. Accelerated, it might disrupt the infant's ongoing state. In another modality two mothers may spend equal amounts of time vocalizing, but one may speak more slowly than the other and the effects on the infant cannot be expected to be equal. Infant tempo (activity level) may in turn affect maternal tempo. In our study we found that the two infants whose tempo was most distinctly slow had mothers who communicated at an accelerated tempo, as if they were attempting to change that of their infants. (*c*) *Distance.* The face-to-face distance kept between mother and infant is not only an important variable in itself, but one that influences the effect of other variables. Rapid vocalizations from a distance may be less imposing than rapid vocalizations made close to the infant. Certain behaviors can be classified as "close" behaviors—for example, leaning forward, moving into the infant's line of vision, kissing, touching, holding, and adjusting. Others may be more effective at a distance, and are "distance" behaviors—vocalizing, smiling, looking, bobbing, and facial and hand gestures. The characteristics of a mother's distancing may play a role in shaping the interaction behavior in her baby.

4. *Patterns of behaviors.* One of the most interesting questions concerned the patterns of behaviors mothers used to elicit responses from their infants. Some mothers seemed to have a tendency to cluster certain behaviors together in a regular functional unit. The form of the cluster might vary from time to time, and the final behavior that appeared to trigger the infant's response could no longer be considered the stimulus by itself. The importance of the cluster in eliciting his response became more obvious as one analyzed the interaction behaviors.

The context or background for the behavior, the cluster within which it was embedded, as well as its timing in the building up of behaviors, might better explain its trigger effect in producing a contingent response. Certainly, these factors seemed to be more important in understanding our data than were more simplified looks at one modality in the mother to a similar modality in the infant.

Ethological descriptions could encompass the patterns of behavior, as well as the context of their occurrence. We felt and do feel the need for an analytic method that can sort out the patterns we recorded at a descriptive level. Patterns of behavior in a cluster analysis, with some measure of their substitutability for each other, might lead to a better way of documenting individual differences and their outcomes. This kind of analysis will be the goal of future research.

The opportunity to observe the development of these five pairs over 20 weeks impressed us with the need for rule learning in a mother-infant dyad. Each member seemed to need to "learn" the nuances of behavior patterns of the other member of the dyad. Although the psychic energy for learning about the other member must be mobilized during pregnancy and around delivery for the mother, an "imprinting" model, as suggested by Bowlby (1968) and others (Klaus, 1972), seems too simple to explain a developing relationship. There seemed to be rules for interaction which were constantly being altered by each member of the dyad, and flexibility and change were necessary for maintaining optimal interaction.

One of the most important rules was concerned with the mother's sensitivity to the baby's capacity for attention and nonattention. In the early weeks this resembled a homeostatic model. We felt that these early weeks provided her with an opportunity for learning the rules about his homeostatic needs in attention and nonattention, as well as in purely physiological parameters such as feeding, temperature control, elimination, or restriction of disturbing activity. If her own needs interfere with a sensitivity to his, it might be reflected at this level in their interaction. We hope to develop a system for recording and analyzing mother-infant interactions which will establish her capacity to attend to her infant's needs at this level, which may be of diagnostic value in determining the degree of potential pathology or strength in the relationship. The parallel between the attention, nonattention model and homeostatic functioning of most systems of the infant's body raises the question of how learning in one such mode can be transferred to another mode. If there is an inability to learn reciprocity in this mode, might it not affect the infant's psychological functioning in other modalities?

There are many opportunities for rule learning for the mother. She not only learns the limits for expecting attention and responses from him, but must learn which of her behaviors set up an expectancy of interaction, which "hold" him, which produce his responses, which echo his, and which activate or deactivate him in relation to further goals. The timing of these is important (Chapple, 1970; Kimberly, 1970; Wilson & Lewis, 1971), but the qualitative aspects of each of her behaviors may be equally important. The type of stimulus, its force, its rhythm, its location, and its duration were powerful qualities in setting the tone of reactions in the infant. Although this may look as if it were "unlearned" behavior in some mothers, the failure to learn it by other mothers may demonstrate the fact that it can be a kind of rule learning. The individuality of each member of the dyad determines the flexibility in the number of rules necessary, and also sets the limits on the variability within each rule that still allow the goal to be achieved.

Another rule is that the mother use her periods of interaction to "model" the baby to become more and more complex. She times the complexity of her models to his stage of development. For example, in the early weeks imitation of his activity is limited and enlarged upon by her. This must serve as a feedback mechanism for him (Bruner, 1971), but one that enlarged upon his awareness of his behavior. He becomes aware of his action, visualizes her imitation of it, and reproduces it for himself again. As he does so, he has the opportunity to add on to it, either by serendipity or by modeling his behavior to match her enlarged version. Either way, he increases its scope. When simple imitation no longer serves her purpose, she provides more than imitative behavior with new goals for him, which leads him into new clusters of behavior and new kinds of learning. The timing of such imitative reinforcement and her sensitivity to his capacity for attention and learning must depend on her having learned this "rule" about him—that concerning his capacity to accept visually her feedback and to use it as a method for further acquisition. The shaping of his curves of attention by sensitive use of behavior on her part might then reflect his ability to "learn" how to attend, and the interdependence of this ability on the sensitivity of his environment.

This interdependency of rhythms seemed to be at the root of their "attachment" as well as communication. When the balance was sympathetic to the needs of each member of the dyad, there was a sense of rhythmic interaction which an observer sensed as "positive." When the balance was not equalized, and one member was out of phase with the other, there seemed to be a "negative" quality in the entire interaction. At the periods of new acquisitions (e.g., at 8 and 12 weeks) when the infant was out of phase, the mother reflected the stress she felt in not being able to communicate. As she readjusted or waited for the infant's readjustment, subsequent weeks reflected the reestablishment of a kind of synchrony between them. Sander (1970) says that "each new thrust of activity in the growing infant requires a new period of interactional adjustment with the caretaking environment to reach stable coordination on the bases of new changes [p. 330]." The smoothness with which these dyads made such adjustments reflected the depth of their attachment and probably contributed a further opportunity for learning about each other member. Certainly, the strength of the interdependency of the dyad seemed to be more powerful in shaping each member's behavior than did any other force—such as the individual member's style or wish of the moment.

The infant also learns many rules—about his environment and about himself. As he learns how to interact with and master his own physiological needs he frees himself to attend to his external world. In learning how to achieve this kind of control, he learns the rudiments of "ego" function.

We have not answered our questions about the evolution of individuality, or about the relative contribution of each member of the dyad to the interaction. But we have raised questions about how they may be assessed in future studies.

Acknowledgments

The authors wish to express their gratitude to Dr. Jerome S. Bruner for his inspiration, and for the opportunity to work at the Center for Cognitive Studies, Harvard University. In addition, Mrs. Roberta Kelly was of primary importance as a research assistant in her work with the mothers and babies, in analyzing the films, and in providing moral and intellectual support for the project in its earliest years. Drs. Colwyn Trevarthan and Martin Richards were instrumental in helping us differentiate the details of the two modes of interaction with objects and with familiar persons. Their analysis of infant behavior in the object mode is forthcoming. Most important of all, we are deeply indebted to the faithfulness and patience of the five mothers who were willing to bring their babies to us weekly for 5 months, and were brave enough to be filmed as they interacted with their babies at such a critical period in their lives. We hope the fruits of this study will be just reward for their dedication.

References

Aaronson, E., & Tronick, E. Perceptual capacities in early infancy. In J. Elliot (Ed.), *Human development and cognitive processes*, New York: Holt, Rinehart & Winston, 1970.

Birdwhistell, R. L. *Introduction to kinesics.* Department of State, Foreign Service Institute, Washington, D.C., 1962.

Bower, T. G. Visual world of infants. *Scientific American*, 1966, **215**: 80–92.

Bowlby, J. The nature of the child's tie to his mother. *International Journal of Psychoanalysis*, 1958, **39**: 350–73.

Brackbill, Y. A., Adamo, G., Crowell, D. H., & Gray, M. L. Arousal level in neonates and preschool children under continuous auditory stimulation. *Journal of Experimental Child Psychology*, 1966, **4**, 178–88.

Brazelton, T. B. Neonatal Behavioral Assessment Scale, National Spastics Society Monograph, London: Heineman, 1973.

Bruner, J. S. The uses of immaturity. Paper presented at Harvard Graduate School of Education, 1971.

Bruner, J. S., May, A., & Koslowski, B. *The Intention to Take*: A film. New York: Wiley, 1972.

Chapple, E. D. Experimental production of transients in human interaction. *Nature*, 1970, **228**, 630–33.

Condon, W. S., & Ogston, W. D. A segmentation of behavior, *Journal of Psychiatric Research*, 1967, **5**, 221–35.

Gesell, A. Cinemanalysis: A method of behavior study. *Journal of Genetic Psychology*, 1935, **47**, 3–15.

Gewirtz, J. L. A distinction between dependence and attachment in terms of stimulus control. Paper presented at a meeting of the Society for Research in Child Development Conference, Santa Monica, Calif., March, 1969.

Kestenberg, J. S. The role of movement patterns in development, I. Rhythms of movement. *Psychoanalytic Quarterly*, 1965, **36**, 1–36.

Kestenberg, J. S. The role of movement patterns in development, II. Flow of tension and effort. *Psychoanalytic Quarterly*, 1965, **36**, 517–63.

Kestenberg, J. S. The role of movement patterns in development, III. Control of shape. *Psychoanalytic Quarterly*, 1965, **36**, 356–408.

Kimberly, R. P. Rhythmic patterns in human interaction. *Nature*, 1970, **228**, 88–90.

Klaus, M. H., Jerauld, R., Kreger, N. C., McAlpine, W., Steffa, M., & Kennell, J. H. Maternal attachment: The importance of the first postpartum days. *New England Journal of Medicine*, 1972, **286**, 460–63.

Piaget, J. *The origins of intelligence in the child*. London: Routledge, 1953.

Piaget, J. *The child's construction of reality*. London: Routledge, 1955.

Prechtl, H., & Beintema, O. *The neurological maturation of the full term newborn infant*. London: Heinemann, 1964.

Sander, L. W. Regulation and organization in the early infant-caretaker system. In R. Robinson (Ed.), *Brains and early behavior*. London: Academic Press, 1970. Pp. 313–31.

Schnierla, T. C. Aspects of stimulation and organization in approach/withdrawal processes underlying vertebrate behavioral development. In D. Lehrman, R. Hinde, & E. Shaw (Eds.), *Advances in the Study of Behavior*, New York: Academic Press, 1965, **1**, 1–74.

Sharpless, S., & Jasper, H. Habituation of the arousal reaction. Monograph from Department of Experimental Psychology, McGill University, Montreal, 1959.

Tronick, E. Personal communication, 1972.

Twitchell, T. E. Normal motor development. *Journal of the American Physical Therapy Association*, 1965, **45**, 419–23.

Twitchell, T. E. Voluntary movements in reaching. Personal communication, 1971.

Watzlawick, P., Beavin, H. J., & Jackson, D. The pragmatics of human communication. New York: Norton, 1967.

White, B. L., Castle, P., & Held, R. Observations on the development of visually guided directed reaching. *Child Development*, 1964, **35**, 349–64.

Wilson, C. D., & Lewis, M. A developmental study of attention: A multivariate approach. Paper presented at the meeting of the Eastern Psychological Association, New York, April 1971.

CHAPTER 4

Variability of Growth and Maturity in Newborn Infants

J. M. Tanner

Institute of Child Health and the University of London

Newborn infants vary greatly in size, shape, and physical maturity. The standard deviation of birth length, for example, is about 4% of the mean birth length; the standard deviations of height at age 5, and at adulthood, are also approximately 4% of their means. The range of newborn weight, in comparison with its mean, is also similar to the ranges at 5 and 18 years in similar comparison. The brain is no exception; the range of brain weight in newborns is about 200 to 500 grams, and its standard deviation is about 13% of its average (Larroche, 1968).

Thus it is quite wrong to think of newborns as identical buds, from which in the fullness of time flower the variegated colors of the preschool assembly. The newborn already has had a long and eventful history. At birth he is in a highly dynamic state of change and development, quite apart from the episode of birth itself. Indeed, birth should not be over-emphasized. Although several physiological alterations take place at or soon after birth as a direct consequence of emergence into a new environment, very many developmental events, from the replacement of fetal by adult hemoglobin (Jonxis, 1965) to the appearance of conditioned responses (Dargassies, 1966; Papousek, 1961), seem quite indifferent to the fact of birth; their progression has to await the striking of some differently regulated biological clock.

Thus newborns, just like 6-year-olds or 14-year-olds—although perhaps not so obviously—represent a wide variety of degrees of physiological maturity; there is variation in advancement and retardation of growth, as well as in absolute size. On the Dubowitz scale (see below) the range amounts to the equivalent of 3 to 4 weeks of age, even in infants all born at exactly 40 weeks' gestation.

Whether these variations in size, shape, and maturity have an effect on the infant's caregiver we do not at present know; but clearly they may have. We might perhaps expect size itself to have a smaller effect than shape and body composition (although I have been following the growth of a child with cerebral gigantism whose 2-year-old size at 6 months played havoc with his mother's caregiving behavior, for she felt she was carrying around an enormity, like Alice

77

with the Pig-Baby). Infants characteristically put on subcutaneous fat rapidly after birth, and variations in the plumpness (especially in strategic places such as the cheeks and bottom) may well affect the caregiver's responses. Similarly, variation in the amount of muscle may be important, especially in relation to the caregiver's view of the baby's masculinity or femininity (remember the folk tales of Starke Hans and the Infant Hercules).

Besides these possible effects, of which the caregiver may be only marginally aware (as in the similar case of sexually attracted adults), there is in our culture an effect of which the mother is all too conscious. This is the amount of weight gained by the baby during the first months after birth. Babies are expected to gain weight (preferably in exact accordance with the tables published by baby food manufacturers) and an insufficient gain is in itself a signal critical to, and sometimes critical of, the mother. We should therefore additionally bear in mind the variations in weight gain during infancy.

In this chapter, then, I discuss: (1) variation in birth weight and length; (2) variation in physical maturity at birth; (3) variation in shape and body composition of newborns.

VARIATION IN BIRTH WEIGHT AND LENGTH

Probably in newborns, as in children, length is a more satisfactory measure of body size than weight, which encompasses too many dissimilar tissues. However, length has been rather difficult to measure in the newborn until the recent introduction of the Harpenden neonatometer, and for this reason it has not been required as routine in most countries (Sweden and Switzerland being exceptions). Even where it is measured this is often done in a way that makes accuracy impossible. In the future, however, research studies on infants should certainly be organized in such a way that they have newborn values for length (and skinfolds; see below) as well as weight.

For birth weight, however, there are enormous numbers of statistics. It is defined as the weight of the newborn taken within the first hour after birth, before significant postnatal weight loss has occurred. (The next convenient point to measure weight after this time is at 4 weeks postnatal). Birth weight is affected by: (1) length of gestation; (2) parity (first, second, third, etc. in birth order); (3) sex; (4) maternal uterine and systemic characteristics, some hereditary; (5) socio-economic circumstances and habits of the mother.

Length of Gestation

The average length of gestation, traditionally measured from the first day of the last menstrual period (hence on average 14 days prior to actual fertilization) is 280 days, or 40 weeks. However, there is considerable individual variation about this figure (even when mistakes and inaccuracies in determining gestational age are set aside), and lengths of gestation from 259 days (37 completed weeks) to

293 days (42 completed weeks) are by international agreement regarded as normal. Babies born within these limits are called *term* babies. Babies born earlier are called *preterm* babies, and those born later *postterm* babies.

Until a few years ago, all babies under the weight of 2.5 kg were designated "premature," whatever their gestation period or physiological state. This definition (promulgated by the WHO in 1948) did a lot of harm and has now been dropped; the word premature has completely disappeared from scientific use. Babies weighing less than 2.5 kg are called low-birth-weight babies; this low birth weight may be due to their being preterm babies or to their being babies who are pathologically small for their length of gestation. These latter are defined as babies below the third centile, or two standard deviations, on standards for birth weight which allow for length of gestation (32 weeks onward), sex, and parity of mother (e.g., Tanner & Thomson, 1970). They are called *light for dates* (LFD) babies. The prognosis for future development of babies who are preterm but not LFD is considerably better than for those who are LFD. In the United Kingdom it is estimated that about one-half to two-thirds of the babies under 2.5 kg are LFD; the remainder are preterm but not LFD. Preterm babies can of course be LFD also; about one-third are (Farr & Mitchell, 1969). In Sweden, the percentage of babies under 2.5 kg who are LFD seems to be lower (Hedberg & Holmdall, 1970).

In Figures 1a and 1b the Tanner-Thomson birth weight standards are given, showing the increase of weight with gestation. The maximum rate of weight growth (peak weight velocity) is reached, in well-nourished fetuses, at about 34 postmenstrual weeks. From 34 to 36 weeks the rate of growth slows down slightly, and from 36 to 40 weeks it slows very distinctly (Figures 2 and 3). This appears to be due to the influence of the maternal uterus (see below) whose available space is becoming fully occupied. Twins slow down earlier, when their combined weight is approximately that of the 36-week weight of a singleton fetus (McKeown & Record, 1952, 1953; Naeye, Benirschke, Hagstrom, & Marcus, 1966).

Figure 2 serves to show the variation in weight and length during the first year; but variation among children in *rate* of growth (velocity) cannot be envisaged from a "distance" chart such as this.

Parity

Firstborn children are on average about 0.10 kg lighter at birth than second-, third- and later-born (Figure 1). Firstborns grow a little faster than others once out of the confines of the uterus, however, and so they make up the deficit by the end of the first year (Ministry of Health, 1959).

Sex

Boys are larger than girls from at least 35 weeks onward and by 40 weeks average about 0.15 kg more in weight and 1.1 cm more in length.

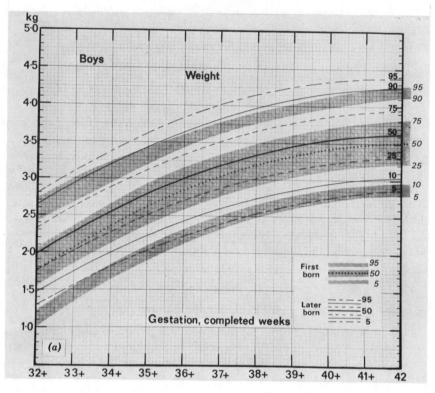

FIGURE 1a.

Maternal Uterine and Systemic Environment

The slowing down of growth after 34 or 36 weeks appears to be due to the maternal environment. It occurs in well-nourished fetuses, although less in them than in ill-nourished ones (see below). Newborns whose growth has been the most held up in the uterus have an increased velocity of growth after birth, representing a "catch-up" similar to that which occurs in malnourished children when their nutritional deficit is corrected (Prader, Tanner, & Von Harnack, 1963; Tanner, 1963). The upper chart in figure 4 illustrates this. The growth of children who were 5 to 6 lb, 6 to 7 lb, and so on at birth was followed up to 3 years. The distance curves have their minimum spread at about 2½ months after birth. This corresponds to the point of maximum postnatal velocity, hence maximum difference between the velocity of the 5-pounders and the 9-pounders (Figure 4, bottom). In these babies the catch-up is finished by about 5 months; all the compensation possible has presumably been achieved, and from then on the larger-born babies increase in weight slightly faster, as expected from geometrical considerations. Thus there is a significant negative correlation

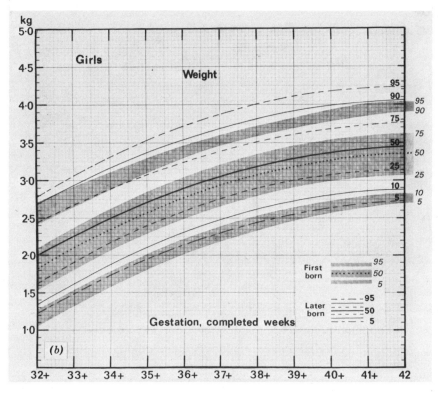

FIGURE 1b. Figures 1a and 1b are standards for birth weight, according to length of gestation, parity, and sex. Further adjustment, not shown here, may be made for maternal size. (Charts prepared by J. M. Tanner and R. H. Whitehouse, Institute of Child Health, University of London, from data by A. H. Thomson, W. Z. Billewicz and F. E. Hytten in J. Obstet. Gynaec. Brit. Cwlth., 75, 903, 1968. Also from Tanner & Thomson, 1970, from data of Thomson, Billewicz, & Hytten, 1968).

between weight at birth and weight increment during the first 6 months after birth; the same is true of birth length and length increment. In babies born to poorly nourished mothers, the catch-up may continue for at least a year (Banik, Nayar, Krishna, Ray, & Tasker, 1972).

This slowing down of growth between 34 and 40 weeks enables a genetically large child developing in the uterus of a small mother to be successfully delivered at the proper time. It operates in other species of mammals also; the most dramatic demonstration was made by crossing reciprocally a large Shire horse and a small Shetland pony (Walton & Hammond, 1938). The pair in which the mother was a Shire had a large newborn foal, and the pair in which the mother was a Shetland had a small foal. But both foals were the same size after a few months. The same occurs in certain cattle crosses (Dickinson, 1960).

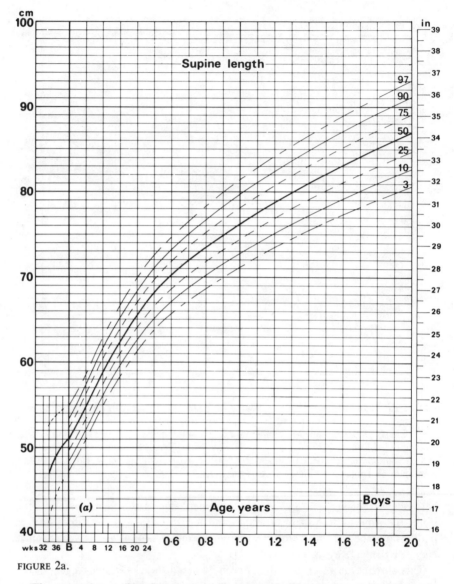

FIGURE 2a.

The control acts therefore by retarding growth. Relatively small babies who are born to restraining mothers, and who have large velocities after birth, must be born at a lesser maturity than the average.

The way in which the maternal control works is not known. Although it is probable that the effect proceeds from the uterus, it is uncertain whether systemic factors are also involved. The placenta at first grows more rapidly than the fetus, but from 30 weeks onward this situation reverses, and the placenta/fetus weight

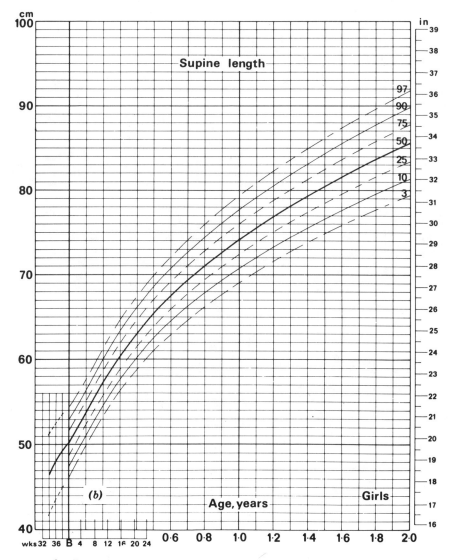

FIGURE 2b. Figures 2a and 2b are standards for growth in length for boys and girls from birth to 2 years. Babies born before 40 weeks should have their values plotted at the appropriate number of weeks gestation with subsequent values plotted in relation to this "conception age." (From J. M. Tanner, in Arneil and Forfar (Eds.), *Textbook of Paediatrics*, Edinburgh: Livingstone, 1973.)

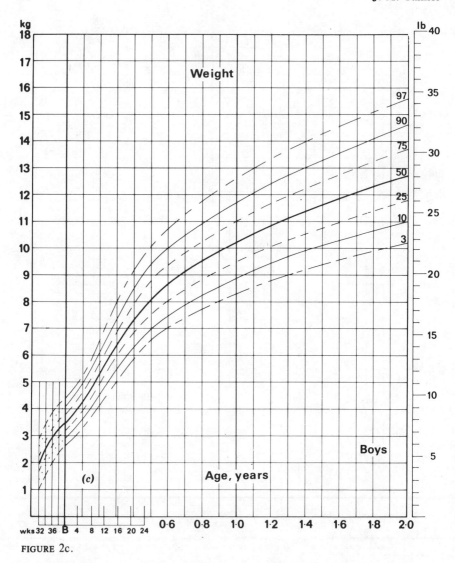

FIGURE 2c.

ratio begins to fall. It may be that the placenta simply cannot increase its capacity to supply nutriments sufficiently to maintain the rapid 34-week weight velocity even in the average fetus. In fetuses growing in mothers with small placentas, the deficit can be even more marked. In mice and guinea pigs hydrodynamic factors seem to be involved, the size of the placenta being dependent on the pressure at which the maternal blood reaches it, and the size of the fetuses in turn depending on the size of the placenta (McLaren, 1965). However, placental morphology

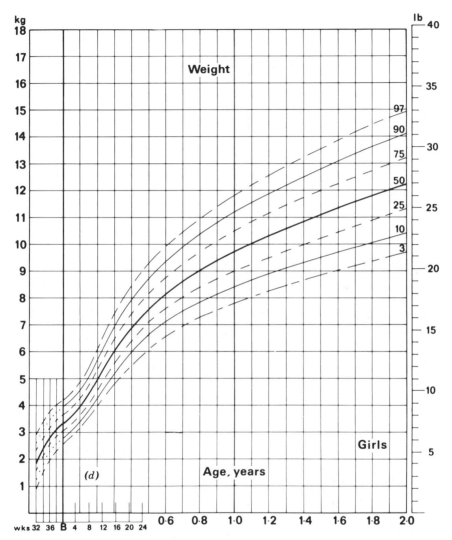

FIGURE 2d. Figures 2c and 2d are standards for growth in weight for boys and girls from birth to 2 years. Babies born before 40 weeks should have their values plotted at the appropriate number of weeks gestation with subsequent values plotted in relation to this "conception age." (From J. M. Tanner, in Arneil and Forfar (Eds.), *Textbook of Paediatrics*, Edinburgh: Livingstone, 1973.)

and physiology differ so much among species that we cannot be sure this finding applies to man.

The maternal restraining effect persists from one pregnancy to the next; some mothers consistently produce rather large babies and others rather small ones.

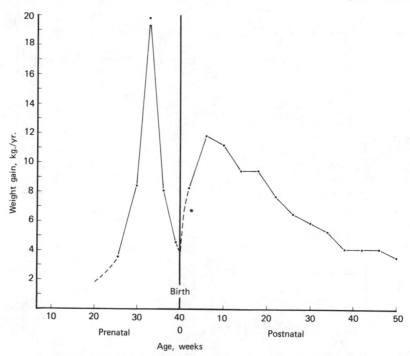

FIGURE 3. Velocity of growth in weight of singleton children. Prenatal curve from McKeown and Record (1952) from birth weights of preterm children. Postnatal data from Ministry of Health (1959). (From Tanner, 1963.)

Thus siblings resemble each other in birth weight, the correlation being about 0.5. This correlation is due chiefly to maternal factors (Robson, 1955), since half-sibs with the same mother have also a correlation of about 0.5, whereas half-sibs with the same father but different mothers have a correlation of only 0.1 (Morton, 1955). Analysis of the birth weight correlation between relatives shows that much of the difference among mothers is inherited (Penrose, 1961; Robson, 1955), although of course it does not show whether this inherited portion is a uterine or a systemic characteristic.

Thus within-family variation in birth weight is considerably less than the variation in the whole population. The within-family standard deviation is about 310 grams, compared with a population standard deviation of about 450 grams. Where possible, the relative size of a newborn should be judged in relation to his siblings' size rather than the size of newborns in general; standards for doing this have recently been given by Tanner, Healy, and Lejarraga (1972). In some series of data (e.g. Aberdeen; Thomson, Billewicz, & Hytten, 1968) but not in others (Sydney middle-class; Tanner, Lejarraga, & Turner, 1972), there is a correlation between the weight of the newborn and the height and weight of the mother. The correlation is low, however; differences in mother's sizes account for only a

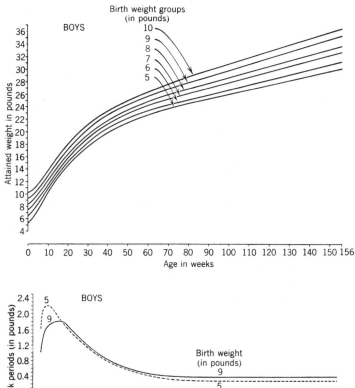

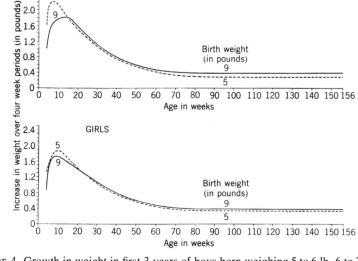

FIGURE 4. Growth in weight in first 3 years of boys born weighing 5 to 6 lb, 6 to 7 lb, and so on. Above, (a) weight for age, boys only. Below, (b) velocity of growth of children weighing 5 to 6 lb and 9 to 10 lb. (From Ministry of Health, 1959.)

small amount of the variation in the birth weights of their children. Some part of the variation in the mother's adult sizes, in developed but socioeconomically heterogeneous populations, reflects the conditions of life of the mothers when they themselves were children. Restrictions on a mother's development in height might be correlated, although only to a slight degree, with restrictions on the size of the uterus.

Although less is known about maternal influences on birth length than on birth weight, available evidence indicates that a similar restraint occurs. The length at birth fails to reflect at all well length at adulthood; the correlation is only about 0.3. This correlation rises rapidly during the first year and the length at age 2 closely foreshadows adult height, with a correlation approaching 0.8 (Tanner, Healy, Lockhart, MacKenzie, & Whitehouse, 1956). Similarly, birth length correlates very poorly with the adult height of the parents (see Table 1), but by 1 year the correlation has risen to levels nearly as high as in adult life (Tanner, Goldstein, & Whitehouse, 1970). Only after birth can the genes of the fetus controlling adult size express themselves; until then the maternal influence predominates. The first year is one of great adjustment in growth pattern; by 1 year of age the child's size has come very much to represent its own adult size status, and thus to resemble the size status of its parents.

TABLE 1   Correlation between Height (or Length) of Child at successive Ages and Midparent Height (Average of Mother's and Father's Heights)[a,b]

Age (years)	Boys	Girls
0.083	0.22	0.28
0.25	0.39	0.34
0.50	0.44	0.43
0.75	0.41	0.41
1.0	0.52	0.41
1.5	0.48	0.46
2.0	0.49	0.46
3.0	0.57	0.47
4.0	0.54	0.49
5.0	0.58	0.55
6.0	0.49	0.49
7.0	0.55	0.49
8.0	0.53	0.49
9.0	0.50	0.50

[a]Pooled data I.C.C. European Studies. From Tanner et al. (1970), where source of data is detailed.
[b] Supine length 0.083 to 2.0 years; stature 3.0 to 9.0 years.

The hereditary factors of the fetus, then, have little effect in controlling size before birth, but are to a large extent responsible for the rapidity and magnitude of the catchup during the first year after birth.

Socioeconomic Circumstances and Habits of Mothers

In developed countries with considerable differences in the socioeconomic circumstances of their citizens, the birth weights and lengths of the less well off are somewhat below those of the very well off. This difference in size persists throughout childhood and is still present in adults. However, in Aberdeen, a town in Scotland with a relatively homogeneous population and exceptionally good antenatal services, social class birth weight differences practically disappeared when maternal size was allowed for (Thomson et al., 1968). In such a town therefore these differences probably do not reflect differences in maternal nutrition during pregnancy, although they may reflect in part the nutritional circumstances of the mother during her own childhood (see also Adams & Niswarden, 1968).

The malnutrition that occurs in underdeveloped countries, and during the wars of developed ones, has been shown to decrease the growth of the fetus in the last 2 to 4 weeks of its development, although not much earlier (Dean, 1950; Grunewald, 1967; Smith, 1947). The weights of newborns are fairly uniform all over the world up to nearly 38 weeks, but thereafter diverge between rich and poor countries.

Smoking by the mother during the last 2 months of pregnancy appears to lower the birthweight, on average about 0.17 kg (Butler & Alberman, 1969; Butler, Goldstein, & Ross, 1972).

VARIATION IN PHYSICAL MATURITY AT BIRTH

Although babies born at 38 weeks postmenstrual age are on average less mature than those born at 40 weeks, simple time *in utero* is not itself a measure of maturity. Fetuses progress at different tempi of growth, just as do children and adolescents, so that even among babies all born at 40 weeks, some are relatively advanced in their development and others relatively delayed.

The problem is to measure the degree of maturity (Mitchell & Farr, 1965). The methods proposed are: (1) radiological appearance: skeletal maturity or "bone age"; (2) neurological function: "neuromaturational age"; (3) "clinical external" characteristics; (4) body shape: "shape age"; (5) biochemical characteristics.

Since different body systems do not all mature at the same rate, different measures of maturity give different results. A fuller discussion can be found in Tanner (1962); in principle all the same problems occur in relation to the newborn as are there considered in relation to the older child.

Radiological Appearance: "Bone Age"

This is a measure of how far the bones have progressed along their course of development. Each bone begins as a primary center of ossification, passes through various stages of enlargement and shaping of the ossified area, acquires in some cases one or more epiphyses, and finally reaches its adult form, with fusion of the epiphysis. The *sequence* of events in a given bone is the same in all individuals, irrespective of whether the bone is advanced or delayed in its ossification in relation to chronological age. Thus a scale of skeletal maturity on bone age may be constructed.

In older children the most convenient and useful area to x-ray is the hand and wrist, but in the infant few hand and wrist centers are present. From birth to about 18 months, a more informative area is the knee and ankle, since the centers (in this context "maturity indicators") at the lower end of the femur and upper end of the tibia are usually present at birth, and four centers in the ankle usually appear during the first few months. The amount of radiation involved in taking such radiographs is very small, indeed equivalent to that necessarily incurred (and as a whole-body radiation) in spending about 3 weeks on a holiday in the mountains. There is no evidence that such a small dose of radiation in man causes any harm.

In older children standards for bone age have been set up on the basis of the hand and wrist appearances (Greulich & Pyle 1959; Tanner, Whitehouse, & Healy, 1962). In the latter method the appearance of each center is scored by matching with a set of standard plates, and the scores are added to give a "skeletal maturity score." This can be compared with scores of the standardizing group of children, and a centile position for skeletal maturity read off a graph just as for height. Alternatively, the score may be converted to a bone age if desired, a bone age of 6 years being by definition the score of the fiftieth centile child at that age.

Unfortunately, infant bone age standards have been much less developed than standards for older children. Much of the literature about the newborn concerns the use of radiographs to estimate the length of gestation. Many of these articles contain a logical inconsistency, since they assume that bone age is exactly correlated with length of gestation instead of varying even at a given gestational age. Underlying the authors' anxiety to estimate the length of gestation, however, is usually a desire to know what chances of survival a given infant has and what treatment should be given, and these are probably more related to true skeletal maturity than to length of gestation or postconceptional age. The still rather crude standards of Vincent and Hugon (1962) may best be used in infants, with locally derived norms.

Skeletal maturity in infants is affected by heredity (Parkin, Neligan, Dee, &

Simpson 1969), fetal nutrition, and maternal nutrition if it is poor. As in later years (see Tanner, 1962), girls are more mature on average than boys. The sex difference becomes apparent at about 30 weeks postmenstrual age (Singh & Venkatachalan,1963; Vincent & Hugon, 1962), and amounts to about 2 "weeks" of bone age at birth, 3 "weeks" at 6 months after birth, and 8 "weeks" at 1 year (Pyle & Hoerr, 1969; Hoerr, Pyle, & Francis, 1962). Thus separate standards have to be set up for girls and boys. This is desirable for another reason also; although in each bone the sequence of changes is the same in all children, there are sex differences between bones in the relative speed with which development occurs (i.e., sex-bone interaction). The manner in which this can be dealt with is outlined in the latest revision of the Tanner-Whitehouse standards (Tanner et al., 1974).

There are differences between races also, black newborns and infants being on average more skeletally mature than whites living in similar or better circumstances (see Tanner, 1962, for references). Differences according to fetal nutrition are inferred from the fact that in monozygotic twins the bone age of the one who is heavier at birth is nearly always in advance of that of the lighter (Parkin et al., 1969). Genetic differences being absent, the differences both in weight and bone age presumably reflect chiefly the "lie" in the uterus of each twin, and are mediated by their relative nutrition. Maternal nutrition can also affect skeletal maturity at birth, but for this to occur the nutrition of the mother must be relatively poor (Tompkins & Wiehl, 1954; Tarleton, Crump, & Horton, 1969).

Neurological Function

Just as a child's bones pass through a sequence of changes during development *in utero*, so also does a child's nervous system. Saint-Anne Dargassies (1966) (see also Amiel-Tison, 1968) has described in detail the changes occurring in the responses to neurological examination from 28 to 41 weeks. The examination is of a clinical type and concerns the infant's posture, mobility, muscle reflexes, and sensory and autonomic nervous system responses to light, heat, cold, vibration, taste, and so on. Dargassies emphasizes that maturation occurs in a definite sequence, and that it appears to be independent of environmental stimuli and of experience, to judge by the progress of newborns delivered preterm. The development of these is neither accelerated nor slowed by extrauterine conditions. Robinson (1966), who studied the development of 10 clear-cut reflexes in children born between 25 and 42 weeks postmenstrual age, reached the same conclusion:

"The gestational ages at which the reflexes could first be elicited were the same whatever the stage of gestation at which the baby was born. This was demonstrated by the longitudinal study of babies born early in gestation. . . .

Neurological maturation in the latter third of gestation is neither accelerated nor retarded by extrauterine influences (other than obviously injurious ones)."

Thus it is possible to construct a scale of "neuromaturational age" (Graziani, Weizman, & Velasco, 1968) for newborns and infants, using a scoring system similar to that used in the construction of scales for bone age and tooth age. Basing their scores on Dargassies and on the examination of the newborn of Prechtl and Beintema (1964) and others, Farr (1968b), Graziani et al. (1968), and Dubowitz, Dubowitz, & Goldberg (1970) have provided such systems. Farr found that a score for "reflex gestational age" estimated the length of gestation to within 2½ weeks of that given by the history of the last menstrual period. Looked at the other way, the scores act as a scale of maturity, given that one takes the length of gestation as correct.

The scale of Dubowitz et al. (1970) is probably the best for use at present. Ten neurological criteria are used, together with 11 clinical external criteria as given by Farr (see below). Each of the 10 items is rated on a 3- to 6-point scale. The total neurological score ranges from 0 to 35, and the whole score from 0 to 70. A diagram of the neurological responses is given. The ratings are shown to be reliable and not influenced by the state of the baby. A graph is given enabling the reader to estimate the "gestational age" from the score, but no population limits are yet available.

It is noteworthy that on this score, comprising both neurological and clinical external criteria, the range for babies born at precisely 40 weeks is about 50 to 62 units, which corresponds to a difference in "neuroexternal maturity age" of 3 to 4 weeks. Clearly, any study of newborns should seek to characterize them by maturity as well as simple age.

Electroencephalogram (EEG) responses to flash of light (*evoked potentials*) have been quite extensively studied from 28 weeks (Dreyfus-Brisac, 1966; Engel & Benson, 1968), and provide a second index of neurological maturation. The time from the flash to the beginning of the EEG response, called the photic latency, decreases as the baby grows older, and Engel and Benson have given data which can be used with virtually no change as a maturity scale for this characteristic in newborns. Figure 5 shows the very large standard deviation of the photic latency at each week of postmenstrual age. They remark that a given baby shows only very small differences in latency on hourly retesting during the day, so the variation is not due to unreliability or within-individual changes but must reflect differences among babies, some of them of maturational origin. They note that preterm infants did not mature quite so fast as term ones, that is to say, did not quite reach the same level by 38 to 40 weeks. (These babies were not followed further, as in the study of Moosa and Dubowitz cited below.)

Girls on average had a shorter latency than boys at all ages from 35 to 42 weeks (Figure 5). This corresponds to girls being about 1 week more mature than boys

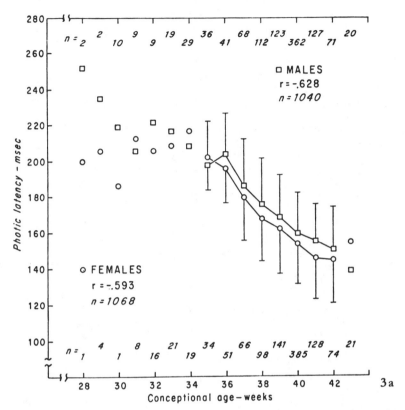

FIGURE 5. Mean plus or minus one standard deviation of latency of evoked potentials to light flash, girls and boys, newborns at 38 to 43 weeks' gestation. (From Engel & Benson, 1968.)

at the time of birth (contrasting with 2 weeks in skeletal maturity). Negroes were said to have on average a shorter latency than whites of the same postmenstrual age, presumably also implying greater maturity. Twins were a little retarded in maturation compared with singletons, but there was no tendency for the heavier twin to be more mature than the lighter in this characteristic. No such tendency was seen in nerve conduction velocity either (see below) (Schultz, Michaelis, Linke, & Nolte 1968).

Vitova and Horbeck (1972 have studied the development of another EEG characteristic, the response to a flickering light rather than simply to flashes. In this also, changes occur in infancy; the optimal "driving" frequency is 3 cycles/second in newborns and 8 cycles/second in infants. This technique might perhaps be developed to serve as a maturation indicator.

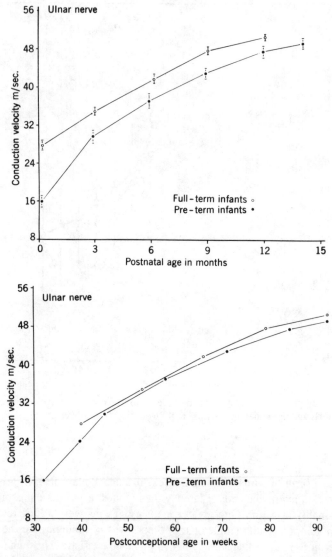

FIGURE 6. Age changes in conduction velocity of ulnar nerves in preterm and full-term infants: (*a*), plotted against age after birth (upper figure); (*b*) plotted against postconceptional age (lower figure). (From Moosa & Dubowitz, 1971.)

The *conduction velocity* of the peripheral nerves gives a further index of neurological maturation (Blom & Finnstrom, 1968; Dubowitz, Whitaker, Brown, & Robinson, 1968; Schultz et al., 1968). There is a more-or-less linear increase in velocity from 30 to 42 weeks postmenstrual age; gradually the rate of increase becomes less (the graph against age being parabolic), and adult rates are reached at about age 2. The measurement is simple and may even be made without waking the infant; an electrical stimulus is given just below the elbow, or the knee, to stimulate the ulnar, or posterior tibial or peroneal nerves, and the twitch of the peripheral muscles is picked up by surface electrodes. The results are reliable and objective. There are insufficient data in the literature to judge whether girls are more mature than boys in this aspect of neurological function, but unpublished results of Dubowitz indicate that they probably are, on the order of 1 week to 10 days. The arm is a little ahead of the leg in conduction rate, hence maturity, a result in agreement with morphological studies on the regional development of the brain and clinical examination of the infant.

Blom and Finnstrom stress the large and reliable differences between newborns even of the same postmenstrual age. Moosa and Dubowitz (1971) studied the subsequent development of nine preterms (not light-for-dates) babies compared with a group of full-term ones (Figure 6). At 40 weeks' conceptional age (i.e., calculated after the first day of the last menstrual period), the conduction velocity in the arms, although not the legs, of the preterm babies was slightly (but significantly) retarded compared with the 40-week full-term babies. However, by 45 weeks both were the same and remained so up to 90 weeks conceptional age, the last point studied. This confirms Dargassies' and Robinson's opinions, that if there was any effect of the external environment on the development of nerve conduction it was minor and transient. Moosa and Dubowitz' article gives a very good example of the correctness of plotting measurements of babies against conceptional or postmenstrual age and the incorrectness of plotting against age after birth, in which the preterm babies fail to catch up in velocity (Figure 6). The former plot should always be made in critical studies of infants, even if all the subjects are full-term, that is, born within the age range of 37 to 41 weeks.

Clinical External Characteristics

Several external characteristics of a newborn vary according to its maturity at birth. These are the texture, color, and opacity of the skin, the presence of edema, the state of the lanugo (fine downy hair), the ear form and firmness, the shape of the genitalia, breasts, and nipples, and the presence of plantar skin creases. Farr (1968a) devised a scoring system for each of these, which was followed with minor modifications by Dubowitz et al. (1970) in the article discussed above.

This examination was designed for obtaining a clinical external maturity score in the newborn, and its applicability naturally lapses soon after birth. The indices of neurological maturity and especially of conduction velocity apply, although with diminishing usefulness, for several months after birth.

Body Shape

The human fetus develops from the head down like most vertebrates; that is to say, its head is always in advance of, or nearer completion than, its body and limbs. This maturity gradient (see Tanner, 1962, p. 74) also applies to the limbs as a whole, the arms being generally more advanced than the legs; but within the limbs, surprisingly, the gradient goes the other way, the periphery being in advance. (Thus hands and feet stop growing before upper arms and thighs.) Thus the newborn has a larger head and a smaller body and limbs than the young child.

The degree of maturity at birth can in principle be judged by seeing how far the process of change toward adult shape has progressed. In the simplest terms this might be the ratio of head circumference to length or even head circumference to weight (except during the period when head circumference is still affected by birth molding). The ratio of crown-rump length to total length also changes with age, as the legs grow more swiftly than the trunk.

The difficulty in using such indices as measures of maturity, however, is basically the same as the difficulty in using simple weight and length. A tall child may be tall either because he is advanced in maturity, or because he is going to be a tall adult, born of tall parents. The measurement of stature does not distinguish these two conditions, and the use by pediatricians of so-called "height age" to compare one child with another in maturity is erroneous. The difficulty arises because children end up with different heights; bone age, by contrast, is a legitimate measure of maturity because all children end up with the same bone age.

Thus change in *shape* reflects maturation better than change in *size;* but the difficulty that children end up with different shapes still persists. An index of shape that is independent (or nearly so) of final shape differences would be a highly useful measure but so far none has been computed.

Biochemical Characteristics

Numbers of biochemical indices change during fetal life and in the first year after birth. Thus in the fetus there is one kind of hemoglobin and in the adult another. The change takes place gradually from about the 36th week to about a month after birth. The newborn of the fortieth week has about 75% fetal and 25% adult hemoglobin. Thus the ratio can be used as an index of a certain type of maturity; however, it is also affected by anemia, even of minor degree, in the infant. Another approach is to estimate the levels of various enzymes in the blood or urine. To date, however, this shows more how great the biochemical variation in newborns is, rather than how a scale of maturity can be constructed. However, substances are being discovered whose excretion is linked to postconceptional age (Townes & Ferrare, 1972).

For newborns analyses of creatinine and cell content of amniotic fluid may be useful for estimation of gestational age (Donnai, Gordon, Harris, & Hughes, 1971) but are seldom available for later research subjects. The same is true of the lecithin/sphingomyelin ratio in the amniotic fluid (Bhagwanani, Fahmy, & Turnbull, 1972).

VARIATION IN SHAPE AND BODY COMPOSITION

Though all newborns may look the same to adults not accustomed to working with them, the facts are quite otherwise. All physical measurements of newborns and infants show variability of the same order (relative to absolute size) as do adults. Shape is no exception to this rule, except perhaps in one particular case. Some of the adult variation in shape arises at puberty as a distinct sex dimorphism; thus variation in the amount of muscle or in the size of the jaw in adult males is relatively greater than in prepubertal ones.

Some variations in shape have been discussed above; the relation of head circumference to body length, or of trunk length to total length is an index of maturity, as well as of different persistent builds.

The shape of the face and head (see Joseph & Dawbarn, 1970) is perhaps of particular significance in eliciting maternal responses. Children who are born LFD often have a rather characteristic face, arrested in a relatively immature stage. The calvaria, or head above the level of the eyes and ears, is relatively large; the center portion of the face is rather small and the jaw is very small. The ears are low-set, the nasal bridge more depressed than usual, and the corners of the mouth often turned down (see Tanner & Ham, 1969). Lorenz (1956) has discussed the features of a baby that make adults call it *herzig* (from *herzen*, to fondle) or *cute*.

"The head must have a large neurocranium, and the eyes must be below the middle of the whole profile. Beneath there must be a fat cheek. The extremities must be short and broad. The consistency of the body ought to be that of a half-inflated football, elastic . . . and finally the whole thing must be small, must be a miniature of something [p. 128]."

The child's buccal fat pad is of considerable importance in forming this picture. It is a very special organ, said to persist even in starvation when all the rest of the body fat is mobilized, and said, on perhaps dubious grounds, to be important for sucking at the breast. Young monkeys do not have it, which (together with the lack of fat on their bottoms), in Lorenz' view, prevents them from looking cuddly. Children differ both in the size of their buccal pad and in the rate at which they lose it.

Fat elsewhere in the body is perhaps also important from the point of view of the mother, as well as from that of the child. Subcutaneous fat begins to be laid down at about the thirtieth week *in utero* and increases in amount until 6 to 9 months after birth (Garn, Greaney, & Young, 1956; Tanner, 1962). It then declines gradually, until about age 5; later it increases once again. Girls have only slightly more fat than boys at birth (Gampel, 1965; Garn, 1958; Vincent & Hugon, 1962), but by 6 months there is in most data a clear sex difference, which persists for the rest of life. This of course concerns the averages only; there is some overlap between male and female distributions. Equally, the statement that the maximum fat is reached at 6 to 9 months applies to near-average babies; some reach their fat peak earlier and some later. Subcutaneous fat may be simply measured by picking up a fold between thumb and forefinger (best over the triceps and under the angle of the scapula) and measuring its width with Harpenden skin fold caliper (Tanner & Whitehouse, 1957). This technique is perfectly feasible in most infants.

At first the distributions of fat measurements are not much skewed, but by about 6 months they become so, with a long tail to the right which characterizes them thenceforth. This may be because at first increase in fat is mainly due to multiplication of fat cells, but during the first year this is increasingly replaced by the packing of fat into existing cells. The degree to which fat may be packed into a cell seems to be exponentially, not normally, distributed. Boys and girls do not differ in the number of fat cells they have, only in the amount of fat in them (Brook, 1972).

The cause of this infantile subcutaneous fat wave and the reason for its biological existence is not at all clear. It does not occur in other primates. This fat seems not to function primarily as a ready source of calories for the human, as does the special brown fat pad in certain other animals, but it may be necessary as a source of fatty acids. If an equivalent of the brown fat pad exists at all in man, it seems more likely to be located in the deep "central" body fat rather than in these superficial areas (Brook, 1972). Perhaps Alastair Hardy was right after all in his evolutionary suggestions, and during the Wader Man phase subcutaneous fat developed to add buoyancy in the shallows and insulation in cold water.

The amount of muscle may also be important to the caregiver, especially as an indication of masculinity in a boy. Singh and Venkatachalam (1963) took radiographs of the calf and forearm of newborns and measured widths of fat, bone, and muscle. The boys had considerably more muscle on average, exceeding the girls by about 7%. (In width of limb bones, the sex difference is only about 3%.) Again there are considerable individual differences, the standard deviation of limb muscle width being about 8% of the mean.

Sex Differences in the Newborn

Finally, it may be useful to summarize what has been said above about differences between girl and boy newborns and infants. Boys are larger, and particularly so in the head and face region. They are considerably more muscular but have slightly less fat as newborns and considerably less fat as 9-month-old infants. They grow faster in length and weight from birth till about 7 months, but then more slowly; boys decelerate in growth faster than girls.

Girls are more advanced in skeletal maturity from about 30 weeks' gestation onward, and in neurological maturity as judged by photic stimulation latency period and probably also by peripheral nerve conduction rate from 35 weeks until some time after birth.

Summary

Variation among newborns in size and shape is just as relatively great as variability in school children or adults. Variation in physiological maturity or "developmental age" is also large, amounting to about 3 to 4 weeks of development among babies all of exactly 40 weeks' gestational age. The factors that affect birth weight and birth length have been detailed.

Methods of assessing maturity in the newborn have been discussed, including skeletal maturation and neurological maturation judged by the latency period of light-evoked potentials, the speed of peripheral nerve conduction, and external clinical characteristics.

Sex differences in size, shape, and maturity of newborns and infants have been detailed; girls are ahead of boys at birth by about 2 weeks in bone age, and 1 to 2 weeks in neurological maturation.

The effects of these variations in size, shape, and maturity on the attitude of the caregiver have not been studied scientifically. It would be strange if they were negligible.

REFERENCES

Adams, M. S., & Niswander, J. D. Birth weight of North American Indians. *Human Biology*, 1968, **40**, 226–234.

Amiel-Tison, C. Neurological evaluation of the maturity of newborn infants. *Archives of Disease in Childhood*, 1968, **43**, 89–93.

Banik, N. D. D., Nayar, S., Krishna, R., Ray, L., & Tasker, A. D. Some observations on low birth weight babies during the first year. *Indian Paediatrics*, 1972, **9**, 95–98.

Bhagwanani, S. G., Fahmy, D., & Turnbull, A. C., Prediction of neonatal respiratory distress by estimation of amniotic-fluid lecithin. *Lancet*, 1972, **1**, 159–162.

Blom, S., & Finnstrom, O. Motor conduction velocities in newborn infants of various gestational ages. *Acta Paediatrica Scandinavica*, 1968, **57**, 377–384.

Brook, C. G. D. *Obesity in childhood*. M.D. thesis, Cambridge University, 1972.

Butler, N., & Alberman, E. D. *Perinatal problems: The second report of the 1958 British Perinatal Mortality Survey*. London: Livingstone, 1969.

Butler, N. R., Goldstein, H., & Ross, E. M. Cigarette smoking in pregnancy: Its influence on birth weight and perinatal mortality. *British Medical Journal*, 1972, **I**, 127.

Dargassies, S. Neurological maturation of the premature infant of 28 to 41 weeks gestational age. In F. Falkner (Ed.), *Human development*, London: Saunders, 1966. PP 306–325.

Dean, R. F. A., The affect of undernutrition on the size of the baby at birth and on the ability of the mother to lactate. *Proceedings of the Royal Society of Medicine*, 1950, **43**, 273.

Dickinson, A. G. Some genetic implications of maternal effects—An hypothesis of mammalian growth. *Journal of Agricultural Science*, 1960, **54**, 379–390.

Donnai, P., Gordon, H., Harris, D. A., & Hughes, E. A. Further studies in the assessment of gestational age by amniotic fluid analysis. *Journal of Obstetrics and Gynaecology of the British Commonwealth*, 1971, **78**, 603–609.

Dreyfus-Brisac, C. The bioelectrical development of the central nervous system during early life. In F. Falkner (Ed.), *Human development*, London, Saunders, 1966. Pp 286–305.

Dubowitz, L. M. S., Dubowitz, V., & Goldberg, C. Clinical assessment of gestational age in the newborn infant. *Journal of Paediatrics*, 1970, **77**, 1–10.

Dubowitz, V., Whittaker, G. F., Brown, B. H., & Robinson, A. Nerve conduction velocity: An index of neurological maturity of the newborn infant. *Developmental Medicine and Child Neurology*, 1968, **10**, 741–749.

Engel, R., & Benson, R. C. Estimate of conceptional age by evoked response activity. *Biologia Neonatorum*, 1968, **12**, 201–214.

Farr, V. Estimation of gestational age: comparison between radiological assessment and maturity scoring. *Biologia Neonatorum*, 1968, **12**, 35–41. (a)

Farr, V., Estimation of gestational age by neurological assessment in first week of life. *Archives of Disease in Childhood*, 1968, **43**, 353–357. (b)

Farr, V., & Mitchell, R. G. Estimation of gestational age in the newborn infant. *American Journal of Obstetrics and Gynaecology, 1968*, **103**, 380–383.

Gampel, B. The relation of skinfold thickness in the neonate to sex, length of gestation, size at birth and maternal skinfold. *Human Biology*, 1965, **37**, 29–37.

Garn, S. M. Fat, Body size and growth in the newborn. *Human Biology*, 1958, **30**, 265–280.

Garn, S. M., Greaney, G. R., & Young, R. W., Fat thickness and growth progress during infancy. *Human Biology*, 1956, **28**, 232–250.

Graziani, L. J., Weizman, E. D., & Valasco, M. S. A., Neurologic maturation and auditory evoked responses in low birth weight infants. *Pediatrics*, 1968, **41**, 483.

Greulich, W. H., & Pyle, S. I., *Radiographic atlas of skeletal development of the hand and wrist.* (2nd ed.) Stanford University Press, California, 1968.

Gruenwald, P. Growth of the human foetus. In A. McLaren (Ed.), *Advances in reproductive physiology*, Vol. II, London: Logos, 1967. Pp. 279–309.

Hedberg, E., & Holmdahl, K. On relationship between maternal health and intrauterine growth of the foetus. *Acta Obstetrica et Gynaecologica Scandinavica*, 1970, **49**, 225–230.

Hoerr, N. L., Pyle, S. I., & Francis, C. C., *Radiographic atlas of skeletal development of the foot and ankle.* Springfield, Ill.: C. C. Thomas, 1962.

Jonxis, J. H. P. The development of haemoglobin. *Paediatric Clinics of North America*, 1965, **12**, 535–556.

Joseph, M., & Dawbarn, C. *Measurement of the facies: A study in Down's syndrome.* S.I.M.P. Research Monographs, No. 3, London: Heinemann, 1970.

Larroche, J. C., The development of the central nervous system during intra-uterine life. In F. Falkner (Ed.), *Human Development* London: Saunders, 1966. Pp. 257–276.

Lorenz, K. Z. In J. M. Tanner & B. Inhelder (Eds.), *Discussions of child development* Vol. I, London: Tavistock Publications. P. 128.

McKeown, T. & Record, R. G. Observations on foetal growth in multiple pregnancy in man. *Journal of Endocrinology*, 1952, **8**, 386–401.

McKeown, R. & Record, R. G. The influence of placental size on foetal growth in man, with special reference to multiple pregnancy. *Journal of Endocrinology*, 1953, **9**, 418–426.

McLaren, A. Genetic and environmental effects on foetal and placental growth in mice. *Journal of Reproduction and Fertility*. 1965, **9**, 79–98.

Ministry of Health. *Standards of normal weight in infancy*. Ministry of Health Report, Public Health, No. 99, London: Her Majesty's Stationery Office, 1959.

Mitchell, R. G., & Farr, V. The meaning of maturity and the assessment of maturity at birth. In M. Dawkins & W. C. MacGregor (Eds.), *Gestational age, size and maturity*, London: Heinemann, 1965.

Moosa, A., & Dubowitz, V. Postnatal maturation of peripheral nerves in preterm and full-term infants. *Journal of Pediatrics*, 1971, **79**, 915–922.

Morton, N. E. The inheritance of human birth weight. *Annals of Human Genetics, 1955*, **20**, 125–134.

Naeye, R. L., Benirschke, K., Hagstrom, J. W. C., & Marcus, C. C. Intrauterine growth of twins as estimated from live-born birthweight data. *Pediatrics*, 1966, **37**, 409–416.

Papousek, H. A physiological view of early autogenesis of so-called voluntary movements. *Plzen.lek. Sb.* Supplement, **3**, 195–198.

Parkin, J. M., Neligan, G. A., Dee, P. M., & Simpson, W. the influence of genetic differences, nutrition and sex on the radiological appearances of the lower limb ossification centres in newborn twins. *Human Biology*, 1969, **41**, 1–12.

Penrose, L. S. Genetics of growth and development of the foetus. In L. S. Penrose (Ed.), *Recent advances in human genetics*, London: Churchill, 1961. Pp. 56–75.

Prader, A., Tanner, J. M., & Von Harnack, G. A. Catch-up growth following illness or starvation. *Journal of Pediatrics*, 1963, **62**, 646–659.

Prechtl, H. F. R., & Beuntema, D. *The neurological examination of the newborn infant.* Clinics Developmental Medicine. Vol. 12. London: Heinmann, 1964.

Robinson, R. K. Assessment of gestational age by neurological examination. *Archives of Disease in Childhood*, 1966, **41**, 437–447.

Robson, E. B. Birth weight in cousins. *Annals of Human Genetics*, 1955, **19**, 262.

Schultz, F. K., Michaelis, R., Linke, I., & Nolte, R. Motor nerve conduction velocity in term, preterm and small-for-dates infants. *Pediatrics*, 1968, **42**, 17.

Singh, R, & P. S. Anthropometric studies of the newborn. *Indian Journal of Medical Research*, 1962, **50**, 794–799.

Singh, R., & Venkatachalam, P. S., Radiographic studies of the newborn with special reference to to subcutaneous fat and osseous development. *Indian Journal of Medical Research*, 1963, **51**, 522–532.

Smith, C. A. Effects of maternal undernutrition upon the newborn infant in Holland 1944–45. *Journal of Pediatrics*, 1947, **30**, 229.

Sterky, G. Swedish standard curves for intra-uterine growth. *Pediatrics*, 1970, **46**, 7–8.

Tanner, J. M. *Growth at adolescence.* (2nd ed.) Oxford: Blackwell Scientific Publications, 1962.

Tanner, J. M. The regulation of human growth. *Child Development*, 1963, **34**, 817–847.

Tanner, J. M., & Thomson, A. M. Standards for birthweight at gestation periods from 32 to 42 weeks, allowing for maternal height and weight. *Archives of Disease in Childhood*, 1970, **45**, 566–569.

Tanner, J. M., Goldstein, H., & Whitehouse, R. H. Standards for childrens' height at ages 2 to 9 years, allowing for height of parents. *Archives of Disease in Childhood*, 1970, **45**, 755–762.

Tanner, J. M., Healy, M. J. R., & Lejarraga, H. Within-family standards for birthweight: A revision. *Lancet*, 1972, **2**, 1314–1315.

Tanner, J. M., Healy, M. J. R., Lockhart, R. D., MacKenzie, J. D., & Whitehouse, R. H. Aberdeen growth study. I. The prediction of adult body measurements from measurements taken each year from birth to 5 years. *Archives of Disease in Childhood*, 1956, **31**, 372–381.

Tanner, J. M., Lejarraga, H., & Turner, G. Within-family standards for birthweight. *Lancet*, 1972, **2**, 193–197.

Tanner, J. M., Whitehouse, R. H., & Healy, M. J. R. *A new system for estimating skeletal maturity from the hand and wrist, with standards derived from a study of*

2,600 healthy British children. Parts I and II, Paris: Centre International de l'Enfance, 1962.

Tanner J. M., Whitehouse, R. H., Marshall, W. A., Healy, M. J. R., & Goldstein, H. A revised system (TW2) for estimating skeletal maturity from hand and wrist radiographs with separate standards for carpal and other bones. 1974. To be published.

Tarlton, G. J., Crump, E. P., & Horton, C. P. Growth and development. VIII. Relation of osseous development in the newborn Negro infants to sex, weight, length, skin colour, and reflex maturity index in the infant, and to such maternal factors as parity, length of gestation period, prenatal nutrition, age, height and socio-economic status. *Radiology,* 1960, **75,** 932–941.

Thomson, A. M., Billewicz, W. Z., & Hytten, F. E. The assessment of foetal growth. *Journal of Obstetrics and Gynaecology of the British Commonwealth,* 1968, **75,** 903–916.

Tompkins, D. & Wiehl, D. G. Epiphyseal maturation in the newborn as related to maternal nutritional status. *American Journal of Obstetrics and Gynaecology,* 1956, **68,** 1366–1376.

Townes, P. L. & Ferrari, B. T. Pepsingen 7 as an indicator of neonatal maturity: Preliminary studies. *Journal of Pediatrics,* 1972, **80,** 815–819.

Vincent, M., & Hugon, J. L'insuffisance ponderale du prémature africain au point de vue de la santé publique. *Bulletin of the World Health Organisation,* 1962, **26,** 143–174.

Vitova, A., & Horbeck, A. Developmental study of the responsiveness of the human brain to flicker stimulation. *Developmental Medicine and Neurology,* 1972, **14,** 476–486.

Walton, A., & Hammond, J. The maternal effects on growth and conformation in Shire horse–Shetland pony crosses. *Proceedings of the Royal Society B, 1938,* **125,** 311.

CHAPTER 5

The Effect of the Infant's State, Level of Arousal, Sex, and Ontogenetic Stage on the Caregiver [1]

ANNELIESE F. KORNER

Stanford University School of Medicine

With the recent impetus in infant research, we have become increasingly aware that the young infant is a great deal more capable of organized responses than has been assumed, and that he is not nearly the passive-receptive organism he has been described as for so long. We are beginning to learn that, by virtue of his earliest characteristics, he is an active contributor to the beginning mother-infant interaction. In this chapter I document from my own research and the research of others how certain characteristics of the infant *do* in fact have an impact on this first relationship and how, for the sake of the infant's optimal development and mother-infant mutuality, certain types of individual differences within the infant *should* affect maternal care. I illustrate these points with evidence from three broad categories of infant characteristics. They are: the infant's state of arousal; the infant's sex; and the infant's ontogenetic stage of development.

EFFECT OF THE INFANT'S STATE OF AROUSAL ON THE CAREGIVER

During the neonatal period and during the subsequent earliest weeks of life, the principal interactions between mother and child, aside from feeding, center around comforting and soothing interventions designed to calm the crying infant. Because crying is such a potent and usually aversive stimulus to the mother, I can scarcely think of any period in the child's later life in which he is more predictably the initiator of interactions with his mother than during the earliest weeks of life. Moss and Robson's (1968) evidence on the sequence of

[1] The author's research was supported by U.S. Public Health Service Grants HD-00825 and HD-03591 from the National Institute of Child Health and Human Development, and was conducted under the auspices of Grant RR 81 of the General Clinical Research Centers Program and the Divisions of Research Resources, National Institutes of Health.

105

mother-infant interaction revolving around the infant's crying, supports this strongly. During two 6-hour observation periods at 1 month, it was the infant who initiated roughly four out of five interactions.

From much of the literature and everyday observation, it is safe to say that babies generally, through their crying, are extraordinarily good elicitors of maternal attention. Judging from our study of individual differences (Korner, 1971), it appears that babies differ significantly from each other in the frequency with which they provoke such attention. In this study we monitored the sleeping and waking states of 32 healthy, full-term, 2- to 3-day-old, bottle-fed neonates during four ½-hour periods during two feeding cycles. Among these states we recorded the frequency and duration of the infants' crying. We found highly significant differences among our subjects both in how frequently and how long they cried ($p < .01$ and, $< .05$, respectively). With such individual differences in crying, it is reasonable to infer that an irritable infant initiates interaction with his mother more frequently than a more placid baby. The overly placid baby who, in the long run, may be in greater need of stimulation, may receive less, purely by virtue of his peacefulness. The newborn may thus be viewed, in part at least, as the determiner of how much stimulation he receives.

Since I refer to data originating from our study of individual differences in newborns repeatedly and in different contexts, I briefly describe the kinds of variables we were interested in and the kinds of procedures we used to collect our data. During the four ½-hour periods of state monitoring, which was done in a quiet treatment room with illumination, temperature, and the position of the baby held constant, we recorded the frequencies and durations of: regular sleep, and irregular sleep, with and without REMs; drowse; alert inactivity; waking activity; crying; and what we called "indeterminate state" when the infant's state was not classifiable. We used Wolff's (1966) behavioral criteria with minor modifications for judging these states. Since we were interested in the influence of hunger and satiation on the infants' states, we scheduled the first ½-hour period just prior to the midday feeding, the next immediately after the feeding, another at midpoint between feedings, and the last one just prior to the next feeding. Within the context of each state, we recorded the incidence of spontaneously occurring behaviors such as reflex smiles, startles, erections, and bursts of rhythmic mouthing. Intermittently, during each of the four ½-hour periods, a camera mounted above the infant took film samples of the infant's behavior. A timer attached to the camera automatically turned the camera on and off, thus taking 16 unselected behavior samples which were identical for each infant in length and in the interval since the last feeding. The 1000 ft. of film obtained on each of the 32 babies was then analyzed with the help of a computer attachment for our projector, which allowed us to analyze the film at a predetermined number of frame units at a time. To date, we have undertaken six film analyses, all revolving around clearly distinguishable and frequently occurring neonatal behaviors such as frequency of motions, kinds of motions, and a variety of spontaneous oral behaviors (Korner, 1973; Korner & Beason, 1972; Korner, Chuck, & Dontchos, 1968; Korner and Kraemer, 1972).

After the session during which the infants' states were monitored and film was taken, a session during which the infant was not handled in any way, another interfeed cycle was used to conduct a variety of sensory stimulation experiments. These experiments tested response to touch, texture, light, sound, and to multiple simultaneous stimuli. The sensory stimuli provided were standard in duration and intensity, and were given only when the infant was in a predetermined prestimulus state.

Observer reliabilities were high throughout, both in the direct observations of the infants and in the film analyses. At the beginning of the study and periodically thoughout, we checked interobserver agreements. Agreements were above 90% in all but two behavior categories. In the film analyses, in order to avoid subtle changes in scoring criteria over time, we not only established interobserver reliabilities, but also score-rescore reliabilities for the same person throughout the period a particular film analysis was made.

Returning to our subject, let me single out those findings of our study involving infant characteristics that must affect the caregiver. Perhaps more subtly than the infant's crying, the infant's high arousal as expressed in wakefulness and restlessness affects the mother-infant interaction. Our study clearly points to significant differences among our subjects in durations of waking activity ($p < .01$), the frequency of shifts in states ($p < .01$), and the frequency of global and of diffuse motions ($p < .01$ for both). Long wakefulness and a high degree of restlessness no doubt evoke more frequent interactions with the mother than quiet sleepiness.

The infant's visual alert state seems to hold a special fascination for mothers. Visual behaviors, such as visual fixation and pursuit, which can be elicited during the visual alert state, are probably the most mature behaviors in the neonate's behavioral repertoire. As Rheingold (1961) suggested, the maturity of this behavior is all the more remarkable when one considers that, by the end of the second month, it is already in the form it will keep throughout life. Undoubtedly, it is the forerunner of the capacity for eye-to-eye contact with the mother, which Wolff (1963), Robson (1967), and Robson and Moss (1970) described as a source of intense pleasure for the mother and as a cornerstone in the development of the mother's attachment to her infant. In one of our neonatal studies, we found reliable differences among newborns in how frequently they spontaneously alert (Korner, 1970), and in another study how readily they respond with alertness to different types of maternal ministrations (Korner & Thoman, 1972). Also, Barten, Birns, and Ronch (1971) found highly significant differences in the capacity for visual pursuit among neonates.

Variations in the neonates' sensory responsiveness certainly should feed into his level of arousal, and by implication into the mother-infant relationship. Birns (1965) tested 30 newborns' responses to a variety of sensory stimuli over four consecutive days. She classified the infants as either slightly, moderately, or intensely responsive over sensory modalities, and they maintained their ranks reasonably well over the 4 days. In our study (Korner, 1970), we found a correlation of .42 between visual pursuit and auditory responsiveness which is significant at the .02 level. This confirms Birns' finding that the infant's sensory response threshold levels tend to be similar over several sensory modalities.

Auditory input, in relation to which the organism is perhaps more defenseless than to visual input, may be a particularly rousing source of stimulation. We are currently attempting to test ascending auditory response thresholds, much in the manner in which Bell, Weller, and Waldrop (1971) assessed ascending tactile response thresholds. We are using a tone which has the sound qualities Eisenberg (1965) found to be particularly suitable for eliciting responses in the neonate. This sound is a noise band rather than a pure tone, with harmonics ranging from 133 to 4600 cycles, and with a rapid rise time. It is a speechlike sound which is emitted by an artificial larynx, which is a handy little object no bigger than 6 in. long and 2 in. wide. This artificial larynx has been electronically altered so as to emit, at will, sounds ranging from 1/10- to 10-second duration in 5-dB increments, beginning at 43 dB and ranging to 88 dB at the infant's ear.[2] The sound is delivered during irregular sleep without REMs through a speaker which is at a distance of 9½ inches from the infant's exposed ear. One of the objects of this study is to assess the infant's self-consistency in response thresholds over time. We are just doing preliminary work on this study, but are surprised to have found already several infants who consistently begin to respond at 53 dB between two interfeed periods and one on two consecutive days. Fifty-three decibels is a very low level of sound. It can readily be seen that an infant with marked auditory sensitivity is subject to environmental bombardment of stimuli, which must affect his level of arousal.

Not only does the infant's general arousal, and particularly his irritability, have an effect on his caregiver, his relative soothability does as well. The mother's capability in soothing her infant is one of the cardinal challenges she faces in the infant's earliest weeks of life, and her success or failure cannot help but leave an impact on her feelings of effectiveness and competence as a mother. Several studies, notably by Bridger and Birns (1963), by Birns, Blank, and Bridger (1966), and studies from our own laboratory (Korner & Grobstein, 1967, unpublished; Korner & Thoman, 1972) have shown that newborns differ significantly from each other in how soothable they are. In one of our studies

[2] I thank Dr. Dorothy Huntington and Ralph Hisey from the Department of Hearing and Speech Sciences at Stanford University School of Medicine for their technical help in designing and building our apparatus for testing auditory response thresholds.

(Korner & Thoman, 1972) in which we imitated common maternal soothing techniques, we made six interventions with crying infants which entailed singly, or in combination, contact and vestibular-proprioceptive stimulation, with or without the upright position. Over interventions we found that infants differed significantly from each other in how soothable they were ($p < .001$) and how much they cried after completion of the soothing interventions ($p < .001$).

So far, I have given illustrations of variations in the infant's states and in the level of his arousal, and how, by implication, these may differentially affect the caregiver. All the examples given involved strictly normal babies. In the case of abnormal infants, the impact of the infant's deviation in state and/or level of arousal on the caregiver need not be inferred, for it has been clearly demonstrated. Brazelton (1961) described a classic case in which a difficult neonate with deviant state patterns demoralized his mother to the point where she became depressed and totally ineffectual. The mother, a young professional woman, was delighted with her pregnancy and eagerly expected the birth of her baby. From the first day on, her infant was capable of only two extreme states. In the first state the infant appeared to be in deep sleep during which his muscle tone was poor; he was difficult to rouse and impervious to any external stimuli. In the second state he screamed continuously and was hyperactive and hypersensitive to any stimulation. Nothing could calm him except restraint and swaddling which made him revert immediately back to the first state of inaccessible, deep sleep. A neurological examination revealed no deficit. The later development of this child was very uneven. The narrow range of this child's states persisted at least until preschool age when his coping mechanisms were limited to either screaming, or withdrawing into a state in which he seemed to neither hear nor see. From the start the mother felt "rejected" by the infant and overwhelmed by the task of mothering, for she was unable to do anything to comfort him in his agitated state and was unable to reach him in his state of withdrawal. The mother became depressed and finally sought psychotherapy which enabled her to see her infant's problems as his own, rather than as a function of what she felt was her mishandling. It is of interest that despite her experience with her firstborn, she had the courage to have a second child who was an easy baby with whom she was capable of having a normal mother-infant relationship.

Another good example of how infants with deviant states of arousal can affect the caregiver is Prechtl's (1963) longitudinal study of eight infants who were born with pre- and paranatal complications, and who all showed what Prechtl calls the "hyperexcitability syndrome." In some ways babies who have this syndrome resemble Brazelton's case. Speaking of infants with the "hyperexcitability syndrome" in general, Prechtl described these infants as "hyperkinetic, often hypertonic, [they] cry more than normal babies, show sudden changes of state from being drowsy and difficult to arouse, to being wide awake, crying and difficult to pacify. . . . Nearly all of their responses are exaggerated and have a remarkably low threshold." It was interesting, with respect to our topic, that Prechtl remarked that, during the neonatal neurological examinations, he and his co-workers were often "annoyed" with these infants "because of their exaggerated reactions and their sudden changes in state."

In discussing the longitudinal data of the eight infants who were followed to the age of 46 weeks, Prechtl indicated that, while none of the mothers realized that their infants showed signs of brain dysfunction, seven of the eight mothers either expressed rejection or were overanxious vis-a-vis their child. In a control group of 10 normal babies, who were followed in the same way, he found only one mother who was overanxious and troubled, while the others had harmonious relationships with their infants. Almost invariably, in spite of the infants' obvious dysfunction, the mothers of the deviant babies tended to blame themselves, thinking that they had mishandled their children in some way.

EFFECT OF THE INFANT'S SEX ON THE CAREGIVER

There is very little doubt, judging from the growing literature, that at a very early age, male and female infants are treated differently by their caregivers. The infant's biological sex thus exerts an influence on parental behavior. A recent study by Thoman, Leiderman, and Olson (1972) suggested that differences in maternal treatment as a function of the sex of the child start right after birth. Primiparous mothers at least talked to and smiled at their baby girls significantly more during feeding than they did with boys. Earlier, Moss and Robson (1968) found that in response to fretting 3-month old infants, mothers were apt to respond to girls by talking, looking, and offering a pacifier, while they tended to hold close their baby boys or to offer them distractions. Lewis (1972), also with a sample of 3-month-old infants, found very similar differential responses in mothers; they vocalized more frequently to girls and they held boys more often than girls. Lewis (1972) concluded that in the interaction between mothers and infants, boys are apt to receive more proximal and girls more distal stimulation.

At the same time, sex differences in infants have been noted in the earliest months of life (e.g., Lewis, Kagan, & Kalafat, 1966; Moss, 1967; Watson, 1969). The question is whether the sex differences noted are entirely a function of differential treatment of the sexes by caregivers, or whether, as Olley (1971) pointed out, differential parental behaviors are also in response to subtle sex differences in the infants. To answer this question, the obvious time to study sex differences is right after birth, when differential maternal treatment has not as yet had a chance to have much impact.

I recently reviewed what little evidence there is of sex differences in newborns (Korner, 1973). The scant evidence may in part be a function of the fact that investigators of neonates often do not analyze their data for sex differences, as if it were unthinkable that such differences might exist. Many studies that assessed sex differences did not yield significant results. Yet there are a few studies which point to sex differences in newborns, particularly in certain target areas. It is the cumulative evidence from these studies, rather than the results of any single study, that makes the hypothesis tenable that innate behavioral sex differences do exist.

Tentatively, the female emerges as more receptive to certain types of stimuli, and as orally more sensitized. At the same time, she is in no way less active or expressive. There is also suggestive evidence that the male may be endowed from birth with greater physical strength and muscular vigor. Let me review the evidence.

There are several studies suggesting that the female may have greater tactile sensitivity. For example, Bell and Costello (1964) found females to be more responsive to the removal of a covering blanket and to an air jet stimulation applied to the abdomen. Wolff (1969), in a longitudinal study of a small sample of infants, observed that girls aged 2 weeks were more sensitive to skin contact than boys. Lipsitt and Levy (1959) found significantly lower electrotactual thresholds in females than in males.

In the visual modality an interesting discrepancy appears, depending on whether sex differences are assessed with respect to active visual behavior or photic receptivity on EEG. The female's response to photic stimulation appears to be significantly faster than that of males. In testing the mean photic latency of Oriental, Caucasian, and Negro neonates, Engel, Crowell, and Nishijima (1968) found significantly shorter latencies in females in each of the three races. By contrast, we were unable to find sex differences in visual tracking of moving objects, in the frequency and duration of the state of alert inactivity (Korner, 1970), or in the visual responsiveness in response to maternal types of ministrations (Korner & Thoman, 1970).

No sex differences have been demonstrated in auditory receptivity. Eisenberg (1972) who has tested the auditory responsiveness of hundreds of neonates under carefully controlled conditions, has found no sex-dependent differences. In our study of individual differences (Korner, 1970), we found no sex differences in response to an 80-dB buzzer. Similarly, Engel et al. (1968) were unable to find such differences in the latency of response on EEGS to acoustic stimulation.

Female neonates also appear to be more responsive to sweet taste, which is the first of several examples that they are what I call "orally more sensitized." Nisbett and Gurwitz (1970) found that when females were given sweetened formula, they increased their consumption of milk significantly more than did males. Females were more responsive to the taste of the formula at each body weight level tested. This finding incidentally has interesting parallels in the animal literature. Consistently, female rats consume more glucose and saccharin solutions than males (Valenstein, Kakolewski, & Cox, 1967; Wade & Zucker, 1969).

While there seem to be no sex differences in the frequency of hand-mouth and hand-face contacts and of finger sucking, or in the efficiency or perseverance of these behaviors (Korner & Kraemer, 1972), all of which are more-or-less activity-related behaviors, we found highly significant sex differences in the style of hand-to-mouth approaches. In one of our film analyses, it was determined for each hand-to-mouth approach whether the hand approached the mouth and the mouth only opened on contact, or whether the mouth approached the hand, with head straining forward to meet the hand. Females engaged in significantly more mouth searching than males ($p < .01$).

When we analyzed for sex differences in the spontaneous behaviors that occurred in the context of various sleep states, we found highly consistent and suggestive sex-related trends which were, however at best of only marginal statistical significance (Korner, 1969). Wolff (1966), who was the first to systematically monitor these spontaneous behaviors, postulated that, since no known stimulus evokes these behaviors, they may represent the discharge of a neural energy potential, which occurs in inverse proportion to the degree of afferent input. In our study we calculated the mean hourly rate of spontaneous startles, reflex smiles, erections, and episodes of rhythmical mouthing in each of three sleep states, namely, regular sleep, irregular sleep, and drowse. In each state the mean hourly rate of startles of males exceeded that of females ($p < .10$). By contrast, females exceeded in reflex smiles and rhythmical mouthing in all the states in which these behaviors occur. Since the overall rate of spontaneous discharge behaviors was almost identical for males and females when erections were excluded, it appears that females make up in smiles and reflex sucks what they lack in startles. If indeed these behaviors represent the discharges of a neural energy potential, it appears that females tend to discharge this potential more frequently via the facial musculatures particularly the mouth region, whereas males tend to discharge it more frequently through total and vigorous body activation.

Our finding that females engage in more frequent reflex smiles than males finds confirmation in observations by Freedman (1971). In our sample, the rate of reflex smiles during irregular sleep was almost triple that of males ($p < .06$). Even though the hourly rate of rhythmical mouthing in females was almost twice that of males, this difference was not statistically significant.

Females seem to exceed males in still another rhythmical oral behavior. Balint (1948) found that females during bottle feedings showed a rhythmical clonus of the tongue more frequently than males.

By contrast to the oral behaviors which, according to Wolff (1966) probably are of central, neural origin, no sex differences have been observed in the frequency or rate of ordinary spontaneous sucking (Hendry & Kessen, 1964; Korner et al., 1968) or of nutritive or nonnutritive sucking (Dubignon, Campbell, Curtis, & Partington, 1969). This type of sucking is strongly influenced by the overriding and sex-unrelated biological function of hunger (Hendry & Kessen, 1964; Korner et al., 1968), and by high arousal (Bridger, 1962).

Bell and Darling (1965) demonstrated that males were able to lift their heads heads higher from the prone position, suggesting that they may be endowed with greater muscular strength. Possibly, the males' greater tendency to startle, with the total body activation this entails, can also be taken as an index of greater muscular vigor.

When it comes to spontaneous active and expressive behaviors, I believe no sex differences have been reported for newborns. Several studies, some of which used large samples of neonates, monitored neonatal activity, and none of them found reliable sex differences in the frequency of motions (Brownfield, 1956; Campbell, 1968; Korner et al., 1968; Pratt, 1932). In one of our film analyses, we scored separately small, small multiple, global, and diffuse motions, and none of these were more relied upon by either sex (Korner et al., 1968). While Moss (1967) found significant differences in fussing by 3 weeks of age, boys being more irritable than girls, no such differences have been demonstrated in crying immediately after birth (Fisichelli & Karelitz, 1963; Korner et al., 1968). Similarly, no sex differences have been found in the reduction of crying in response to maternal types of soothing interventions (Korner & Thoman, 1972).

If we accept from this evidence that there are in fact behavioral sex differences detectable shortly after birth, the question is: What can they possibly be due to and how might they affect the caregiver? As to the first part of this question, aside from possible genetic determinants, the most plausible explanation for these differences is that they are hormonal in origin. As Hamburg and Lunde (1966) have pointed out, the hormones responsible for sexual differentiation *in utero* may sensitize the organism's central nervous system in such a way that sex-linked behaviors emerge at a later time, even when the circulation of these hormones is no longer detectable within the system. As to the second part of this question, I believe that, while sex role expectations and sex role taboos are the primary reasons why males and females are treated differently from birth, the behavioral sex differences of the infants themselves may also exert a subtle influence on the caregiver. For example, the mother's repeatedly reported tendency to provide boys with more proximal, tactile stimulation may be, in part at least, an inadvertent, unconscious compensatory response to the male's lesser cutaneous sensitivity. It may also express an effort on her part to provide containment for her more startle-prone male newborn. Also, the male's greater muscular strength and sturdiness and his bigger size (Garn, 1958) may make the mother less hesitant to handle him, particularly if she is an inexperienced mother.

The female newborn's oral sensitivity probably is not a passing matter. Moss (1967) found that 3-month-old girls mouthed significantly more than boys. In light of the neonatal data, one wonders whether this was spontaneous sucking or an attempt to mouth and incorporate objects. Since infants learn through their mouths, one could ask whether female infants learn more frequently through this channel and whether there are qualitative differences in in this kind of learning between males and females. Judging from Honzig and McKee's (1962) review of several studies, it appears that girls seek comfort through oral means more often than do boys. From age 1 on, girls are both more frequent and more persistent thumbsuckers than boys. Perhaps mothers intuitively sense a girl's affinity for oral comforting. This could at least in part explain why they offer pacifiers to girls more often than to boys (Moss & Robson, 1968).

EFFECT OF THE INFANT'S ONTOGENETIC STAGE OF DEVELOPMENT ON THE CAREGIVER

Probably, more than at any later stage of the child's development, it is the newborn's level of neurophysiological functioning that sets the stage for maternal actions. Immediately after birth, maternal ministrations are usually not as yet geared to socialize, educate, or stimulate the infant toward goals held desirable by the mother; instead, her interventions are evoked by the infant's discomfort, associated with his first attempt to function as an independent organism. It is the infant's crying and other signs of discomfort that dictate maternal actions.

Providing contact-comfort is probably the most common form of maternal intervention designed to calm the newborn. In a recent experimental study, Evelyn Thoman and I demonstrated that frequently it is the vestibular-proprioceptive component entailed in interventions providing contact comfort that is the more potent ingredient in calming the infant than contact per se (Korner & Thoman 1970, 1972). Imitating common types of maternal soothing techniques, we made six interventions in random order with each of 40 crying neonates, equally divided into male, female, bottle- and breast-fed, first- and later-born infants. Each intervention lasted 30 seconds, during which crying time was recorded. The interventions were:

1. The infant was lifted and put to the shoulder with the head supported and with the face just above shoulder level.

2. The infant was lifted horizontally and was cradled in the arms in the nursing position.

3. The infant was held close while he remained lying down. He was not moved in any way.

4. The infant, who had previously been placed in an infant seat, was raised 55° to an upright position.

5. The infant, in the infant seat, was moved to and fro as if in a perambulator.

6. The infant, lying supine, was talked to in a high-pitched female voice. The voice was used as a marker for observation after a preliminary study had shown that the voice had no greater effect than no stimulation at all.

Table 1 shows the mean crying time and the types of stimulation given during each of the six interventions.

Quite clearly, the shoulder position had the greatest soothing effect, and the voice had the least. While contact had a statistically significant effect on the reduction of crying, the interventions entailing vestibular-proprioceptive stimulation, particularly the motion of being put in an upright position, had a much more potent effect.

More remarkable perhaps is the fact that, while soothing the infants, these interventions evoked various levels of visual alertness in them. We were struck by the implications of this, for it suggested that by soothing an infant a mother inadvertently provides him with visual experiences. We assessed the infant's level of alertness on a six-point scale ranging from eyes closed to alert scanning of the visual surroundings. Table 2 shows the mean alerting scores and types of stimulation given during each of the six interventions.

The shoulder position was again the most effective. In fact, 77.5% of the infants responded with bright-eyed scanning in this position. Over interventions, treatments that entailed vestibular-proprioceptive stimulation either by itself or in combination with the upright position had a significantly more potent effect in evoking visual alertness than did contact. In fact, contact alone was not more effective than the female voice, which, preliminary work had shown to have no effect at all.

I believe that the reason why vestibular-proprioceptive stimulation is such an effective form of stimulation for the newborn is that it is mediated by a system,

TABLE 1   Mean Crying Time during Six Interventions

Intervention	Stimulation[a]	Mean Crying Seconds during Intervention	SEM
1. To shoulder	CVU	11.23	1.34
2. To breast	CV	21.25	1.37
3. Held close	C	23.00	1.28
4. Infant seat up	VU	14.80	1.63
5. Infant seat side to side	V	17.65	1.38
6. Female voice	—	26.00	1.02

[a]Stimulation: C = contact; V = vestibular-proprioceptive; U = upright.

TABLE 2   Mean Alerting Scores of Crying Infants during Interventions

Intervention	Stimulation[a]	Mean	SEM
1. To shoulder	CVU	4.500	0.19
2. To breast	CV	2.700	0.27
3. Held close	C	1.725	0.25
4. Infant seat up	VU	3.675	0.27
5. Infant seat side to side	V	3.750	0.23
6. Female voice	—	1.725	0.25

[a]Stimulation : C = contact; V = vestibular-proprioceptive; U = upright.

the functions of which are highly developed at birth. Judging from the work of Langworthy (1933) and Humphrey (1965), the vestibular system begins to become functional at 4 months of gestational age and is fully myelinated and functional at birth. While mothers obviously are not aware that they are relying on ontogenetically mature functions to soothe their infants, they nevertheless do so, probably because they have learned through the centuries that this works for achieving their aims.

There are many other examples demonstrating that the baby's stage of development has a powerful pull on the actions and feelings of the caregiver. One of the best examples is the effect of the emergence of the smile and of eye-to-eye contact in promoting maternal attachment to the infant as described by Robson (1967) and Robson and Moss (1970). The maturation of the infant's visual functions has yet other consequences which *should* but do not always have an impact on the caregiver. White (1969), Stechler and Latz (1966), and Benjamin (1961) independently made the observation that, at the age of about 3 weeks, certain infants show an aversive reaction and turn away from visual displays. It was only Benjamin (1961) who tied this phenomenon in with the usual onset time of infantile colic. Benjamin suggested that, with the maturation of sensory functions by the third postnatal week, infants with low sensory thresholds tend to become overwhelmed by overstimulation, which may be one factor contributing to colic. Benjamin (1961) stressed the importance of a mothering person to intervene at that time as a tension-reducing agent to offset the discomfort of what he considered a maturational crisis.

Moss (1967) in comparing infant and maternal behaviors for 3-weeks-old and three-months-old infants, demonstrated how much the behaviors of both changed during that time interval. It seems unlikely that the mothers of the older babies stimulated and aroused, imitated, talked to, and smiled at infants more out of an intellectual conviction that this is what they should be doing with a 3-month-old. Obviously, it must to a large extent have been the maturational changes in the infants that evoked the changes in maternal behavior.

Sander (1962), in his article, "Issues in Early Mother-Infant Interaction," which is a distillate from the findings of a longitudinal study with Eleanor Pavenstedt, outlined in bold strokes what is involved in the mutual stimulus regulation between mother and child for the first 18 months of life, and how the requirements change with the advent of new developmental acquisitions. Particularly interesting in Sander's scheme is that one can infer that several of his "issues" correspond closely in time and task to Piaget's (1952) stages of sensorimotor development. This again points to the fact that the appropriateness of a mother's response to her infant is largely determined by the infant's level of neurophysiological development.

Summary and Conclusions

In this chapter evidence has been presented demonstrating that the infant's state, his level of arousal, and his ontogenetic stage of development do and should affect the actions of the caregiver. Also, recent evidence of behavioral sex differences in newborns has been reviewed, which may in more subtle ways evoke differential treatment on the part of the caretaker. The point that this evidence highlights more than anything is that an extraordinary degree of flexibility is required for mothers to respond appropriately to the cues of different infants as they are at birth and as they grow and change.

During the first few weeks of life, most maternal ministrations are designed to comfort and to soothe the infant. The mother's function during that time is primarily to aid in regulating the infant's sensory input and his motor responses. In a sense she acts like a shield or an external stimulus barrier. While this is probably important for the development of all babies, it is critical for those infants who are unusually irritable, or who have very low sensory thresholds.

Too often, mothers cannot or will not respond to the infant's cues, either for reasons of their own psychology and needs or because of convictions they hold as to what constitutes "good" childcare. Such factors within the mother can seriously impede the beginning mother-infant interaction and result in a mismatch of the pair. For example, a mother's conviction that even very young babies require a good deal of stimulation may severely hamper an excitable baby's success in achieving any kind of homeostasis. A mother's fear of "spoiling" her infant may make her refrain from soothing efforts which he requires to settle down. Or a mother who, because of her own psychological needs, may wish for a cuddly newborn to whom she can give a lot of contact comfort, may react in disappointment if she happens to have an active, uncuddly baby who resists physical restraint (Schaffer & Emerson, 1964).

It is surprising, although historically understandable, that for so long there has been an almost exclusive emphasis on the parents' effect on the child's development without considering what the child represents as a stimulus to his caregiver. This emphasis on parent effect has been especially strong in the United

States (Bell, 1971; Korner, 1965). There are many reasons for this, one of which is a strong emphasis on environmental factors as being almost exclusively responsible for shaping the development of children. This undoubtedly stems in part from a repudiation of Old World tenets, some of which are based on the assumption that there are inequalities of birth and class. The thought that there might be genetic or biological differences among individuals which could influence development was too close to Old World dogma and had to be rejected until recently. Besides, there was some comfort in the thought that parental actions determine outcome, in spite of the potential guilt-producing aspects of this stance. At least it implied a degree of control over the developmental process which we do not have.

We are just beginning to document the degree to which the child's characteristics affect the caregiver. Particularly, the sequential analyses of behavior interactions between mother and child as used by Bell (1971), Lewis (1972), and Yarrow, Waxler, and Scott (1971) have been illuminating and have demonstrated methodological approaches which make study of these interactions feasible. The place where the mutual dovetailing of response between parent and child is still insufficiently stressed, and where unilateral parent effect is still emphasized too much, is in the clinic. It is precisely there where the child effect is apt to be the strongest, and where, for the sake of therapy, recognition of this fact is apt to be most useful.

References

Balint, M. Individual differences of behavior in early infancy and an objective way of recording them. *Journal of Genetic Psychology,* 1948, **73,** 57–117.

Barten, S., Birns, B., & Ronch, J. Individual differences in the visual pursuit behavior of neonates. *Child Development,* 1971, **42,** 313–319.

Bell, R. Q. Stimulus control of parent or caretaker behavior by offspring. *Developmental Psychology,* 1971, **4**, 61–72.

Bell, R. Q., & Costello, N. Three tests for sex differences in tactile sensitivity in the newborn. *Biologia Neonatorum,* 1964, **7,** 335–347.

Bell, R. Q., & Darling, J. F. The prone head reaction in the human neonate: Relation with sex and tactile sensitivity. *Child Development,* 1965, **36,** 943–949.

Bell, R. Q., Weller, G. M., & Waldrop, M. F. Newborn and preschooler: Organization of behavior and relations between periods. *Monographs of the Society for Research in Child Development,* 1971, **36** (1-2, Serial No. 142).

Benjamin, J. The innate and the experiential in development. In H. Brosin (Ed.), *Lectures on experimental psychiatry.* Pittsburgh: University of Pittsburgh, 1961. Pp. 19–42.

Birns, B. Individual differences in human neonates' responses to stimulation. *Child Development,* 1965, **36,** 249–256.

Birns, B., Blank, M., & Bridger, W. H. The effectiveness of various soothing techniques on human neonates. *Psychosomatic Medicine,* 1966, **28,** 316–322.

Brazelton, T. B. Psychophysiologic reactions in the neonate. I. The value of observation of the neonate. *The Journal of Pediatrics,* 1961, **58,** 508–512.

Bridger, W. H. Ethological concepts and human development. *Recent Advances in Biological Psychiatry,* 1962, **4,** 95–107.

Bridger, W. H., & Birns, B. Neonates' behavioral and autonomic responses to stress during soothing. *Recent Advances in Biological Psychiatry,* 1963, **5,** 1–6.

Brownfield, E. D. An investigation of the activity and sensory responses of healthy newborn infants. *Dissertation Abstracts,* 1956, **16,** 1288–1289.

Campbell, D. Motor activity in a group of newborn babies. *Biologia Neonatorum,* 1968, **13,** 257–270.

Dubignon, J., Campbell, D. Curtis, M., & Partington, M. W. The relation between laboratory measures of sucking, food intake, and perinatal factors during the newborn period. *Child Development,* 1969, **40,** 1107–1120.

Eisenberg, R. Auditory behavior in the human neonate. I. Methodological problems and the logical design of research procedures. *The Journal of Auditory Research,* 1965, **5,** 159–177.

Eisenberg, R. Personal communication, 1972.

Engel, R., Crowell, D., & Nishijima, S. Visual and auditory response latencies in neonates. In B. N. D. Fernando (Ed.), *Felicitation Volume in Honour of C. C. De-Silva,* Ceylon: Kularatne and Company, Ltd., 1968. Pp. 1–10.

Fisichelli, V. C. & Karelitz, S. The cry latencies of normal infants and those with brain damage. *Journal of Pediatrics,* 1963, **62,** 724–734.

Freedman, D. G. Personal communication, 1971.

Garn, S. M. Fat, body size, and growth in the newborn. *Human Biology,* 1958, **30,** 265–280.

Hamburg, D. A. & Lunde, D. T. Sex hormones in the development of sex differences in human behavior. In E. E. Maccoby (Ed.), *The Development of Sex Differences,* Stanford, Calif.: Stanford University Press, 1966. Pp. 1–24.

Hendry, L. S. & Kessen, W. Oral behavior of newborn infants as a function of age and time since feeding. *Child Development* 1964, **35,** 201–208.

Honzig, M. P. & McKee, J. P. The sex difference in thumbsucking. *Journal of Pediatrics,* 1962, **61,** 726–732.

Humphrey, T. The embryologic differentiation of the vestibular nuclei in man correlated with functional development. *International symposium on vestibular and oculomotor problems, Tokyo,* 1965. Pp. 51–56.

Korner, A. F. Mother-child interaction: One or two-way street? *Social Work,* 1965, **10,** 47–51.

Korner, A. F. Neonatal startles, smiles, erections, and reflex sucks as related to state, sex and individuality. *Child Development,* 1969, **40,** 1039–1053.

Korner, A. F. Visual alertness in neonates: Individual differences and their correlates. *Perceptual and Motor Skills,* 1970, **31,** 67–78.

Korner, A. F. Individual differences at birth: Implications for early experience and later development. *American Journal of Orthopsychiatry,* 1971, **41,** 608–619.

Korner, A. F. Sex differences in newborns with special reference to differences in the organization of oral behavior. *Journal of Child Psychology and Psychiatry*, 1973, **14**, 19–29.

Korner, A. F. & Beason, L. M. The association of two congenitally organized behavior patterns in the newborn: Hand-mouth coordination and looking. *Perceptual and Motor Skills*, 1972, **35**, 115–118.

Korner, A. F., Chuck, B., & Dontchos, S. Organismic determinants of spontaneous oral behavior in neonates. *Child Development*, 1968, **39**, 1145–1157.

Korner, A.F. & Grobstein, R. Individual differences in irritability and soothability as related to parity in neonates. Unpublished manuscript, 1967.

Korner, A. F., & Kraemer, H. C. Individual differences in spontaneous oral behavior. In J. F. Bosma (Ed.), *Third symposium on oral sensation and perception: The mouth of the infant*. Springfield, Ill.: C. C. Thomas, 1972, 335–346.

Korner, A. F. & Thoman, E. B. Visual alertness in neonates as evoked by maternal care. *Journal of Experimental Child Psychology*, 1970, **10**, 67–78.

Korner, A. F. & Thoman, E. B. The relative efficacy of contact and vestibular-proprioceptive stimulation in soothing neonates. *Child Development*, 1972, **43**, 443–453.

Langworthy, O. R. Development of behavior patterns and myelinization of the nervous system in the human fetus and infant. *Carnegie Institution of Washington, Contributions to Embryology*, 1933, **24**, 1–57.

Lewis, M. State as an infant-environment interaction: An analysis of mother-infant interactions as a function of sex. *Merrill-Palmer Quarterly*, 1972, **18**, 95–121.

Lewis, M., Kagan, J., & Kalafat, J. Patterns of fixation in infants. *Child Development*, 1966, **37**, 331–341.

Lipsitt, L. P., & Levy, N. Electrotactual threshold in the human neonate. *Child Development*, 1959, **30**, 547–554.

Moss, H. A. Sex, age, and state as determinants of mother-infant interaction. *Merrill-Palmer Quarterly*, 1967, **13**, 19–36.

Moss, H. A., & Robson, K. The role of protest behavior in the development of mother-infant attachment. Paper presented at the meeting of the American Psychological Association, San Francisco, 1969.

Nisbett, R. E. & Gurwitz, S. B. Weight, sex, and the eating behavior of human newborns. *Journal of Comparative and Physiological Psychology*, 1970, **73**, 245–253.

Olley, J. G. *Sex differences in human behavior in the first year of life*. Major area paper, Department of Psychology, George Peabody College for Teachers, Nashville, Tennessee, 1971.

Piaget, J. *The origins of intelligence in children*. New York: International Universities Press, 1952.

Pratt, K. C. Note on the relation of activity to sex and race in young infants. *Journal of Social Psychology*, 1932, **3**, 118–120.

Prechtl, H. F. R. The mother-child interaction in babies with minimal brain damage. In B. M. Foss (Ed.), *Determinants of Infant Behavior*, Vol. II. London: Methuen, 1963. Pp. 53–59.

Rheingold, H. L. The effect of environmental stimulation upon social and exploratory behavior in the human infant. In B. M. Foss (Ed.), *Determinants of Infant Behavior*, Vol. I. New York: Wiley, 1961. Pp. 143–177.

Robson, K. S. The role of eye-to-eye contact in maternal-infant attachment. *Journal of Child Psychology and Psychiatry*, 1967, **8**, 13–25.

Robson, K. S., & Moss, H. A. Patterns and determinants of maternal attachment. *The Journal of Pediatrics*, 1970, **77**, 976–985.

Sander, L. W. Issues in early mother-child interaction. *Journal of the American Academy of Child Psychiatry*, 1962, **1**, 141–166.

Schaffer, H. R., & Emerson, P. E. Patterns of response to physical contact in early human development. *Journal of Child Psychology and Psychiatry*, 1964, **5**, 1–13.

Stechler, G., & Latz, E. Some observations on attention and arousal in the human infant. *Journal of the American Academy of Child Psychiatry*, 1966, **5**, 517–525.

Thoman, E. B., Leiderman, P. H., & Olson, J. P. Neonate-mother interaction during breast-feeding. *Development Psychology*, 1972, **6**, 110–118.

Valenstein, E. S., Kakolewski, J. W., & Cox, V. C. Sex differences in taste preferences for glucose and saccharin solutions. *Science*, 1967, **156**, 942–943.

Wade, G. N., & Zucker, I. Hormonal and developmental influence on rat saccharin preferences. *Journal of Comparative and Physiological Psychology*, 1969, **69**, 291–300.

Watson, J. S. Operant conditioning of visual fixation in infants under visual and auditory reinforcement. *Development Psychology*, 1969, **1**, 508–516.

White, B. L. Child development research: An edifice without a foundation. *Merrill-Palmer Quarterly*, 1969, **15**, 49–79.

Wolff, P. H. Observations on the early development of smiling. In B. M. Foss (Ed.), *Determinants of infant behavior*. Vol. I. London: Methuen, 1963. Pp. 113–134.

Wolff, P. H. The causes, controls and organization of behavior in the neonate. *Psychological Issues*, 1966, **5**(1), Monograph 17.

Wolff, P. H. The natural history of crying and other vocalizations in early infancy. In B. M. Foss (Ed.), *Determinants of infant behavior*. Vol. IV. London: Methuen, 1969. Pp. 113–138.

Yarrow, M. R., Waxler, C. Z. & Scott, P. M. Child effects on adult behavior. *Developmental Psychology*, 1971, **5**, 300–311.

CHAPTER 6

Organization of Sleep in Prematures: Implications for Caregiving

C. Dreyfus-Brisac
Unité de Recherches Biologiques Néonatales

Sleep disorders are one of the main problems of infancy and are particularly prevalent and prolonged in prematurely born children. These problems of the infant may disturb family life, and have important implications for the infant's subsequent development.

Is it possible, by a better knowledge of sleep development, to improve caregiving for prematures, both in the hospital and later at home?

Our aim in this chapter is (1) to point out the peculiar organization of sleep cycling in prematures; (2) to discuss some implications in caregiving for prematures, in relation to sleep cycling; and (3) to provoke discussion on possible modifications in the care of the baby to minimize such disorders.

SLEEP STATES IN PREMATURE AND TERM INFANTS

It is often difficult to differentiate sleep from the waking state in prematures. About 25 years ago, for example, Gesell and Amatruda (1947) indicated that in early prematurity body mobility may be present in sleep, whereas it may be absent during wakefulness. Since that time systematic observations on the wakefulness and sleep patterns of prematures have been made by different investigators particularly by Parmelee, Bruck, and Bruck (1962), studying the influence of temperature on sleep and mobility.

Polygraphic recordings, including electroencephalograms, (EEGs), electrocardiograms (ECGs), records of respiratory rate and of myographic activity, combined with careful observations, have considerably enriched our knowledge and understanding of the ontogenesis of sleep (Dittrichova, 1966; Dreyfus-Brisac, 1966, 1968, 1970; Monod & Dreyfus-Brisac, 1965; Parmelee, Wenner, Akiyama, Stern, & Flescher, 1966; Parmelee, Wenner, Akiyama, Schultz, & Stern, 1967; Parmelee, Akiyama, Schultz, Wenner, Schulte, & Stern, 1968; Petre-Quadens, 1967; Weitzman & Graziani, 1968). From all the data collected, we may ask whether it is possible to determine the state of sleep of a premature and to decide what is the best time to handle him.

In *full-term newborns*, three states can be differentiated quite easily (Anders, Emde, & Parmelee, 1971). These are *wakefulness, active sleep* (also called REM, paradoxical, or irregular sleep), and *quiet sleep* (NREM or regular sleep). In other work, the State 1 described by Prechtl, Akiyama, Zinkin, and Grant (1968) corresponds to quiet sleep, State 2 to active sleep, and States 3, 4, and 5 to wakefulness.

Wakefulness is easily recognized as occurring when the baby is quiet, with eyes open and moving horizontally, or blinking, and when gross body movements are accompanied by crying and eyes open. Polygraphic records show a tonic electromyograph (EMG) pattern of chin muscle and a low-voltage EEG pattern (Figure 1). If gross body movements and crying occur with eyes closed, the minimal duration of gross body movements and/or crying required to classify this state as wakefulness differs among different investigators. Artifacts generally obscure the polygraphic recording during such periods.

In *active sleep* rapid eye movements (REMs), irregular respiration, and facial and localized body mobility are present. Polygraphic records show that tonic EMG activity of the chin is absent, and phasic bursts of EMG may appear as a

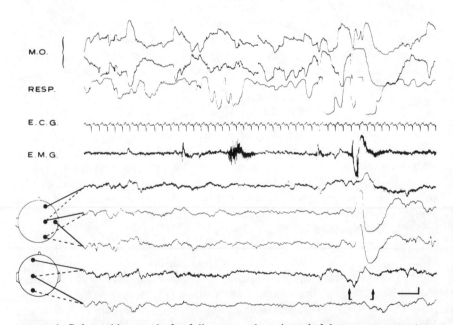

FIGURE 1. Polygraphic record of a full-term newborn in wakefulness, eyes open (eyes closed only between the two arrows). In this and the following figures: M.O., electrooculogram; Resp., respiratory rate recording; ECG, electrocardiogram, EMG, electromyogram at chin level. Below: right and left leads of electroencephalogram; Calibration: 1 second, 50 microvolts.

result of movements. The EEG pattern is of low voltage, low voltage superimposed by slow waves, or sometimes slow waves (Figure 2).

In *quiet sleep* all the events are reversed. However, the EEG, which is generally a *trace alternant*, may also be made up of continuous slow waves (Figure 3).

Two kinds of active sleep are described by some authors: one as a transition between wakefulness and quiet sleep, and the other occurring between quiet sleep and active sleep or between active sleep and wakefulness (Monod & Pajot, 1965; Petre-Quadens, 1966). However, this distinction has not been confirmed by Ashton and Connolly (1971) in studies of cardiac and respiratory rates.

More detailed behavioral classifications have been introduced for full-term newborns. Among them, the classifications of wakefulness introduced by Wolff (1968) are not easily applied to prematures. However, Emde and Koenig (1969) have described 12 states which are also recognized in premature infants: sleep NREM and REM, drowsy NREM and REM, sucking NREM and REM, crying awake and crying REM, alert inactive and alert active, fussy awake and fussy REM.

Fussy REM and crying REM usually interrupt an ongoing sleep REM state shortly before an infant awakes. Drowsy REM is considered a special form of REM state with eyes open and a higher level of arousal. Crying awake and alert active states correspond to wakefulness although no indication is given whether the eyes

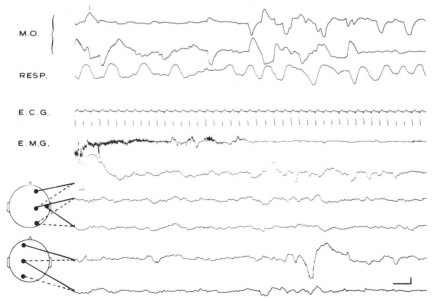

FIGURE 2. Polygraphic record of a full-term newborn in active sleep.

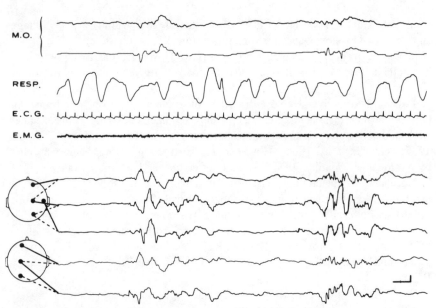

FIGURE 3. Polygraphic record of a full-term newborn in quiet sleep.

are open. The alert inactive state is characterized by ocular movements of pursuit as described by Wolff. This ocular fixation and pursuit may be stimulated by particular visual patterns, as Fantz and Nevis (1967) have shown in waking full-term newborns.

Sleep and wakefulness in *prematures* differ markedly from that of full-term newborns. In premature infants, active sleep and quiet sleep are poorly organized, and the respective periods of each state (wakefulness, active sleep, and quiet sleep) are of shorter duration. Sterman and Hoppenbrouwers (1971) prefer to differentiate states of prematures without any reference to sleep. They distinguish behavioral quiescence, behavioral activity, and REM state. Before 28 weeks of conceptional age (CA), there is an absence of differentiation of sleep states (Dreyfus-Brisac, 1968). The state of this nonviable premature could be considered an indefinite one characterized only by its recurrent mobility, and may be compared to that of chick embryos described by Hamburger (1965).

After 32 weeks of CA, or perhaps slightly earlier, different behavior patterns begin to appear which resemble wakefulness, active sleep, and quiet sleep. However, these three states are not fully developed at this age and are not completely similar to those of full-term neonates (Dreyfus-Brisac, 1970).

In our work we have considered as wakefulness: (1) periods with eyes open, moving horizontally with or without diffuse body movements, with or without crying; these criteria are generally accepted; (2) periods with eyes closed and diffuse body movements with or without crying, lasting at least 2 minutes; this duration has been arbitrarily chosen. Inversely, we have considered as sleep: (1) periods of quietness with eyes open without any movement or blinking; (2) periods similar to those described above in Item (2) but lasting less than 2 minutes; such periods are considered as sleep, for they occur very frequently during periods of active sleep and do not seem to interrupt the sleep cyclicity.

Active sleep (Figures 4 and 5) is not fully developed before 35 weeks, and *quiet sleep* (Figure 6) does not attain a complete degree of organization until 37 weeks. Before 35 weeks of CA, rapid eye movements are rare, and periodic respiration may predominate (Figure 6). Nonetheless, these two states of sleep with some atypical components may be recognized as early as 31 weeks.

The development of these various states does not progress evenly. Some phenomena may appear at a given CA and disappear later. This is the case with periodic respiration which does not exist in very early prematurity (before 30 weeks) and generally disappears after 38 weeks, but which occupies 25% of the time between 30 and 35 weeks (Parmelee, Stern, & Harris, 1972). Certain phenomena may occur simultaneously for a few weeks, as is the case with REMs and chin clonic movements, which may occur simultaneously at 30 to 32 weeks and never occur later in the same state of sleep (Figure 4).

A dynamic concept of the progressive organization of sleep is useful and seems more adequate than the former concept of a progressive reduction of active sleep.

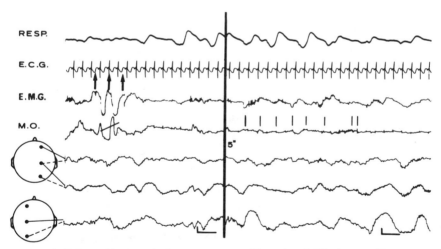

FIGURE 4. Polygraphic record of a premature at 32 weeks of CA, born at 30 weeks of Gestational Age (G.A.). Chin clonic movements are indicated by arrows; eye movements by vertical lines. [Reproduced from Monod and Dreyfus-Brisac (1965) with the permission of the publisher]

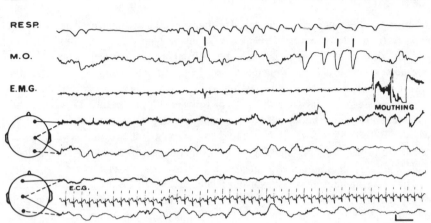

FIGURE 5. Polygraphic record of the same infant at 35 weeks of CA in active sleep. Vertical lines indicate eye movements. [Reproduced from Monod and Drefus-Brisac. (1965) with the permission of the publisher.]

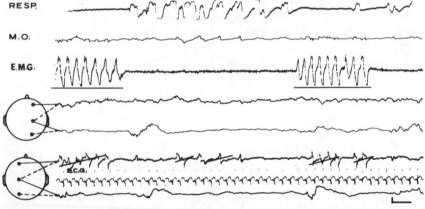

FIGURE 6. Polygraphic record of the same infant at 35 weeks of C.A. in quiet sleep. Two sequences of chin clonic movements occur (underlined). Artifacts on the EEGraphic Fronto central lead. [Reproduced from Monod and Dreyfus-Brisac, 1965, with the permission of the publisher.]

It is difficult to choose the most significant criterion with which to assess a state of sleep. Different methods have been used (Dreyfus-Brisac, 1970; Parmelee, Akiyama, Stern, & Harris, 1969). Choosing some criteria in advance can be unnecessarily limiting. Monod and Garma (1971) found that the most useful criteria to differentiate between quiet and active sleep in prematures were (1) the EEG (discontinuous in quiet sleep, continuous in active sleep; (2) REMs (absent in quiet sleep and present in active sleep); and (3) mobility. Even with these measures, many periods cannot be classified and are simply considered transitional sleep. Parmelee, however, considers that regular or irregular respiratory rates are the best indicators of sleep states. In our work we have shown that the chin EMG is not a good indicator (Eliet-Flescher & Dreyfus-Brisac, 1966).

We have found that sleep of prematurely born infants attaining full-term CA is not as well organized as the sleep observed in the full-term newborn. We have also observed a lower percentage of regular respiration and of low-voltage EEG patterns, as well as a more rapid cardiac rate and more irregular respiratory rhythms (Figures 7 and 8) (Dreyfus-Brisac, 1970).

EXTERNAL INFLUENCES ON SLEEP OF PREMATURES

Are there any methods for improving sleep in prematures? Temperature modifies behavior during sleep (Parmelee, Bruck, & Bruck, 1962). In prematures a higher percentage of quiet sleep was obtained at temperatures of 32 to 34°C, even if the rectal temperature remained between 35 and 36.5°, which is lower than in full-term newborns in the same thermal environment.

Periods of "quiet sleep" in this study did not correspond exactly to what is now called quiet sleep, since it included periods with facial movements. Nevertheless, it appears that periods of "quiet sleep" so defined are longer at neutral temperatures than at lower or higher temperatures. Periods of

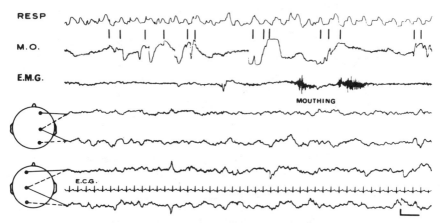

FIGURE 7. Polygraphic record of the same infant at 39 weeks of C.A. in active sleep. Vertical lines indicate eye movements. [Reproduced from Monod and Dreyfus-Brisac, (1965) with the permission of the publisher.]

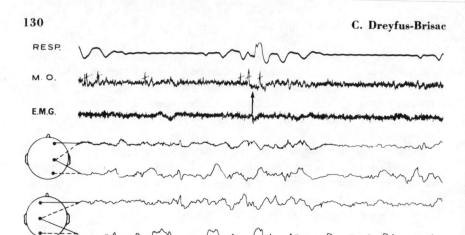

FIGURE 8. Polygraphic record of the same infant at 39 weeks of C.A. in quiet sleep. Artifacts occur on oculogram (Line 3). [Reproduced from Monod and Drefus-Brisac (1965) with the permission of the publisher]

wakefulness, gross body movements, and limb mobility are increased when temperature is below to the neutral one.

Feeding does not seem to influence sleep in prematures. This influence is also questionable for full-term infants during the first day of life. Irwin (1932) has suggested that body activity is more marked just before feeding than just after, but this was not confirmed by Prechtl, Akiyama, Zinkin, & Grant (1968). In prematures, Parmelee et al. (1962) stated that hunger did not influence periods of quietness or activity. Polikanina (1966) drew the same conclusion and noted furthermore that prematures are not awakened by hunger.

We came to the same conclusion but were concerned with the question whether the manipulations to which the baby was subjected for recording purposes could mask the influence of hunger. This criticism, however, cannot be made of Parmelee et al. (1962). It appears that feeding and hunger do not markedly influence the sleep cycle in prematures.

The influence of lighting has not been studied systematically; Evsukova (1971) recorded full-term newborns at 1, 3, 5, 7, and 10 days of age for 2 hours, twice a day, in the morning and at night. The modification of day sleep was much more important than that of night sleep between 1 and 10 days. Paradoxical sleep, which occupied 77.7% of day sleep before 4 days, occupied only 43.5% thereafter; quiet sleep increased from 22 to 56.3%. In night sleep the percentages of active and quiet sleep were approximately 65 and 35%, respectively, and showed no significant modification.

Many other factors may affect the influence of lighting in such an experiment. Sander, Julia, Stechler, and Burns (1972) state that day-night differentiation of activity measured during two 12-hour periods appeared later in nursery caregiving conditions than in home caregiving. This difference was probably due to extrinsic influences, among which was illumination.

It may be expected that other factors may also interfere (schedule of demand feeding, multiple or single caregiving, temperature level, sound). Unfortunately, similar studies have not been made of premature infants.

What are the best times for feeding and handling infants? Should they be awakened in active sleep or in quiet sleep? Which sleep is the deepest? To try to answer these questions, we have reviewed all the periods of crying occurring during 27 records made of 12 infants under particularly satisfactory conditions. The incubator temperature was regulated by a servocontrol, the skin temperature being maintained at 36°C. The rectal temperature was between 35 and 37°C.

Eleven records were made at 28 to 31 weeks of CA, and 16 at 32 to 38 weeks of CA. The records revealed 158 periods of crying, sometimes no longer than 5 or 10 seconds. We have analyzed the relationship of these crying episodes to the different events used to discriminate between active and quiet sleep. With respect to the events of quiet sleep 22 occurred during periods of discontinuous tracing (among them, four just preceded a change to continuous tracing), and none occurred during periods of chin clonic movements. Contrarily, most of the periods of crying (136) occurred in periods of continuous tracing (four just preceded a change to discontinuous tracing), and 66 were closely related to REMs. Thus it appears that most of the periods of crying occur simultaneously with two criteria belonging to active sleep.

All studies on newborns and infants are in agreement that active sleep is "lighter" than quiet sleep. In the early descriptions active sleep was called light sleep. The presence of crying in the first period of active sleep described by some investigators as drowsiness (Watanabe & Iwase, 1972), as well as in the second period of active sleep following quiet sleep is an argument for classifying these two periods together.

Do other events help in the evaluation of the quality of sleep in infants? Spontaneous skin potential responses (SPR) are present beginning at 28 weeks CA and occur during periods of active sleep in prematures and full-term newborns (Curzi-Dascalova, 1971; Curzi-Dascalova, Pajot, & Dreyfus-Brisac, 1970). This is in accord with Bell's (1970) finding of greater skin potential variablilty during REM periods. The characteristic patterns of autonomic regulation of heart rate and respiration pattern during active sleep is another argument in favor of designating it as light sleep. Sleep always begins with a period of active sleep (called drowsy REM by Emde and Koenig, 1969), although it is not always as clear in prematures as in full-term newborns, inasmuch as wakefulness in prematures is not yet well-established. Furthermore, active sleep precedes awakening in most of the cases.

THE PREMATURE AND ITS ENVIRONMENT

The study of responsiveness and reactivity in sleep also helps to evaluate the quality of sleep and the relationships between the premature and his environment. Different methods are available for exploring the impact of sensory stimulations on infants. These include autonomic reactivity, behavioral responsiveness, and evoked potentials.

Autonomic reactivity in prematurely born children has not been extensively studied, although Polikanina (1966) states that stimuli can change the respiratory pattern. Cardiac reactivity does not appear to exist in prematures (Monod & Garma, 1971).

Behavioral responsiveness changes with maturation (Schmidt & Birns, 1971). Changes in behavioral response to a given stimulus (a click) have been studied by Monod and Garma (1971) in active and quiet sleep from 30 weeks of CA. Both diffuse and localized motor responses are described. Among the localized motor responses, limb movements, facial movements, palpebral movements (blinking), and eye movements have been studied. The percentage of responses during the total sleep time decreases slightly with maturation: 29% at 32 weeks, 21% at 37 to 39 weeks—this decline being significant in four children out of seven. This decline in behavioral response is much more apparent in quiet sleep, shifting from 26 to 9% and does not occur in active sleep. Responsivity is higher in active than in quiet sleep, whatever the CA. On the contrary, palpebral responses increase significantly in active sleep. The changes of behavioral responsivity are higher in active than in quiet sleep for clicks, as well as for tone bursts. Monod and Garma also point out that their results must be considered with some reserve. They state that the ambient continuous noise level in an incubator reaches 80 dB, which is very high compared to that of the normal ambience of full-term newborns examined in a crib.

Evoked potential studies have determined the progressive diminution of the latencies and the progressive modifications of the form and polarity of this particular aspect of neural activity with increasing CA (Akiyama, Schulte, Schultz, & Parmelee, 1969; Ellingson, 1964; Engel, 1967; Hrbek, Hrbkova, & Lenard, 1969; Weitzman & Graziani, 1968). Another fact seems extremely important: responses can be elicited only with stimuli given at long intervals (Ellingson, 1966). At this point we do not know whether this is due to fatiguability of the central nervous system or to long refractory periods.

These neurophysiological and behavioral data give us some important information regarding sleep in prematures: (1) sleep cycles are poorly organized in prematurely born children, even when they attain 40 weeks CA; (2) active sleep is lighter than quiet sleep; and (3) afferent stimuli are not integrated as they are in full-term infants.

Early interruption of intrauterine life modifies significantly the environment of the premature. Curiously, the high ambient noise is similar *in utero* and in the incubator (Henshall, 1972), although the pulse noise is missing. This has led some investigators to use the heartbeat as a sedating noise (Bertini, Fornari, & Venturini, 1970). Permanent lighting, unmodified by succession of day and night, is one of the most important changes imposed on the premature after birth.

A premature birth deprives the fetus of the influences of the maternal sleep cycle and of other aspects of maternal cyclicity (Payne & Bach, 1965). Studies of the relation between maternal sleep and intrauterine infant mobility have shown that the number of fetal movements is higher in periods of paradoxical sleep (characterized by REM bursts) and waking than during NREM sleep, and still higher in periods of a particular state of pregnant women: States 2 and 3 of sleep with spindles and isolated ocular movements (Petre-Quadens, 1969).

Two mobility cycles have been described for human fetuses in utero. The shorter one (30 to 50 minutes) seems to be an intrinsic rhythm of the fetus. The slower one (80 to 110 minutes) is unique to the uterine environment of extra fetal origin, and is in direct relation to the maternal sleep cycle. Curiously, the periodicity of these two cycles are essentially the same at different gestational ages (Sterman & Hoppenbrouwers, 1971).

Besides the maternal sleep-wake cycle, other influences are missing for the premature, for example, neurohumoral secretions of the mother may regulate some activity in infants. Among the secretions investigated in prematures and newborns, we know from Shaywitz, Finkelstein, Hellman, and Weitzman (1971) that growth hormone secretion is not related to states of sleep as they are later.

Somesthesic afferences which surround the totality of the body of *in utero* fetus are absent while the force of gravity is present. This may influence the development of muscle tone. After birth, the premature receives afferences only rarely, being fed by tube and not diapered; moreover, oral stimulation present in the uterine environment is missing.

How does the premature react to these important changes? At this point we do not know if he is able to feel them or if he is only a passive subject in the new, quiet artificial environment.

The possible emotional and sensory disruption and deprivation of prematures were first considered by Rothschild (1967) as being a contributing cause to the high incidence of emotional disturbances among prematurely born persons. We have discussed (Dreyfus-Brisac, 1970) the possible responsibility of sensory deprivation in the poor organization of sleep of prematures. Sensory deprivation influences the anatomical and functional development of the brain, as well as enrichment of environment. We are interested in the experiences of prolonged sensory deprivation in cats submitted to subtotal deafferentation (Vital-Durand & Michel, 1971). These animals, 6 to 18 months after the deafferentation, were inactive most of the time, although they were not in a typical state of REM or NREM sleep. The percentage of REM sleep was normal, and the time spent in

NREM sleep and wakefulness was decreased. Forty percent of the total time consisted of a particular state, corresponding to alternating short periods of waking and drowsiness, and the state of deep NREM sleep was not attained most of the time. It seems pertinent to consider the similarity of such a state with the transitional sleep of prematures. In addition, McGinty (1969) states that kittens reared in isolation have a percentage of active sleep which is reduced much below the adult level.

To consider fully the environment of the premature, we must also ask, on the contrary, if the new environment is too complex. Afferences received by prematures affect different organs of sense. It has been shown in young animals (Garma & Verley, 1969; Scherrer, Verley & Garma, 1969) that the speeds of conduction are heterogeneous and can be neither integrated nor filtered. Extrauterine life, in a complex environment, may create a state of maladaption in the human premature. Studies of sensory evoked potentials should be made, studying the comparison of latencies and refractory periods for different immature afferent systems.

A third hypothesis is that *over*stimulation enhances development. We know that mobility is greater in young animals than in older. Could these body movements help to improve the organization of the *schema corporel*? Are they too numerous? Korner (1968) has pointed out that such abundant spontaneous jerks may be the most important afferents in prematures. It has also been suggested (Roffwarg, Muzio, & Dement, 1966) that REMs deliver signifiant functional stimulation to the cortex, and that REM mechanisms (which are already active in prematures) serve as an endogenous source of stimulation, furnishing great quantities of functional excitation to higher centers. Such a mechanism could also contribute to provoke overstimulation, although the number of eye movements in prematures is lower than in full-term newborns (Dreyfus-Brisac, 1970).

The importance of environment and of ecological factors appears in many species (Jouvet-Mounier, 1968). Early weaning, as well as early birth, modify sleep cycling. In some animals (ruminants) the cycle may be abruptly modified by birth (Ruckebusch, 1971). From this discussion it is apparent that many hypotheses exist, and currently we just do not know how to explore further the affectivity and personality of prematures. Studies of conditioned reflexes or habituation, as well as the neurophysiological measures outlined above, would probably help. However, comparisons with animals favor the hypothesis that the premature infant is understimulated and not overstimulated.

INFLUENCE OF PREMATURITY ON LATE
ORGANIZATION OF SLEEP

What is the influence of prematurity on late organization of sleep? It is well known that prematurely born infants often present later sleep distrubances. This may be secondary to different influences, among which the anxiety of the family is certainly of great importance.

A development study of sleep spindles (Metcalf, 1969) has shown that the evolution of electrographic patterns of sleep are not delayed by a premature birth. On the contrary, the onset of sleep spindles and achievement of mature spindle quality occur approximately 4 weeks earlier in prematurely born infants than in full-term infants. Metcalf concludes that the impact of experience on an innate maturational process is demonstrated by this earlier appearance of spindles. Such an advance does not appear later in the organization of sleep cycles. (Parmelee, Akiyama, Schultz, Wenner, Schulte, & Stern, 1968). This discrepancy between the two phenomena may be due to the difference in maturation rate between the sleep cycle (which is slow) and that of the spindles, which is rapid, and also to the different degrees of complexity of the two events. Another example of dissociation of simple and complex phenomena is found at 40 weeks CA. The EEG of a prematurely born baby attaining 40 weks CA is similar to the EEG of a full-term newborn (Samson-Dollfus, 1955), although the length of bursts in *trace alternant* is statistically greater in premature infants reaching term than in normal full-term infants (Parmelee et al., 1969). Thus the basic organization of sleep is very different in these two types of infants.

DISCUSSION AND CONCLUSION

Would the premature benefit from more stimulation? At what age can he take advantage of these stimulations? Which kinds of stimuli are best? Are some moments better than others to stimulate him? Would it be useful to modify the environment of the premature? Would it be better to attenuate the transition between life in an incubator and in a crib?

We know that:

1. Active sleep is a lighter sleep state than quiet sleep. This is demonstrated by events occurring during active sleep (SPR, crying), and also by the existence of spontaneous awakenings occurring only through REM periods (Emde & Koenig, 1969). It may be suggested from such data that if it is necessary to awake prematures for any care, this should be done during active sleep. Inversely, short periods of crying do not necessitate any care and should not provoke anxiety or fear in caregivers.

2. Active sleep and quiet sleep are both necessary in newborns. The need for REM sleep is not as prominent in newborns as it is in adults (Anders & Roffwarg, 1969b). They have found that following total deprivation of sleep the percentages of REM and NREM sleep are not modified. When a newborn is awakened during any state of sleep, he goes back to the same state; however, repeated awakenings provoke prolonged wakefulness (Anders & Roffwarg, 1969a). Unfortunately, this phenomenon has not been studied systematically in prematures.

3. Responsiveness to external stimuli exists as early as an infant is viable, that is, 28 weeks CA. If the premature is in a sensory deprivation state, stimuli should be given to him as early as possible. Oral and facial stimulations are perhaps particularly useful for anatomical (early maturation of the fifth cranial nerve) and functional reasons. If motor stimuli are important afferents, limitation of movements, often required in intensive care units, is perhaps detrimental. On the contrary, in case of overstimulation, this restriction of motion would be helpful.

Surprisingly, sound in the incubator is as high as *in utero* noise, but it should be remembered that the frequency band may be different, and that this shift may have an effect.

4. The presence of a circadian rhythm differentiates intrauterine from extrauterine life. The permanent lighting in the nursery contributes to this absence of rhythm. We believe that an external artificial rhythm should be imposed on prematures. Studies should be made to try to ascertain the influence of discontinuous lighting on development, as well as to determine the best duration for periods of light and darkness. While it appears that feeding is not an important event for a premature, it is possible that some manipulations are more important and useful than others.

5. Finally, a comparison between prematures and pathological full-term newborns shows that the poor organization of cycling in prematures is not similar to that of pathological newborns. In the latter infants, a more-or-less severe disorganization of the sleep cycle may occur (Monod, Eliet-Flescher, & Dreyfus-Brisac, 1967; Schulman, 1969; Schulte, Lasson, Parl, Nolte, & Jurgens, 1969). Anomalies of sleep cycling in pathological term infants are essentially: (1) a lack of relationship between the different criteria of active and quiet sleep (2) a reduction in the number of REMs; and (3) an absence of the usual modifications of respiratory and cardiac rates during the different states of sleep (Monod et al., 1967). Of all the criteria mobility seems disturbed the least, but the reorganization of the sleep cycle generally occurs within a short time. The relationship between the different physiological events improves progressively. A secondary prolonged insomnia is frequent. Monod et al. (1967) states that among 30 pathological newborns with a sleep record made after the fifteenth day of life, 13 were asleep less than 55% of the total recording time. This occurred only in three cases among 32 pathological infants recorded before the fifteenth day of life.

In conclusion, sleep studies of prematurely born children raise many problems. Careful studies of the influence of the environment on the development of prematures are now necessary.

Acknowledgments

We are much indebted to Dr. N. Monod and Dr. L. Garma for creative discussions during the preparation of this chapter, and to Dr. N. Spears who kindly reviewed the manuscript.

References

Akiyama, Y., Schulte, F. J., Schultz, M. A., & Parmelee, A. H. , Jr. Acoustically evoked responses in premature and full-term newborn infants. *Electroencephalography Clinical Neurophysiology*, 1969, **26**, 371–380.

Anders, T. F., & Roffwarg, H. P. The effect of selective sleep state deprivation on the human newborn. *Psychophysiology*, 1969, **6**, 264–265. (a)

Anders, T. F., & Roffwarg, H. P. The effects of total sleep deprivation on the human newborn. *Psychophysiology*, 1969, **6**, 265. (b)

Anders, T. F., Emde, R., & Parmelee, A. (Eds.), *A manual of standardized terminology techniques and criteria for scoring of states of sleep and wakefulness in newborn infants.* Los Angeles: U.C.L.A. Brain Information Service, N.I.N.D.S. Neurological Information, 1971.

Ashton, R., & Connolly, K. The relation of respiration rate and heart rate to sleep states in the human newborn. *Developmental Medicine and Child Neurology*, 1971, **13**, 181–187.

Bell, R. Q. Sleep cycles and skin potential in newborns studied with a simplfied observation and recording system. *Psychophysiology*, 1970, **6**, 778–786.

Berges, J., Lezine, I., Harrison, A., & Boisselier, F. Les séquelles neuropsychiques de la prématurité. *Revue Neuropsychiatrie Infantile*, 1969, **17**, 719–779.

Bertini, M., Fornari, F., & Venturini, E. Observations on neonate sleep under the influence of a heart beat sound. In M. Bertini (Ed.), *Psicofisiologia del Sonno e del Sogno*. Milano: Vita e Pensiero, 1970. Pp. 3–14.

Curzi-Dascalova, L. Activité électrodermale spontanée au cours du sommeil d'enfants de 24 à 41 semaines d'âge conceptionnel: Etudes polygraphiques. Thèse 3° Cycle, University of Paris, 1971.

Curzi-Dascalova, L., Pajot, N., & Dreyfus-Brisac, C. Activité EDG spontanée et stades de sommeil chez les enfants prématurés: Etude polygraphique. *Revue Neurologique*, 1970, **123**, 231–239.

Dittrichova, J. Development of sleep in infancy. *Journal of Applied Physiology*, 1966, **21**, 1243–1246.

Dreyfus-Brisac, C. Ontogénése du sommeil chez le prématuré humain: Etude polygraphique. In A. Minkowski (Ed.), *Regional development of the brain in early life*. Oxford: Blackwell, 1966. Pp. 437–457.

Dreyfus-Brisac, C. Sleep ontogenesis in early human prematurity from 24 to 27 weeks of conceptional age. *Developmental Psychobiology*, 1968, **1**, 162-169.

Dreyfus-Brisac, C. Ontogenesis of sleep in the human premature after 32 weeks of conceptional age. *Developmental Psychobiology*, 1970, **3**, 91–121.

Eliet-Flescher, J., & Dreyfus-Brisac, C. Le sommeil du nouveau-né et du prémature. II. Relations entre l'EEG et l'EMG mentonnier au cours de la maturation. *Biologia Neonatorum*, 1966, **10**, 316–339.

Ellingson, R. J. Cerebral electrical responses to auditory and visual stimuli in the infant. (human and subhuman studies). In P. Kellaway & I. Petersen (Eds.), *Neurological and electroencephalographic correlative studies in infancy.* New York: Grune and Stratton, 1964. Pp. 78–114.

Ellingson, R. J. Methods of recording cortical evoked responses in the human infant. In A. Minkowski (Ed.), *Regional development of the brain in early life.* Oxford: Blackwell, 1966. Pp. 413–435.

Emde, R. N., & Koenig, K. L. Neonatal smiling and rapid eye movement states. *Journal of the American Academy of Child Psychiatry* 1969, **8**, 57–67.

Engel, R. Electroencephalographic responses to sound and to light in premature and full-term neonates. Lancet, 1967. **87**, 181–186.

Evsukova, J. J. Formation of circade rhythms of sleep in newly born babies. *Voprossi Okhranemia Materinstvo i Detstva*, 1971, **1**, 3–8.

Fantz, R. L., & Nevis, S. Pattern preferences and perceptual cognitive development in early infancy. *Merrill-Palmer Quarterly of Behavior and Development*, 1967, **13**, 77–108.

Garma, L., & Verley, R. Aspect ontogénètique des états de veille et sommeil chez les mammifères. *Revue Neuropsychiatrie Infantile*, 1969, **17**, 487–504.

Gesell, A., & Amatruda, C. J. *The embryology of behavior.* New York: Paul Hobber, 1947.

Hamburger, V. IV. Emergence of nervous coordination: Origins of integrated behavior. *Developmental Biology*, 1965, Suppl. 2, 251–271.

Henshall, W. R. Intrauterine sound levels. *American Journal of Obstetrics and Gynecology*, 1972, **112**, 576–577.

Hrbek, A., Hrbkova, M., & Lenard, H. C. Somato-sensory, auditory and visual evoked response in newborn infants during sleep and wakefulness. *Electroencephalography and Clinical Neurophysiology*, 1969, **26**, 597–603.

Irwin,O. C. The distribution of the amount of mobility in young infants betwen two nursing periods. *Journal of Genetic Psychology*, 1932, **44**, 429–445.

Jouvet-Mounier, D. Ontogénèse des états de vigilance chez quelques mammifères. Thèse Doctorat Es-Sciences, University of Lyon, 1968.

Korner, A. F. REM organization in neonates *Archives of General Psychiatry, 1968,* **19** 330–340.

McGinty, D. J. Effect of prolonged isolation and subsequent enrichment on sleep patterns in kittens. *Electroencephalography and Clinical Neurophysiology*, 1969, **26**, 335.

Metcalf, D.R. The effect of extrauterine experience on the ontogenesis of EEG sleep spindles. *Psychosomatic Medicine* 1969, **31**, 393–399.

Monod, N., & Dreyfus-Brisac, C. Les premières étapes de l'organisation du sommeil chez le prémature et le nouveau-né. In *Le sommeil de nuit normal et pathologique: Etudes électroencéphalographiques.* Paris: Masson, 1965. Pp. 116–148.

Monod, N., Eliet-Flescher, J., & Dreyfus-Brisac, C. Le sommeil du nouveau-né et du prématuré. III. Les troubles de l'organisation du sommeil chez le nouveau-né pathologique: Analyse des études polygraphiques. *Biologia Neonatorum*, 1967, 11 216–247.

Monod, N., & Garma, L. Auditory responsivity in the human premature. *Biologia Neonatorum*, 1971, **17**, 292–316.

Monod, N., & Pajot, N. Le sommeil du nouveau-né et du prématuré. I. Analyse des études polygraphiques (mouvements oculaires, respiration et EEG chez le nouveau-né à terme). *Biologia Neonatorum*, 1965, **8**, 281–307.

Murray, B., & Campbell, D. Sleep states in the newborn: Influence of sound. *Neuropädiatrie*, 1971, **2**, 335–342.

Parmelee, A. H., Akiyama, Y., Schultz, M. A., Wenner, W. H., Schulte, R., & Stern, E. The electroencephalogram in active and quiet sleep in infants. In P. Kellaway & I. Petersen (Eds.), *Clinical electroencephalography of children.* Stockholm: Almqvist and Wiksell, 1968. Pp. 78–88.

Parmelee, A. H., Akiyama, Y., Stern, E., & Harris, M. A. A periodic cerebral rhythm in newborn infants. *Experimental Neurology*, 1969, **25**, 575–584.

Parmelee, A. H., Bruck, K., & Bruck, M. Activity and inactivity cycles during the sleep of premature infants exposed to neutral temperatures. *Biologia Neonatorum*, 1962, **4**, 317–339.

Parmelee, A. H., Stern, E., & Harris, M. A. Maturation of respiration in prematures and young infants. *Neuropädiatrie*, 1972, **3**, 294–304.

Parmelee, A. H., Wenner, W. H., Akiyama, Y., Schultz, M., & Stern, E. Sleep states in premature infants. *Developmental Medicine and Child Neurology*, 1967, **9**, 70–77.

Parmelee, A. H., Wenner, W.H., Akiyama, Y., Stern, E. & Flescher, J. Electroencephalography and brain maturation. In A. Minkowski (Ed.), *Regional development of the brain in early life.* Oxford: Blackwell, 1966. Pp. 459–476.

Payne, G. S., & Bach, L. M. Perinatal sleep-wake cycles. *Biologia Neonatorum*, 1965, **8**, 308–320.

Petre-Quadens, O. On the different phases of the sleep of the newborn with special reference to the activated phase or phase D. *Journal Neurological Science*, 1966, **3**, 151–161.

Petre-Quadens, O. Ontogenesis of paradoxical sleep in the human newborn. *Journal of Neurological Science*, 1967, **4**, 153–157.

Petre-Quadens, O. Contribution à l'étude de la phase dite paradoxale du sommeil. Thésis, University Library, University of Brussels, 1969.

Polikanina, R. I. *Development of the higher nervous activity in prematurely born babies during the early post-natal period of life.* Leningrad: Meditsina, 1966.

Prechtl, H. F. R., Akiyama, Y., Zinkin, P., & Grant, D. K. Polygraphic studies of the full-term newborn: I. Technical aspects and quantitative analysis. In M. Bax & R. C. MacKeith (Eds.), *Studies in infancy: Clinics in developmental medicine.* Spastics Society. London: Heinemann, 1968. Pp. 2–21.

Roffwarg, H. P., Muzio, J. N., & Dement, W. C. Ontogenetic development of the human sleep-dream cycle. *Science*, 1966, **152**, 604–619.

Rothschild, B. F. Incubator isolation as a possible contributing factor to the high incidence of emotional disturbance among prematurely born persons. *Journal of Genetic Psychology*, 167, **110**, 287–304.

Ruckebusch, Y., & Barbey, P. Les états de sommeil chez le foetus et le nouveau-né de la vache *(Bos taurus)*. *Compte-rendus Société Biologie*, 1971, **165**, 1176–1184.

Samson-Dollfus, D. *L'EEG du prematuré jusqu'à l'âge de 3 mois et du nouveau-né a terme.* Paris: Thèse Medicine Foulon, 1955.

Sander, L. W., Julia, H. L., Stechler, G., & Burns, P. Continuous 24 hour interactional monitoring in infants reared in two caretaking environments. *Psychosomatic Medicine*, 1972, **3**, 170–282.

Scherrer, J., Verley, R., & Garma, L. Time, flow and velocity in early life. In L. Jilek & S. Trojan (Eds), *Ontogenesis of the brain*. Prague: University Karlova, 1969, Pp. 303–309.

Schmidt, K., & Birns, B. The behavioral arousal threshold in infant sleep as a function of time and sleep state. *Child Development*, 1971, **42**, 269–277.

Schulman, C. A. Alterations of the sleep cycle in heroin addicted and "suspect" newborns. *Neuropädiatrie*, 1969, **1**, 89–100.

Schulte, J. F., Lasson, U., Parl, U., Nolte, R., & Jurgens, U. Brain and behavioral maturation in newborn infants of diabetic mothers. II. Sleep cycles. *Neuropädiatrie*, 1969, **1**, 36–43.

Shaywitz, B. A., Finkelstein, J., Hellman, L., & Weitzman, E. D. Growth hormone in newborn infants during sleep-wake periods. *Pediatrics*, 1971, **48**, 103–110.

Sterman, M. B., & Hoppenbrouwers, T. The development of sleep-waking and rest-activity patterns from fetus to adult in man. In M. B. Sterman, D. J. McGinty, & A. M. Adinolfi (Eds), *Brain development and behavior*. New York: Academic Press, 1971. Pp. 203–227.

Vital-Durand, F., & Michel, F. Effets de la désafférentation périphérique sur le cycle veille-sommeil chez le chat. *Archives Italiennes de Biologie*, 1971, **109**, 166–186.

Watanabe, K., & Iwase, K. Spindle-like fast rhythms in the EEGs of low-birth weight Infants. *Developmental Medicine and Child Neurology*, 1972, **14**, 373–381.

Weitzman, E. D., & Graziani, L. Maturation and topography of the auditory evoked responses of the prematurely born infant. *Developmental Psychobiology*, 1968, **1**, 79–89.

Wolff, P. H. The causes, control and organization of behaviour in the neonate. *Psychological Issues*, Monograph. New York: International Universities Press, 1966.

Wolff, P. H. The serial organization of sucking in the young infant. *Pediatrics*, 1968, **42**, 943–956.

Wolff, P. H., & White, B. L. Visual pursuit and attention in young infants. *Journal of Child Psychiatry*, 1965, **43**, 473–484.

CHAPTER 7

Developmental Changes in Compensatory Dyadic Response in Mother and Infant Monkeys[1]

LEONARD A. ROSENBLUM[2] and KENNETH P. YOUNGSTEIN

State University of New York, Downstate Medical Center

CAREGIVING IN NONHUMAN PRIMATES

In nonhuman primates, as in man, the helpless status of the newborn and the prolonged period of infantile dependency require immediate, appropriate, and sustained caregiving for the newborn and developing infant. In most species it is the biological mother that primarily provides this care, although others in the social or family group may share in the task (Mitchell, 1969; Rosenblum, 1968). In terms of the macaque genus, for which the most abundant data exist, young infants may elicit care and protection from adolescent females, nonmother adult females, and even adult males under varying circumstances. There can be little doubt that the appearance of a newborn infant in a group evokes great excitement and prolonged interest in most of its members, although under normal circumstances the social stucture of the group may prevent many individuals from overt behavior directed at the infant. In the pigtail macaque, for example, the mother generally prevents all but her closest companion or older offspring from coming close to her young infant (Rosenblum, 1971a). When this type of social constraint is not present, however, very dramatic responsiveness to young infants can be seen in animals other than the biological mother. Harlow, Harlow, and Hansen (1963), for example, indicate that in rhesus some females, as long as 9 months after the birth and immediate removal of their own newborns, adopted separated 1- or 2-month-old infants presented to them in isolation. Not only were these females apparently capable of establishing quite normal mother-infant relationships with these infants, but they eventually even showed quite

[1] This research was supported by Grant #MH-15965, from the National Institute of Mental Health. The authors wish to thank Ms. Barbara Turner for her assistance in carrying out this study.

[2] This research was conducted while Dr. Leonard A. Rosenblum was the recipient of Research Scientist Development Award #K5, MH-23685.

substantial lactation. We have observed similar behavior in our studies of the effects of mother-infant separation in monkeys. In bonnet macaques we often observe that when the mother of a 4- to 6-month-old infant is removed from the group, the infant moves toward and is adopted by another member of the group, usually an adult female but occasionally the adult male. These foster mothers are generally without young of their own, but occasionally adoption by a female with an infant of her own occurs. These adoptions are usually quite strong, with pronounced periods of nipple contact and full protection of the infant. It is of interest in the current context that such adopted infants engage in a relationship whose obvious manifestations of attachment (e.g., contact time) closely resemble those previously observed with the biological mother prior to her removal (Rosenblum & Kaufman, 1967).

In the most general terms, however, the maternal responsiveness to infants in nonmothers is relatively variable and often incomplete or poorly organized (Rosenblum, 1972). We actually know quite little at present of the neural, hormonal, and experiential conditions that influence the readiness to provide care and protection of infant nonhuman primates. In the normal case, however, it appears that it is just prior to parturition that the female's consistent responsiveness to a newborn and the birth materials emerges most strongly. In an early study, Tinklepaugh and Hartman (1930) attempted to observe the reactions to the birth of another female's infant in a young primiparous female whose own pregnancy was approaching term. Three weeks prior to her own delivery, this female was placed in a cage with another female who was just about to give birth. When the latter delivered, the primipara (about 26 days prior to term) showed no real interest in either the new infant or any of the materials ejected during the birth process. However, when the same female only 3 days prior to her parturition was housed beneath another female during the latter's labor and delivery, she was observed to show considerable interest, licked the amniotic fluids and blood that she could retrieve, and devoured avidly a portion of the afterbirth which she also succeeded in obtaining. In a recent study of maternal responsiveness in squirrel monkeys (*Saimiri sciureus*), we also found that only females in the last 2 weeks of pregnancy respond *fully* and *consistently* to a young infant (Rosenblum, 1972).

INITIATION OF MATERNAL CAREGIVING

It is in the parturition process itself that we see the beginnings and some essential features of the mother's response to her newborn. In macaques the approaching parturition at the end of the 5½ months of pregnancy is usually signaled by the mother beginning to touch and manually explore the outer portions of the vagina, with repeated sniffing and licking of the fingers. The actual contractions of labor are usually accompanied by the female periodically assuming a squatting posture while tightly clasping some portion of the environment against which to strain. During the period of hours across which labor may continue, the female alternately paces, squats, and rests. Finally, as the baby's face and head appear, the mother under normal circumstances begins first to touch, grasp, and often to pull on the infant's head. After the infant is completely expelled, it is usually set against the ventral surface of the mother to which it clings, primarily by means of strong clasping reflexes of all four limbs.

Within about 15 minutes of the delivery of the infant, the female begins to pass the placenta and essentially the same exploratory, grasping, and pulling process is repeated. However, once delivered, in most instances the placenta is treated quite differently than the infant. While the infant is temporarily ignored, the mother begins the grueling task of devouring the placenta. As Tinklepaugh and Hartman (1930) report, "Her behavior does not suggest the eating of a delicacy, so much as it does the performance of a task under compulsion [P. 89]." Although usually the placenta is completely consumed, the cord itself is rarely eaten. The female commonly stops after biting into a small portion of the placenta end of the cord, and the latter is allowed to dry and break away.

Although an obvious necessity, it is in these moments after birth that one observes the first dimensions of the infant's capacity to elicit differential solicitude on the part of the mother. Two objects, smelling and tasting apparently alike, are emitted in rapid succession from the birth canal. One is immediately clutched to the breast, the other immediately consumed. What basic stimulus characteristics of the newborn infant—breathing, movement, size, shape—mediate this initial distinction, we do not know, but it is clear that they must elicit appropriate responses from the very outset if infant survival is to be insured.

THE INFANT'S ELICITATION OF CAREGIVING

Turning back to the infant, it is in these first moments of life that we begin to see the interdigitation of the mother's responsiveness to her infant and the infant's own response capacities. After manually bringing the infant forward to her ventrum, the mother does not engage in specific behaviors designed to produce appropriate placement or orientation of the infant. It is up to the infant to orient toward her in the ventral-ventral position and eventually to move upward into an appropriate position for nursing. It is the apparently strong righting reflexes and negative geotropic responses of the healthy newborn (Mowbray & Cadell, 1962) that produce these desired ends, not any form of directed orienting behavior on the part of the mother. If the infant's reflex system is somehow disturbed due to injury, illness or even prematurity, thus making it unable to achieve appropriate orientation on its own, a mother quite contentedly clasps her completely disoriented infant for long periods of time. In our laboratories, for example, we observed the birth of an infant who in the course of delivery fell from an upper bar about 6 feet to the floor of its pen. Postmortem examination revealed that this infant, although it lived for about 18 hours, received a severe brain injury from this fall. The infant during its brief life moved sporadically but was quite uncoordinated, and its mother carried it dorsal-ventral and upside down for long periods both before and after it died.

RESPONSE TO DEAD INFANTS

Perhaps the most dramatic displays of generalized maternal protectiveness coupled with apparently nonadjustive maternal response can be observed when newborns or infants die. It is quite common for macaque mothers to protect (often quite aggressively), transport, and even groom dead infants and stillborns (Figure 1). In most cases, for the first day or two following the death, the mother is constantly with the corpse, with a gradual decrease in protection and interest lasting over many days and often not ceasing until the body is extremely decomposed. During this period of protecting the dead infant, it is set before the mother as she rests, carried by its limbs, tail, body, or head as the mother moves, and periodically explored, turned about, picked at, and groomed. All this

FIGURE 1. Bonnet female grooming her dead neonate on the floor of the pen.

behavior occurs without any obvious attempt to sustain the infant at the ventrum or at the breast. The dead offspring is responded to as part infant and part object. In several instances in our laboratory, by the end of the first or second day, particularly after the delivery of a stillborn, portions of the body were eaten by the mother while the remainder was still protected. It may be noted that infants are rarely eaten when death occurs after the first week or two of life, perhaps because some degree of individual identification of the infant has occurred by that time. Thus some characteristics of the infant, even in death, elicit major aspects of maternal protection and care; what is suggested here, however, is that in these animals at least, the mother makes possible, but does not herself create, the early forms of the mother-infant relationship as we normally observe them.

INFANT CHARACTERISTICS AND MATERNAL CAREGIVING

The nature of the infant's actual contribution to the observed dyadic relationship, the focus of this volume, has concerned many workers in the study of nonhuman primate development. The infant's changing behavior with a nonresponsive and constant mother surrogate (Harlow & Zimmerman, 1959); the developing behaviors of normal mothers and infants as the infant matures (Kaufman & Rosenblum, 1969); the role of environmental complexity in influencing mothers' and infants' responses to each other (Jensen, Bobbitt, & Gordon, 1968); and the detailed statistical analysis of the shifting contributions of mothers and infants in regulating their unfolding relationship (Hinde & Spencer-Booth, 1968) have all been carried out with observations of macaques under controlled laboratory conditions.

In all these and related studies, except for the artificial surrogate work with its own unique features, the very subtle interweaving of maternal and filial behavior in normal dyads can obscure the specific features of each partner's contribution to the observed pattern. It is also difficult to assess those elements of each partner's behavior that actually can elicit and regulate the other's component responses. Several studies have been made, which allow further determination of the role of some of the infant's behavior through the use of disabled infants (see also Chapter 11, on response to blind infants). Lindburg (1969) for example, studied the development of mother-infant relations in rhesus infants with thalidomide-induced limb malformations which prevented normal clinging. Lindburg found that, despite this disability, the course of the relationship was essentially normal, except that mothers compensated for the infants' inability to cling by supporting them during locomotion even as they grew older (this maternal behavior normally disappears by about 3 weeks). The mothers also showed manual cradling of their infants at the ventrum far longer than normal controls. Thus the general supportive behavior of the mother was sustained in response to an infant that failed to show normal development of self-support, and with the infant's remaining reflexes and ability intact, the maternal compensatory behavior allowed the infant to survive. In a now classic study in the same realm, Rumbaugh studied the reaction of squirrel monkey mothers to infants experimentally prevented from clinging (Rumbaugh, 1965; see also Rosenblum, 1968). It should be noted that in this species, unlike the macaques, the normal infant, at birth, climbs onto the mother's back and except for periods of nursing remains perched in that position. The mother squirrel monkey normally seems relatively uninterested in her young infant and neither supports, grooms, or interacts with it overtly to any great degree. However, Rumbaugh restrained the arms of young squirrel monkeys with adhesive tape, thus making them unable to support themselves on their mothers' backs. A mother, after repeatedly assuming a posture that ordinarily would result in the infant's climbing on her, actually picked up the debilitated infant and, cradling it in both hands or arms, scampered off bipedally. When the tape was removed from the infant's arms and the infant returned to its mother, the mother did not attempt to pick it up manually but presented for the normal dorsal carry. Thus Rumbaugh (1965) was led to conclude that the apparent indifference of the squirrel monkey mother toward her normal infant under appropriate conditions of infant need can change to "a very concerted active pattern [p. 174]." We have no notion from these studies, of course, whether an infant prevented from clinging for long periods could actually survive in this species. Nonetheless it does appear that the squirrel monkey mother has a degree of adaptability in her behavior which is not normally observed. Further, it is made clear from this type of experimental study that these adjustments of maternal behavior, in some measure at least, are influenced by changes in the stimulus qualities and behavioral characteristics of the infant at a given point in time.

THE RESPONSE TO EXPERIMENTALLY DEBILITATED INFANTS

In an attempt to delineate further the differential role of mother and infant in the developing dyadic relationship in nonhuman primates, we carried out a study in which mother and infant macaques were first anesthetized and then returned to their dyadic partners. Through the use of this technique, applied at different infant ages, a partner may be provided with most static stimulus features of the other dyad member, but when the latter can neither initiate nor respond. This allows more discrete evaluation of the specific components of response engaged in by each member in the absence of the normal interactive network. This technique also provides controlled, repeated opportunity to determine the flexibility and adaptiveness in infant and maternal roles, and the capacity for reciprocity and compensation available in the repertoire of each member.

Method

The subjects used in this study were bonnet macaques (*Macaca radiata*) drawn from the colony at the Primate Behavior Laboratory of the Downstate Medical Center. Two groups, each containing four mother-infant dyads were used. Group 1 contained the dyads with the four youngest infants, 6 to 7 months of age, of which two were male and two were female; Group 2, contained the older infants, all male, which were 16 to 19 months of age; see Table 1. The two groups were housed in identical pens approximately 7 ft wide, 12 ft deep, and 7 ft high (see Figure 2). The side and back walls of the pens were covered with ceramic tiles, and the front wall contained two large one-way-vision observation screens. The tops of the pens were covered with strong wire mesh. Within each pen, running along the back wall and extending 6 ft forward on each side, was an 18 in.-wide, U-shaped shelf, 3 ft from the floor. In addition, an upper bar was suspended 2 ft from the ceiling near the back wall. In the front wall was a large door which allowed human access to the pen, and a small guillotine door through which the animals could enter and leave for handling, cleaning, and experimental treatment. The tile floor of the pen was covered with San-i-cel bedding and was changed once a

TABLE 1   Weight in Kilograms and Ages of the Members of Groups 1 and 2

Subject	Age (weeks)	Weight (kg)
Group 1		
A Mother		6.25
a Infant, female	23	1.00
B Mother		6.75
b Infant, female	23	1.00
C Mother		4.00
c Infant, male	21	1.25
D Mother		5.00
d Infant, male	21	1.25
Group 2		
A Mother		5.40
a Infant, male	62	1.80
B Mother		6.80
b Infant, male	71	2.50
C Mother		6.70
c Infant, male	75	2.50
D Mother		5.30
d Infant, male	75	2.40

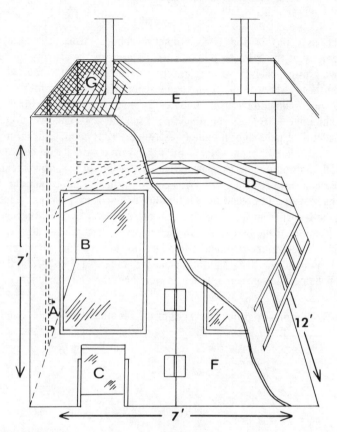

FIGURE 2. Diagram of the animal pens. *A*, Automatic drinking spouts; *B*, one-way vision
observation mirrors; *C*, guillotine door; *D*, aluminum shelves; *E*, upper bars; *F*, Entrance
door; and *G*, heavy wire mesh.

week. Feeding took place late each afternoon, and water was available *ad
libitum*.

It was the purpose of this study to test the responses of the awake member of
the dyad (i.e., either mother or infant) in the normal pen and group setting when
its dyadic partner was rendered unresponsive through anesthetization for a
specified period of time. Fortunately, a drug ideally suited for this type of work
had recently become available and was used in this study. This rapid-acting
general anesthetic is ketamine hydrochloride (Ketalar, Parke-Davis). Based on
pilot determinations, using a concentration of 50 mg/ml and intramuscular
injection, a dosage of 15 mg/kg produced sustained immobility in both infants
and mothers for the 30-minute trials utilized in this study. Recovery after the

anesthetization period was extremely rapid, with virtually normal behavior appearing within an hour of initial injection. No enhancement or inhibition of the drug effects has been seen with limited repeated dosages.

Inasmuch as anesthetization required handling and injection of each animal apart from the direct effects of the drug, and also necessitated capture of both dyad members and their brief separation, it was necessary to assess these handling effects apart from the impact of anesthetization per se. Hence it was necessary to run separate handling control trials. Furthermore, in order that both experimental and handling control conditions could be compared with respect to the normal ongoing behavior of the dyad, a normative, nonmanipulated condition was also necessary. Thus three types of observations were made in the course of this study, normative control (NC), handling control (HC), and the anesthetization, experimental condition (EC). Each mother and each infant was observed twice in each condition with the order of conditions balanced across dyads. In order to control for changes in behavior throughout the course of the study and to link the NC observations as closely as possible to the EC and the HC conditions with which they were to be compared, NC observations immediately preceded every EC and HC session. Each group was tested once each morning and once each afternoon, 4 days a week, with different dyads the focus of observation in the two daily sessions, and only one HC and one EC condition carried out each day. The rapid recovery time from the use of the drug noted earlier, facilitated this testing schedule.

Each day's testing began with a 1000-second NC observation of the dyad to be studied. Following the NC observations the group was captured, and the dyad to be observed that session was separated from the group. The animals used in this study were quite accustomed to capture, and thus the agitation and capture time were minimal. Animals that were not to be the focus of observation were returned to their pens immediately. The mother and infant to be tested were then separated from one another and placed in individual carrying cages. For HC conditions the treated partner was given an injection of sterile saline solution equal in amount to its dosage of Ketalar. It was then placed back in the carrying cage. For EC conditions the animal was treated in the same manner but actually injected with the drug. On these drug trials, when the treated partner was immobile, approximately 3 minutes, the noninjected member of the dyad was returned to its pen. On the HC trials the nontreated partner was returned after a similar interval. Sixty seconds after the introduction of the noninjected partner (the subject of observation), the treated partner was placed back in its pen. On EC trials the injected animal was placed on the floor of the pen via the guillotine door, and on HC trials it was simply released in the usual manner. Observations of the noninjected member began as soon as the injected animal was returned and the pen door closed.

Observations were made using a check sheet and a 20-second cumulative time sampling technique. For this purpose, within each successive 20-second interval, demarcated in separate columns on the check sheet, the observer indicated the occurrence or nonoccurrence of each of a number of behaviors listed on the check sheet. The observer also indicated, when appropriate, whether the subject of observation was the initiator or recipient of the behavior in question, and which partner was involved.

Eighteen behaviors were listed initially, but many failed to occur with sufficient frequency to merit separate consideration here. The following categories, adapted in part from Kaufman and Rosenblum (1966), represented the primary foci of our analyses: (a) Any form of contact (AFC): This primary category was composed of five constituent elements, each separately recorded: (1) passive contact, in which two animals remained in physical contact with one another without engaging in any other specific behavior; (2) ventral contact, a behavior scored for either mother or infant whenever the infant was in ventral contact with the mother, with or without nursing; (3) support-cradle, a rather variable behavior which involved the mother holding or supporting the infant in any fashion including cradling, dragging, or carrying in any way; (4) social exploration, which involved close visual, oral, or olfactory inspection and/or tentative manipulation of the body of another animal; and (5) grooming, in which one animal carefully picked through and/or brushed aside the fur of another with one or both hands. (b) Other level: Considering the pen to comprise four levels, ceiling, upper bar, shelf, and floor, this category was scored whenever mother and infant were at different levels of the pen. (c) Locomotion: This category was scored whenever the subject moved more than one body length, while not obviously engaged in some other scored behavior element. (d) Play: This category included all forms of social play, including those involving contact (rough-and-tumble play) and merely chasing.

The same check sheets and behavior categories were utilized for observations in all types of sessions. Each check sheet contained ten, 20-second columns. Inasmuch as NC observations preceded each HC and EC condition, to keep total observation time equal under each condition, NC observation sessions were half as long as HC or EC sessions. As noted earlier, the NC condition involved 1000 seconds of observation (5 check sheets), whereas the EC and HC sessions each involved 2000 seconds of observation (10 check sheets).

Interobserver reliability was assessed 10 times during the course of the study. In each case both observers followed the same animal simultaneously for ten 20-second intervals. The reliability sessions included NC, HC, and EC, with both mothers and infants as the foci of observation. In order to assess the reliability of observation within the basic time sample unit, correlations of interobserver agreement were tabulated using the Tetrachoric R assessing agreements of occurrence and nonoccurrence in each interval. Correlations of agreement on all categories exceeded .95.

Results and Discussion

As indicated earlier, two of the infants in Group 1 were females, whereas all other infants in the study were males. Preliminary statistical analyses revealed no sex differences in any category, and thus for all analyses described below females and males of Group 1 are treated together.

Looking first at the undisturbed (NC) behavior of the dyad, we can gain an initial assessment of the level of attachment behavior seen in the mothers and infants of the two age groups. As reflected in the right-hand column of Figure 3, Group-1 mothers and infants spent significantly more time in contact with one another than did the older dyads in Group 2. Separate analyses of variance of both mothers' and infants' scores show the same significant trend. Overall, Group-2 dyads were observed in some form of contact during approximately 73% of the time intervals observed, whereas group-2 dyads were only in contact during approximately 35% of the normative intervals. It should also be noted that

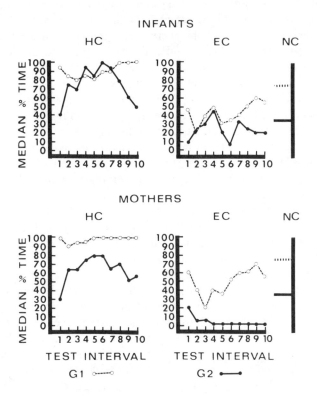

FIGURE 3. Contact scores (total dyadic AFC) in mothers and infants under normative control (NC), handling control (HC), and experimental conditions (EC).

in Group 1 ventral contact, the most intimate form of dyadic contact, represented 65% of the total contact scores (i.e., total AFC), whereas less than 40% of the AFC scores in the older group involved this close form of contact. Similarly, reflecting the same general trend toward decreasing attachment with age of infant, Group-2 dyads spent significantly more time at other levels of the pen away from one another than did Group-1 dyads. The older infants and their mothers were observed on separate levels of the pen during 40 to 50% of the intervals, whereas the younger infants were separated from their mothers in this fashion during only 16 to 18% of the observations. Following the same basic trend, the members of the older dyads showed significantly more independent locomotion than the younger infants and their mothers. These trends are basically in keeping with previously collected normative data (Rosenblum, 1971b) which indicate that the most rapid decline in mother-infant contact occurs during the first 4 to 6 months of the infant's life, reaching a low-level plateau at about 8 months and gradually declining thereafter.

In the most general terms, the HC condition served to enhance tremendously all indications of dyadic attachment in both the younger and older groups. Neuman-Keuls analyses indicate that there were significantly higher dyadic AFC scores in the HC condition than in either the NC or EC sessions. As a further reflection of the general agitation in the dyads as a direct result of handling, the proportion of AFC that involved ventral contact rose to 87% of the scores in Group 1, and 74% of the AFC scores in Group 2. This increase in observed dyadic attachment behavior appeared regardless of whether the infant or the mother was sham injected. In the HC condition (see Figure 3), in the younger infants there was an immediate, and in the older infants an only slightly delayed, attainment of contact between the members of the dyad. This generally was the result of both older and younger infants racing to the mother at the start of the session. Older dyads then showed a more rapid decrease in contact toward the end of the 2000 seconds of observation. Thus the general response to handling and sham injection of either partner was a marked and generally sustained increase in dyadic contact, a picture in rather marked contrast to that observed when anesthetization accompanied the handling.

Response to anesthetized partners was often quite dramatic, particularly in the case of the younger, Group-1 dyads. When the anesthetized young infant was returned to the pen, the observer was often threatened violently and the unconscious baby virtually pulled from his hands. In several cases the mothers of Group 1 rapidly proceeded to drag the unconscious infant toward the back of the pen and then attempted to lift it to the shelf (see Figure 4). Whether remaining with the infant on the floor of the pen, or after succeeding in transporting it to the shelf, the mothers of young infants spent relatively long periods of time near and in contact with them, hovering over them protectively (see Figure 5). In contrast, mothers of the older infants (Group 2) rarely made much more than an initial passing contact with their unconscious infants in the first minutes of the session

FIGURE 4. A mother bonnet lifting her unconscious young infant to the shelf of the pen.

and usually failed to achieve further contact thereafter. Mothers of younger infants even succeeded on occasion in pulling the infants up to their ventrums, whereas the mothers of older infants did not receive a single ventral contact score throughout any experimental trial.

Return of the unconscious mother also evoked quite striking reactions, again particularly in Group 1. The young infants generally rushed to the unconscious mother shortly after the observer's hand was removed and the door closed. Obviously unable actually to move the mother to a "safer" location, these infants nonetheless spent long periods of time in various forms of contact with her (see Figure 6). Indeed, although significantly less total time was spent in any form of contact (AFC) with the unconscious mother than under the HC or NC conditions, 79% of the time Group-1 infants achieved contact with the mother, they succeeded in making ventral contact (see Figure 7). Group-2 infants also responded, although somewhat more hesitatingly, to the unconscious mother, and achieved only about half the total AFC score of their younger counterparts. It is striking, however, that even in these older infants nearly half the time that contact was achieved the infant managed to work its way onto the mother's ventrum (see Figure 8).

In statistical terms, dyads in both groups showed significantly less total AFC between dyad members under the EC than under the HC and NC conditions, although Group 1 showed significantly more such contact than Group 2. Of

FIGURE 5. A mother bonnet protecting her unconscious young infant on the shelf of the pen.

FIGURE 6. A young bonnet infant contacting its unconscious mother on the floor of the pen.

154

FIGURE 7. A young infant in ventral contact with its unconscious mother.

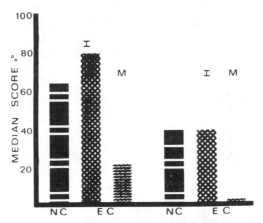

FIGURE 8. Ventral contact between mothers and infants in the normative control (NC) and experimental (EC) conditions. Group 1 is depicted on the left, and Group 2 on the right, of the graph. *I* indicates scores for infants when mothers were unconscious, and *M* indicates scores for mothers when infants were unconscious.

particular significance in assessing the infant's and mother's response to the unconscious partner in the two groups was the following: In Group 1 there was no significant difference in the AFC score obtained when it was the mother or the infant that was unconscious (see Figure 9). The median infant score when the mother was unconscious was 44.3%, while that of the mother with an unconscious infant was 50.3%. Thus in the younger group there was considerable reciprocity in response between mother and infant when the dyadic partner was unable to behave normally. In Group 2, with much older infants, however, no such reciprocity appeared to exist. Whereas the older *infants* achieved AFC scores of 26% when the mother was unconscious, the *mothers* achieved significantly lower scores of only 4% when the infant was unresponsive (see Figure 9). Furthermore, as reflected in Figure 8, in Group 1, 22% of the mothers' AFC scores involved ventral contact, whereas no such scores were recorded for the mothers of older infants. Looking at the other reflection of dyadic attachment behavior, that is, the other-level scores, both groups showed a significant increase in other-level during the EC condition, concomitant with a decrease in total dyadic AFC. However, whereas infant scores for other level did not differ significantly between the two groups, the mothers of older infants showed significantly higher overall scores of other level than did the mothers of the younger infants.

It is also of interest to note that in keeping with previous studies of the reaction of bonnet macaque infants to total separation from the mother (Rosenblum & Kaufman, 1967), as indicated in Figure 10, infants of both groups showed a significant increase in contact with other females in the group during

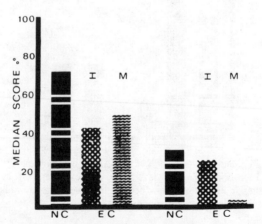

FIGURE 9. Contact scores (total dyadic AFC) between mothers and infants in the normative control (NC) and experimental (EC) conditions. Group 1 is depicted on the left, and Group 2 on the right, of the graph. *I* indicates scores for infants when mothers were unconscious, and *M* indicates scores for mothers when infants were unconscious.

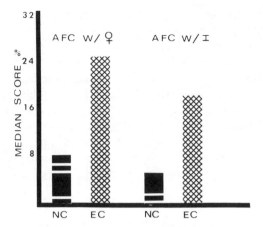

FIGURE 10. Infant contact (AFC) with other females and other infants of their groups during normative control (NC) and experimental (EC) conditions.

the EC condition. Although there was also an increase in contact with other infants in the group during EC, these scores approached but did not attain statistical significance. It is our contention that raising bonnet macaque infants in stable conspecific groups within which they receive considerable positive interaction from the first days of life onward makes possible another form of adaptive response to disability on the part of their mothers, that is, an apparent readiness to move toward and transfer filial responsiveness to other appropriate members of the group (Rosenblum, 1971b). It should be noted that adult bonnet macaques continue to show strong social attachments, and that the mothers of both groups showed a strong tendency to increase their contact with other females in the group when their infants were rendered unconscious during EC sessions.

The technique used in this study enables us to examine several dimensions of both maternal and filial behavior not readily discernable in the normally functioning dyad. The approach is not without certain shortcomings, however. Quite obviously, prolonged debilitation of one dyad member, with the unique developmental information such an approach provides (see Chapters 10 and 11) is not feasible through the anesthetization method. It is also the case that overly frequent short-term repetitions are likely to provide adverse drug and perhaps handling reactions, severely altering the ongoing development of behavior in complex ways. It should also be noted that it is not only the awake dyad member that may react to the presence of the unconscious animal. Other adult and infant group members may also be affected. In a previous pilot study (Rosenblum, Merril, & Mercer, 1966), in which the breeding male of a bonnet macaque group was present with the females, whenever the mother of the unconscious infant was not nearby the male contacted and groomed the infant and protected it zealously. In the present study, when infants were unconscious, they were infrequently attended to and never molested by others in the group. The mothers, however, were actually attacked on occasion while lying unconscious on the floor. Strangely enough, these aggressive responses were most prominently displayed toward the most subordinate mothers of each group and directed at them by the most dominant females. Perhaps the disrupted communication of subordinance and dominance between the pair triggered these outbursts. In any event such general social responses to the disabled member, although potentially of great interest in their own right, can disrupt attempts to evaluate the intradyadic relations.

A THEORETICAL MODEL OF COMPENSATORY DYADIC RESPONSE

What we can suggest from this and related studies, however, is the beginning of a rough formulation of the systematic developmental changes in the mothers' and infants' normal contributions to the dyadic relationship, the degree of reciprocity of these components at various infant ages, and the potential for compensatory behavior of which each partner is capable. We suggest that the contribution made by infant and mother decreases normally over time, but more rapidly in mother than in infant; the most rapid decreases occur in the first 3 to 6 months of life, approaching a gradually declining plateau at about 4 to 6 months in the mother and 8 to 10 months in the infant. It is relevant to note that an early theoretical formulation of changing mother and infant "contact needs" in the normal dyad followed somewhat similar lines (Harlow et al., 1963). In our own formulation we suggest furthermore that each partner's capacity to compensate for the lack of appropriate contribution from the other, which we have termed "compensatory potential," decreases in a similar but linear fashion after about the second to third month of the infant's life. This initial and limited formulation, based as it is on a complex of normative data of previous studies (Rosenblum, 1971b) and only two age points in the current study, may be seen graphically represented in Figure 11. Note that, although the mother's overt component drops off rather rapidly, in the early months her compensatory potential is very great. For the infant, after the first few months there is relatively little maternal component for which it can compensate. This model suggests furthermore that by about the end of the first year of life each partner loses the capacity to compensate for a failure on the part of the partner to respond. Thus in the current study, in Group 2, when the mother was unconscious we saw little change in the overt contact time (i.e., AFC); by this age such behavior almost entirely represents the infant's component of the dyadic behavior. When the infant was unconscious, the mother

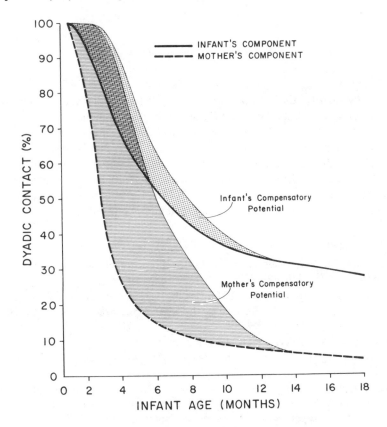

FIGURE 11. Theoretical curves for the model of the infant's and the mother's normal contribution to dyadic contact and each partner's capacity to compensate for a lack in the other's normal contribution.

was no longer capable of compensating for the lack of infant response, and with her own component already close to zero, little or no dyadic contact was observed.

In somewhat more explicit mathematical terms, this model suggests that both the infant's and the mother's components of the normally observed dyadic relation follow a Gaussian decay function of the general form $A_1 E^{-A_2 t^2}$, in which A_2 for the infant's function is less than A_2 for the mother's, thus producing a slower decay in the infant's component. Furthermore, if $X_i(t)$ and $X_m(t)$ are the components of dyadic behavior contributed by the infant and mother at time t, and we let $S_{mi}(t)$ be the observed contact time between mother and infant at time t when m is awake the model is:

$$S_{mi}(t) = X_m(t) + C_{mi}(t)X_i(t)$$

Similarly

$$S_{im} (t) = X_i (t) + C_{im} (t) X_m (t)$$

C_{mi} is the percent of $X_i (t)$ that animal m assumes when animal i is unconscious at time t: similarly, C_{im} is the percent of $X_m(t)$ that animal i assumes when animal m is unconscious at time t: C_{mi} and C_{im} are linear decay functions.[3]

Needless to say, such mathematical formulations may seem pretentiously precise in light of our current paucity of information. Nevertheless, attempting to partition dyadic attachment and contact behavior into its component elements and the testing of some of the implications of this initial model may assist us in formulating and interpreting subsequent research of this type on different ages, species, and dyads observed in different, potentially influential environments.

References

Harlow, H. F., & Zimmermann, R. R. Affectional responses in the infant monkey. *Science*, 1959, **130**, 421–432.

Harlow, H. F., Harlow, M. K., & Hansen, E. W. The maternal affectional system of rhesus monkeys. In H. Rheingold, (Ed.), *Maternal behavior in mammals*. New York: Wiley, 1963. Pp. 254–281.

Hinde, R. A., & Spencer-Booth, Y. The study of mother-infant interaction in captive group-living rhesus monkeys. *Proceedings of the Royal Society, B, 1968*, **169**. Pp. 177–201.

Jensen, G. D., Bobbitt, R. A., & Gordon, B. N. Effects of environment on the relationship between mother and infant pigtailed monkeys *(Macaca nemestrina)*. *Journal of Comparative and Physiological Psychology*, 1968, **66**, 259–263.

Kaufman, I. C., & Rosenblum, L. A. A behavioral taxonomy for *M. nemestrina* and *M. radiata:* Based on longitudinal observations of family groups in the laboratory. *Primates*, 1966, **7**, 205–258.

Kaufman, I. C., & Rosenblum, L. A. The waning of the mother-infant bond in two species of macaque. In B. M. Foss (Ed.), *Determinants of infant behaviour*. Vol. IV London: Methuen, 1969. Pp. 41–59.

Lindburg, D. G. Behavior of infant rhesus monkeys with thalidomide-induced malformations: A pilot study. *Psychonomic Science*, 1969, **15**, 55–56.

Mitchell, G. D. Paternalistic behavior in primates. *Psychological Bulletin*, 1969, **71**, 399–417.

Mowbray, J. B., & Cadell, T. E. Early behavior patterns in rhesus monkeys. *Journal of Comparative and Physiological Psychology*, 1962, **55**, 350–357.

Rosenblum, L. A. Mother-infant relations and early behavioral development in the squirrel monkey. In L. A. Rosenblum & R. W. Cooper (Eds.), *The squirrel monkey*. New York: Academic Press, 1968. Pp. 207–233.

[3] The authors wish to thank Dr. Joel Stutman for his assistance in translating the proposed model into an appropriate mathematical formulation.

Rosenblum, L. A. Infant attachment in monkeys. In R. Schaffer (Ed.), *The origins of human social relations.* New York: Academic Press, 1971(a). Pp. 85–113.

Rosenblum, L. A. The ontogeny of mother-infant relations in macaques. In H. Moltz (Ed.), *Ontogeny of vertebrate behavior.* New York: Academic Press, 1971(b). Pp. 315–367.

Rosenblum, L. A. Sex and age differences in response to infant squirrel monkeys. *Brain, Behavior and Evolution,* 1972, **5** 30–40.

Rosenblum, L. A., & Kaufman, I. C. Variations in infant development and response to maternal loss in monkeys. *American Journal of Orthopsychiatry,* 1968, **38,** 418–426.

Rosenblum, L. A., Merrill, S. A., & Mercer, Z. J. Infant effects on the mother-infant relationship in *M. radiata.* Unpublished manuscript, 1966.

Rumbaugh, D. Maternal care in relation to infant behavior in the squirrel monkey. *Psychological Reports,* 1965, **16,** 171–176.

Tinklepaugh, O. L., & C. G. Hartman. Behavior aspects of parturition in the monkey *(Macacus rhesus). Comparative Psychology,* 1930, **11,** 63–98.

CHAPTER 8

Some Factors Influencing the Attraction of Adult Female Macaque Monkeys to Neonates [1]

GENE P. SACKETT and **GERALD C. RUPPENTHAL**
University of Washington

The early life experiences of most primate species include a period of close physical ties between infants and their mothers. Research on this relationship has concentrated on normative descriptions of mother-infant interaction, or has studied the effects of maternal characteristics on offspring behavior (e.g., Bowlby, 1969; Hinde, 1971). Few experimental studies have been concerned with the effects of infant characteristics on the mother, although correlational data (e.g., Mitchell, 1968), studies of handicapped or disabled infants (e.g., Chapters 10 and 11), and observations of maternal competence by females reared under conditions of social deprivation (e.g., Arling & Harlow, 1967) suggest that attributes of neonates may have major effects on the quality of caregiving behavior.

This article reviews a series of experiments concerned with identifying sources of maternal motivation. The subjects were monkey species that originated in either India (*Macaca mulatta,* the rhesus monkey) or the Malaysia-Indonesia Archipelago (*Macaca nemestrina*, the pigtail monkey). These studies measured preferences for neonates relative to other types of social stimuli, as indexed by approach and proximity of adult female subjects to live monkey stimuli. The factors studied for their potential influence in determining neonate attractiveness included (1) characteristics of infants as stimuli, (2) age and parity of adult female subjects, (3) mother-infant separation, (4) conditions under which the mother had reared her infant, and (5) conditions under which the mother herself had been raised.

[1] Many of the studies reviewed here were supported by U.S. Public Health Service grants RR-0167 and MH-11894 from the National Institutes of Health to the University of Wisconsin Regional Primate Center and Primate Laboratory. Other studies, and manuscript preparation, were supported by grant RR-00166 from the National Institutes of Health to the Washington Regional Primate Research Center and grant HD-02274 from the National Institutes of Health to the Washington Child Development and Mental Retardation Center.

THE SELF-SELECTION CIRCUS TEST

Most of the data presented here were collected in a self-selection circus (Figure 1). This apparatus is constructed from aluminum channels forming a six-sided outer perimeter. Six outer choice compartments surround a central start compartment. Choice compartments are separated from each other by opaque Masonite walls, and are separated from the start compartment by vertically sliding, clear Plexiglas walls. The front walls of each choice compartment are also Plexiglas. The choice compartment floors contain pressure switches which activate clocks and counters when the subject steps onto the floor area. This yields a measure of duration and frequency of entry into each compartment. Solenoid-operated vacuum cylinders, suspended above the circus, can be

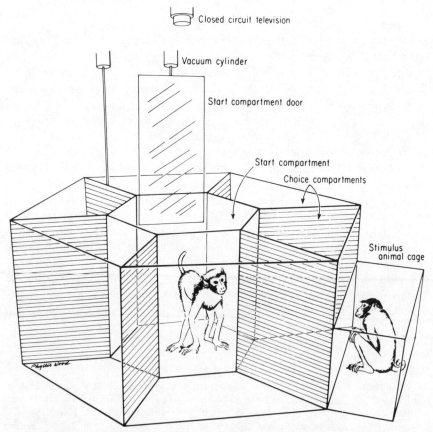

FIGURE 1. The self-selection circus apparatus used to study social stimulus preferences in the studies reviewed in this article.

programmed to raise the Plexiglas doors separating start from choice compartments.

A stimulus animal cage can be hooked onto the outside of each choice compartment. The clear Plexiglas front of this cage gives the subject an unobstructed view of the stimulus animal from the start or choice compartment areas. A closed-circuit television system, mounted above the circus, allows an observer to view the subject's behavior during a test.

In the work reported here, different types of stimulus monkeys were randomly assigned to stimulus animal cages. The standard test procedure involved (1) placing the subject in the start compartment through an unused choice compartment area, (2) a 5-minute *exposure* period when the subject could see the stimulus monkeys but could not approach them because the inner Plexiglas walls were closed, and (3) a 10-minute *choice* period started by raising the inner Plexiglas walls. During the choice period the subject could enter and reenter any choice compartment, or could remain in the central start area.

The number of seconds spent in a choice compartment near a given type of stimulus indexed relative preference for that stimulus animal. While in the choice compartment the subject had close visual, auditory, and olfactory contact with the stimulus monkey, but physical interaction was not allowed. Thus choices were made on the basis of the way a particular stimulus monkey looked, sounded, or smelled. Further, as no attempt was made to influence the behavior of stimulus animals, choices could also have been based on particular behaviors of the stimulus monkeys or on behavioral interactions between the subject and the stimulus animals.

NORMATIVE STUDIES: VALIDATION OF THE PREFERENCE TECHNIQUE

Own-Species Attraction

Sackett, Suomi, and Grady (1970) studied choices by macaque monkeys for adult female stimulus animals of three species: namely, rhesus (*M. mulatta*), pigtail (*M. nemestrina*), and stumptail (*M. speciosa*). The subjects were all wild-born adults of these same three species. The physical appearance of these stimuli, as they appeared to subjects in the circus stimulus animal cages, is illustrated in Figure 2. The data (Figure 3) revealed that each species had its maximum choice time (compartment entry duration) and orientation time (head pointed toward a particular stimulus monkey from any area in the circus) toward its own species (all $p < .01$, except pigtail orientation where $p = .07$). Thus adult wild-born male and female macaque subjects showed strong attraction toward females of their own species.

A parallel study was run on 26 rhesus monkey infants ranging in age from 25 days through 9 months. All subjects had been separated from their mothers at

FIGURE 2. The three types of adult females used to study own-species preferences. Top, rhesus; middle, pigtail; bottom, stumptail.

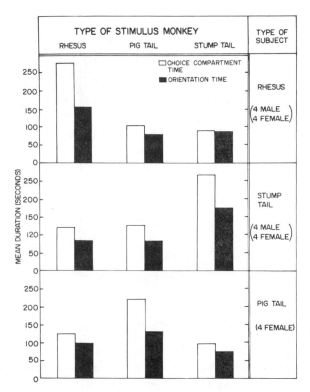

FIGURE 3. Choice compartment entry time and orientation time by rhesus, stumptail, and pigtail subjects choosing among adult females of their own and the other two species.

birth and were raised in wire cages with their only social stimulation from seeing, hearing, and smelling, but not touching, agemates. These infants had no contact with any adult or juvenile monkeys prior to their circus tests. The results (Figure 4) revealed a clear preference for adult rhesus females over the other two types of stimulus females.

In addition to the data presented in Figure 4, three pigtail infants under 2 months of age, which had been reared in wire cages with both pigtail and rhesus neonates in the room, all had maximum orientation time toward the pigtail female stimulus animal. One stumptail baby, tested at 1.5 months of age, was the only infant that preferred the stumptail female.

These data suggest a biological basis for inferring that infant characteristics have important species-specific effects on the behavior of monkey mothers. Although the reason why socially naive, motherless, infants prefer the adult female of their own species is not as yet known, it seems clear that even very

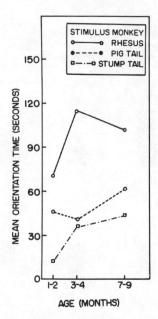

FIGURE 4. Orientation time by partial isolate rhesus neonates and infants for adult females of their own and two other macaque species.

early in life macaque neonates are able to detect and to react with approach behaviors toward adult females of their own species. Thus specific factors involving adult female appearance, odor, or behavior may be prepotent in determining the direction of an infant monkey's choice of stimuli. Such behavioral tendencies increase the probability that the infant will have a strong impact on the adult female of its own species.

A third circus study assessed preferences by the same 26 wire-cage-raised rhesus infants tested in the own-species preference experiment (Suomi, Sackett, & Harlow, 1970). The two types of stimulus monkeys in these tests included an adult female and an adult male wild-born rhesus. All 26 infants in the age range 1 to 10 months had their maximum orientation toward the female. This again suggests that there is a strong, biologically based tendency in monkey infants to be attracted toward an appropriate, adult female stimulus.

Other support for the hypothesis that basic behavioral tendencies of monkey neonates play an important role in the initiation of attachment to an *appropriate* maternal object is found in work by Mitchell (1972). His studies of the birth process in rhesus monkeys show that almost immediately after emergence from the birth canal the newborn clings to the mother and climbs upward onto her ventral surface. Of major interest are two observations. (1) Some infants even deliver themselves by grasping the mother's leg and pulling themselves from the birth canal; and (2) in many, if not most, instances the mother makes little or no attempt to aid the neonate in its upward climb to her chest and nipple area. Further observations made while monkey mothers were engaged in rapid locomotion suggest that very little aid is given to assist the neonate in clinging—rather, almost all the work is done by the baby.

These factors seem to be determined largely by neonate clasping, grasping, and negative geotropic reflexes. They illustrate the fact that basic, biologically determined, response tendencies have a major impact on the initiation of important behaviors underlying the development of mother-infant ties.

Own versus Other Infant Preference

This experiment gave 16 wild-born monkey mothers a choice among their own infant and three other familiar infants. The infant stimuli were 8 months old when these circus tests were conducted. Each mother had been separated from her baby for 1 week prior to the test. On the average, these mothers spent 127 seconds in the choice compartment next to their own infant, with only 68 seconds as the average choice time for the other three infants ($p < .001$). Thus wild-born females found their own infants more attractive than other familiar infants.

EFFECTS OF THE ADULT FEMALE'S REARING HISTORY

Female rhesus monkeys have been subjected to a variety of rearing experiences which could have potential effects upon their maternal motivation and their ability to rear infants. Sackett (1968) has presented a detailed review of these rearing procedures and a summary of effects on later behavior. The rearing variables discussed in this article are included in the following groups: (1) *feral*, wild-born animals captured as juveniles or young adults and brought into a laboratory environment; (2) *mother-peer*, monkeys born in a laboratory and raised by their mothers in cages, pens, or large compounds where they had physical contact with agemates and with other adults; (3) *peer*, animals separated from their mothers at birth and raised in cages with physical access to agemates; (4) *partial isolates*, monkeys separated from their mothers at birth and raised in wire cages with visual, auditory, and olfactory, but no physical, access to other monkeys; and (5) *surrogate mother*, monkeys separated from their mothers at birth and raised in cages with an artificial "mother" which provided food and "contact comfort," but with no visual or physical access to agemates during the early part of infancy.

For macaque monkeys several important maturational phases and events occur during the first 7 to 9 months of life. These include an initial period of close contact and dependence on the mother, a subsequent period of increasing independence from the mother in feeding and social interaction with agemates, and a period of intense play interactions. Feral and mother-peer conditions provide opportunities for all these maturational events; peer rearing includes no maternal component; and partial isolation or surrogate rearing includes neither a maternal nor a play phase during the usual period for these events. After the first 9 to 12 months of life, most of the animals in all the groups considered here experienced a great deal of social contact with agemates; thus the period of social deprivation was generally confined to early infancy.

Female rhesus and pigtail macaques become reproductively mature at approximately 3.5 to 4 years of age. In the studies reported below, all adult female subjects were known to be reproductively mature, and most were 5 years of age or older.

Effects of Rearing Conditions on Nulliparous Females

Figure 5 presents preference data for neonates or for adult rhesus females that had not delivered a baby nor been pregnant prior to circus testing. The circus choice stimuli were an adult female rhesus monkey, a cloth surrogate, an empty choice compartment, and a rhesus neonate under 30 days of age. The scores are averages of the percentage of total choice compartment time spent next to the adult female and to the neonate stimuli. All groups had a reliable preference for the adult female (all $p < .05$), with the exception of peer-raised subjects, who preferred the neonate ($p = .05$). Thus nulliparous females reared with mother and peer experience, or reared under conditions of maternal and peer deprivation, were more attracted to the agemate adult stimulus than to a neonate.

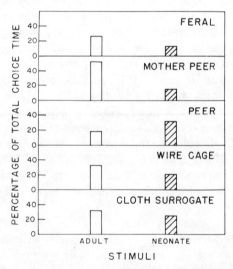

FIGURE 5. Preference for rhesus adult females versus neonates shown by nulliparous adult female rhesus monkeys reared during infancy under five different conditions.

This outcome, and the apparent anomaly in preference for a neonate by peer-reared monkeys, is discussed after presentation of the next study.

Effects of Rearing Conditions and Parity

Figure 6 presents the results of circus tests for feral-born and partial isolate or surrogate laboratory-reared rhesus females (Sackett, Griffin, Pratt, Joslyn, & Ruppenthal, 1967). The groups included monkeys that (1) had not given birth to a baby nor been pregnant, (2) had one infant prior to testing, or (3) had more than one infant. The rhesus choice stimuli were all unfamiliar to the subjects. These stimuli included an adult female, a 3-year-old female, a 1-year-old female, and a neonate under 30 days of age.

Nulliparous feral subjects had no preferences among these stimuli. Primiparous ferals had their maximum choice time with the neonate, but this did not differ reliably from time spent near the adult. However, both of these stimuli were preferred to the 3- and 1-year-olds ($p<.01$). Multiparous ferals had a very large preference for the neonate ($p<.001$). Laboratory-born subjects preferred the adult female regardless of their parity (all $p<.05$).

The data from the last two studies suggest that unfamiliar neonates are not attractive to nulliparous rhesus females. Feral females that have been mothers

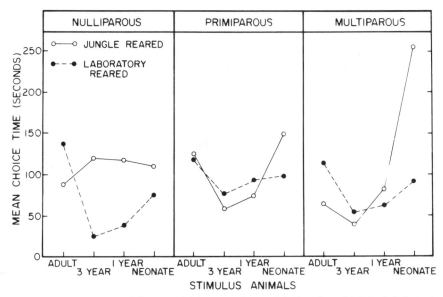

FIGURE 6. Preferences of feral- and laboratory-born adult females which had delivered different numbers of previous infants. The stimuli were adult, 3-year-old, 1-year-old, and neonate female rhesus monkeys.

find neonates attractive; but nonmothered, laboratory-raised, females are not attracted to neonates even after having several babies of their own.

The exception to these findings was the neonate preference shown by nulliparous peer-reared animals. Although the reason for this is not clear, it could be due to the fact that early in life peer-raised monkeys are not in close contact with an adult female—rather, they form close ties with other young infants. Thus an imprintinglike phenomenon could explain the preferences of feral-, mother-peer-, and peer-raised monkeys, whose choices correlate with the type of individual that provided intimate physical contact during the first months of life. This hypothesis receives some support from a study by Sackett, Porter, and Holmes (1965) showing that 3.5 - to 4-year-old partial isolates, which had experienced human contact during the first weeks of life, preferred a human to a monkey in a circus choice situation. Mother-peer- and peer-raised animals, which experienced monkey contact as infants, preferred a monkey to a human.

The data for primiparous and multiparous ferals indicate that their initial preference for unfamiliar adults is reversed after rearing an infant. Thus for feral females successful infant rearing leads to a decline in relative attractiveness of adult peers and a shift toward neonates. However, laboratory-born partial isolate and surrogate subjects do not show a shift after giving birth to infants. These females were largely unsuccessful in rearing infants (Arling & Harlow, 1967), being characterized as either indifferent or abusive toward their babies. This maternal inadequacy is apparently reflected in their relative lack of maternally motivated choice behavior in the circus test situation.

CONDITIONS UNDER WHICH THE MOTHER REARED HER INFANT

Several studies assessed effects of the conditions under which rhesus females raised their own infants. In these studies circus choices were given between the female's own infant and other familiar infants. Two basic conditions were employed for infant rearing. The Harlow playpen situation (Harlow & Harlow, 1969) consisted of four living cages containing a single mother-infant pair in each cage. The infants could leave this cage by a small door in one wall and enter a play area to interact with toys and other monkeys, but the mothers were confined to the $3 \times 3 \times 3$ ft living cage throughout the rearing period. In a second situation groups of four mother-infant pairs lived togehter in a $10 \times 12 \times 8$ ft social pen. This pen contained no physical barriers, so all animals could interact with each other at will.

Multiple Mothering, Repeated Separations, and Motherless Mothering

In the first study to be presented, three feral-born groups containing four females each lived with their infants in playpen units during the first 8 months of the infants' lives (Griffin, 1966). The mothering conditions included (1) a *normal control* group, whose members lived continuously with their infants until the first and final separation occurred at the end of Month 8; (2) a *multiple-mother* group, in which each adult female was separated from her current infant every 2 weeks, with a new infant given to her during the next 2-week period; and (3) a *separation control* group, in which infants were separated from their mother for 2 hours every 2 weeks, and then returned to the same mother. A fourth group consisted of eight partial isolate or surrogate-raised motherless mothers, who reared their infants in the playpen under the same conditions as the normal control feral group. All these laboratory-born females were inadequate in maternal care, showing less nursing and ventral contact than feral-born mothers, and more maternal punishment and abuse.

Own-Infant Attraction ● At 8.5 months, 2 weeks after the final separation of all mothers from their infants, the mothers were given circus choices from among their own infant and the three other infants from their playpen group. In the multiple-mother group, one of the four infants was the mother's biological offspring, but each of these mothers had spent no more time with this infant than with the other three infants in the group. Figure 7 shows the results.

Motherless mothers did not prefer their own infants, spending significantly more time in choice compartments with other babies ($p < .01$). Further, no particular infant was preferred by these motherless mothers as a group. Multiple

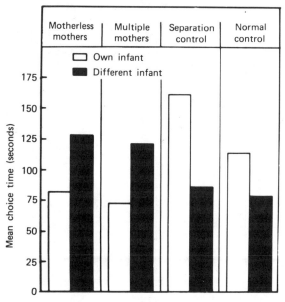

FIGURE 7. Preferences of feral- and laboratory-raised rhesus monkey mothers for their own versus other familiar 8-month-old infants.

mothers did not prefer their biological offspring. Rather, all four multiple mothers had their maximum choice time with one particular infant, thus accounting for their significantly higher choice time with the other infant than with their own offspring ($p < .01$). The separation ($p < .001$) and normal ($p < .05$) control mothers preferred their own infants, with the former showing a particularly large attraction toward their own babies.

These data suggest several conclusions. (1) Feral-born mothers who rear multiple infants exhibit preferences based on individual infant characteristics. They do not show any particular attraction toward their biological offspring, although such an attraction could have been based on the infant's odor at birth or similarities between the mother's odor and that of her offspring. (2) Maternally inadequate motherless mothers do not prefer their own babies, even though they have lived with them for 8 months and have been separated for only a short time. (3) Feral-born females who raise their own infants do prefer them after a 2-week separation, with an especially large preference shown by females that experienced short multiple separations from their infants during the rearing period.

Own-Mother Attraction · Figure 8 presents data parallel to those of the last study, but in this case the infants were subjects, choosing from among their own and other mothers. Offspring of motherless mothers preferred their own mothers ($p < .01$), even though their mothers did not prefer them. As expected, multiply

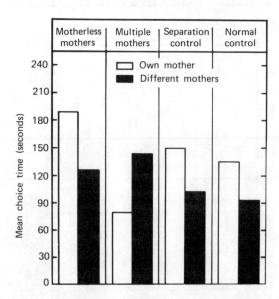

FIGURE 8. Preferences of infant offspring of feral- and laboratory-raised rhesus monkey mothers for their own mothers versus other familiar adult females.

mothered infants did not prefer their own mother, which was only one of four females with which they had lived during the first 8 months of life. One of these mothers, however, was preferred by all four infants, which resulted in reliably greater choice time for other mothers ($p = .05$). Separation and normal control group offspring had a reliable preference for their own over other familiar mothers (both $p < .05$). These data suggest that (1) maternal inadequacy is not sufficient to produce avoidance of the mother, (2) offspring of feral-born mothers do recognize and prefer their own mothers 2 weeks after separation, and (3) infants reared by several mothers are differentially attracted to them on the basis of some, as yet unknown, characteristic (s) of these adult females as individuals.

A subsequent study compared these same groups in a four-choice circus test. The stimuli were two adult and two 9-month old infants. In tests of the mother subjects, one of the infants was the female's offspring and one was an unfamiliar infant, while one of the adult female stimuli was familiar and the other was a stranger. When infants were subjects, one of the adult females was the infant's mother and the other was an unfamiliar adult, while one of the infant stimuli was familiar and the other was a stranger.

Choices by Adult Females · The lower half of Figure 9 shows that rhesus adult females, permanently separated from their babies after rearing them for 8 months, did not prefer infants to adults 1 month after separation. Multiple mothers, separation controls, and motherless mothers all had reliable preferences for adult females over 9-month old infants (all $p < .01$). Normal control females, which had not been separated from their babies during the rearing period, exhibited no reliable choice difference between adult and infant stimuli. Familiarity had no differential effect on choice times in any of the groups.

Contrasting the data on preferences for own versus other infants (Figure 7) with data on preference for infants versus adults (Figure 9, bottom section) suggests that infant attractiveness is a function of at least two basic factors: (1) specific characteristics of the infant, namely, that the infant be the female's own offspring; and (2) the context in which the choices are made. Thus given a choice among several infants the female prefers her own; but given a choice between infants and adults, the female prefers adults or exhibits no preference, even when one of the infant stimuli is the female's own recently separated offspring.

Choices by Infants · Figure 9 (upper part) gives the data for preferences of 9-month old infants for an adult female versus infant stimuli. Offspring of separation and normal control feral mothers preferred infants to adults ($p < .01$), even when one of the adults was the subject's own mother. Thus contextual cues in the choice situation seem as important for the choices of adequately mothered infants as they were for the feral-born mothers of these infants. Infants raised by multiple mothers exhibited no differential preference between infants and adult females. However, offspring of inadequate motherless mothers preferred adults

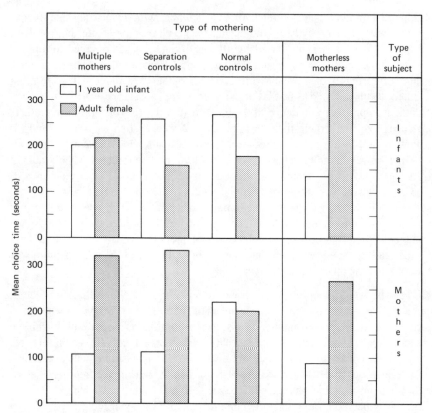

FIGURE 9. Preferences of feral- and laboratory-raised mothers (lower panel) and their infants (upper panel) for 1-year-old infants and adult females. One of the infant stimuli was the mother's own baby, and one of the adult female stimuli was the infant's own mother.

to infants ($p<.001$), and spent reliably more time near their own mothers than near either a familiar or unfamiliar peer or an unfamiliar adult (all $p<.01$). Thus for inadequately mothered individuals a specific social stimulus—the inadequate mother herself—seems to be especially attractive.

Taken together, the last four studies show that (1) all mothers recognize their own infants if they have reared them for 8 months from birth, and all infants recognize their own mothers; but (2) whether the mother prefers its own infant to other infants or adults, and whether the infant prefers its own mother to other adult females or agemates, depends on the specific choice stimuli available and the maternal behavior characteristics of the mother during the rearing period. These data suggest that adequate maternal caregiving yields older infants that are relatively independent of their mothers and mothers that are more motivated toward approaching adults than infants, while inadequate mothering produces infants that remain dependent upon their mothers at an age when adequately mothered infants exhibit strong motivation toward agemates.

EFFECTS OF CONFINED REARING SPACE

In free-ranging environments rhesus monkey babies live in kinship groups containing grandmothers, mothers, and juvenile and infant males and females. Under these conditions infants have many opportunities to interact with animals other than their own mothers, and adult and older juvenile females may interact closely with neonates and infants. Under most laboratory rearing conditions mothers are generally confined with their infants in small cages, thereby limiting the number of animals the infant and mother can interact with, and forcing close mother-infant physical contact for a longer time period during infancy than is ordinarily the case under field conditions.

Confinement effects were tested in feral-born females who raised their infants in the Harlow playpen situation ($n = 12$), or in a larger social pen situation in which four mother-infant pairs had physical access to each other during the first 8 months of the infants' lives ($n = 8$). In addition, a set of four motherless mother-infant pairs, raised under playpen conditions, were studied to replicate the preference data presented in the previous section.

Table 1 presents the average percentage of total circus choice time spent by these mothers with their own versus other infants, and the average percentage of total choice time spent with an unfamiliar adult female versus an unfamiliar infant. These tests were conducted 2 to 3 weeks after the mothers were separated from their infants.

TABLE 1   Preferences for Own versus Other Infants and for an Unfamiliar Infant and Adult Female by Feral- and Laboratory-Born Rhesus Females That Reared Their Infants in the Physically Confined Playpen Apparatus, and by Feral-Born Females That Reared Their Infants in a Large Social Pen[a]

Mothering Situation	Type of Mother	Choice Stimuli			
		Familiar Infants		Strangers	
		Own	Other	Adult Female	Infant
Playpen	Motherless mother	30	58	64	30
Playpen	Feral	46	30	36	47
Social pen	Feral	78	8	24	58

[a]The data are percentages of total choice time in the familiar infant and in the stranger circus test situation.

As in previous studies, motherless mothers did not prefer their own infants, exhibiting a reliable preference for other infants ($p = .05$). These inadequate mothers also had a reliable preference for the unfamiliar adult over the unfamiliar infant ($p < .05$).

Feral-born animals rearing their babies in the confined playpen situation had a small but reliable preference for their own over another infant ($p < .05$), but did not show a reliable difference between choices for an unfamiliar infant and unfamiliar adult. Feral-born mothers who raised their infants in a social pen group preferred their own infants ($p < .001$) and showed a large preference for an unfamiliar infant over an unfamiliar adult female ($p < .01$).

These data suggest that rearing babies under conditions of restricted physical space, with no opportunity for the mother to interact physically with other adult females, produces a marked reduction in attractiveness of infants as stimuli. However, rearing infants under conditions that allow both the mother and her infant to interact with many other animals produces females with strong maternal motivation 2 to 3 weeks after terminal separation from their infants.

EFFECTS OF INFANT'S AGE AT SEPARATION

This experiment studied choices by multiparous feral-born pigtail monkey females for unfamiliar adult females, 2.5-year-old juvenile females, and neonates under 30 days old (Ruppenthal & Sackett, 1972). The independent variable was the age of the infant at separation from its mother. One experimental group contained four females permanently separated within a few minutes after their babies were born. Four other experimental conditions ($n = 4$ per group) involved mothers who lived in enclosed $3 \times 3 \times 3$ ft cages with their babies for 2 weeks, 1 month, 2 months, or 6 months after the infant's birth. A control group of eight females, which had not been pregnant nor lived with any infant available to them for 6 months, was also tested. Experimental group subjects had their three circus tests 1 hour, 24 hours, and 7 days after infant separation. Control group subjects had their second test 24 hours after Test 1, and had a third test 7 days after Test 1. The results are shown in Figure 10.

On the day of separation, reliable neonate preferences were shown by females separated at birth ($p = .05$) after living with their babies for 2 weeks ($p < .001$), and after living with their babies for 1 month ($p < .05$). Animals separated from their 2-month-old infants had equal choice times for the adult female and neonate, while mothers separated from 6-month-old infants and control group females preferred the adult female stimulus (both $p < .05$) and had their lowest choice time with the neonates. Thus, on the day of separation, when maternal motivation should be high, neonates were not attractive to mothers that had lived in confinement with their babies for 2 or 6 months.

On the day after separation, neonate preferences were shown only by mothers

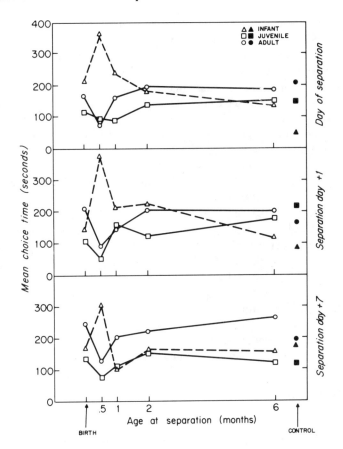

FIGURE 10. Preferences of pigtail adult females for an adult female, 3-year-old juvenile, and 30-day-old infant as a function of the age at which the subject was separated from her own infant. A control group of adult females had not been pregnant nor lived with an infant for at least 6 months prior to these tests.

separated when their babies were 2 weeks ($p<.001$) or 1 month ($p<.05$) old. Females separated at birth preferred the adult female ($p<.05$); those separated at 2 months had equal choice time for the adult and neonate stimuli; while those separated at 6 months had reliably lower choice time for the neonate than for the adult or juvenile stimuli ($p<.01$).

Seven days after separation the only females to prefer a neonate were those separated at 2 weeks ($p<.001$). All other experimental groups preferred the adult female stimulus (all $p<.025$), while the control group still failed to show any evidence of attraction toward neonates.

These data suggest several conclusions about maternal motivation in pigtail monkey females. First, the termination of a full-term pregnancy and/or the act of giving birth produces a transient neonate preference. Second, long periods of confinement with an infant do not enhance maternal motivation; rather, neonate attractiveness appears to be depressed under such conditions. Third, multiparous pigtail monkey females that have not lived with a baby for at least 6 months show no evidence of neonate attraction. This contrasts with the data for multiparous feral rhesus shown in Figure 6, and suggests that there may be species differences in factors underlying maternal motivation even between animals as similar, behaviorally and physiologically, as pigtail and rhesus macaques. Finally, only females that had spent 2 weeks from birth with their babies showed a strong and *persistent* influence of that experience on their attraction toward neonates.

This pattern of results suggests that for laboratory-housed pigtail monkey females hormonal factors are largely responsible for neonate preferences. The 2- to 4-week postpartum period involves rapid and profound hormonal changes, especially in prolactin levels. Further, this is a time when infant clasping, grasping, and nursing reflexes become very strong (Castell & Sackett, 1972), and much more milk is ingested during a 24-hour day than in the previous 2 weeks. Thus the fact that separation at 2 weeks, and to a lesser extent at 1 month, produced the only evidence for strong neonate attraction suggests a basic physiological, rather than experiential, explanation for when neonates as stimuli will elicit strong approach responses from adult females.

EFFECTS OF AGING

A series of experiments on partial isolate and surrogate-reared motherless mothers suggests that maturation may play a major role in determining the attractiveness of infants as stimuli. Rhesus females are reproductively mature between 3.5 and 4 years of age. To assess effects of maturity, reproductively active females of different ages were given two circus tests. The stimuli in Test 1 were an adult female, a 3-year-old female, a 1-year-old female, and a neonate. In Test 2 the stimuli included an adult female, an empty choice compartment, a cloth surrogate mother, and a neonate. The two tests were conducted 14 months apart. Some subjects received both tests, while others had only one. To compare the two studies, data were analyzed in terms of the percentage of total choice time spent with the adult female versus the neonate.

Data for all subjects' tests are shown in Figure 11. Separate analyses of variance on each test revealed significant interactions of subject age with stimulus type (both $p<.01$). Females under 8 years of age preferred the adult female (both $p<.025$), 8-year-olds had a strong attraction toward neonates (both $p<.001$), while females over 8 years of age had no reliable preference among the adult and neonate stimuli. Unfortunately, these comparisons are confounded because some subjects received both tests while others had only one test.

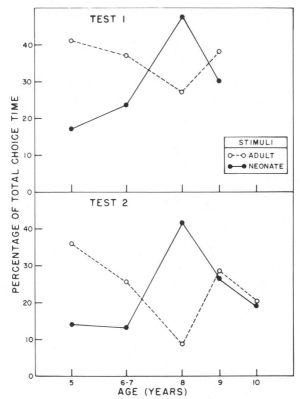

FIGURE 11. Preference for an adult female versus a neonate by laboratory-born adult female rhesus monkeys of different ages. Some subjects received both tests, while other subjects had only Test 1 or Test 2.

Figure 12 presents data for females that received both tests. Subjects within the panels of this figure are the same individuals, while subjects between panels are different individuals. As the tests were given 14 months apart, each subject was more than 1 year older on her second test. The lower panel shows that subjects who were 5 years old on Test 1 and 6 to 7 on Test 2 preferred the adult on both tests (both $p<.01$). The panel second from the bottom reveals that females who were 6 to 7 years old on Test 1 preferred the adult ($p<.025$), but these same females at age 8 preferred the neonate ($p<.01$). The panel second from the top shows that females that were 8 on Test 1 preferred the neonate ($p<.025$), with no significant preference between the neonate and adult shown on Test 2 when these animals were 9 years old. The top panel, showing data for females tested at ages 9 and 10, reveals no reliable preference between the adult and neonate on either test. Thus the age of 8 years appears to represent an especially sensitive period for neonate attraction in rhesus females.

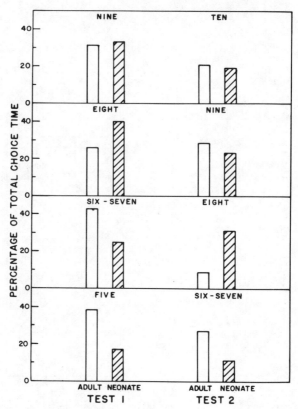

FIGURE 12. Preference for an adult female versus a neonate shown by the same rhesus female subjects at two different ages. Subjects in each panel are the same individuals tested after a 14-month interval. Subjects between panels are different individuals. Age in years at the time of testing is indicated within each panel above the data bars.

A major confounding factor in this study concerns the effects of parity. Under the breeding procedures used for animals tested in this study, older females were more likely to have had previous offspring than younger ones. To assess parity effects we divided the subjects on Tests 1 and 2 into nulliparous females and females that had had one or more babies prior to testing. Unfortunately, there were no nulliparous 8-year-olds studied on Test 1. Separate analyses of variance were conducted on Tests 1 and 2, and the data are presented in Figure 13. Although the figure shows data for multiparous 8-year-old females on Test 1, these values did not appear in the Test-1 analysis.

Both tests yielded a reliable age X parity X stimulus-type effect (both $p<.01$).

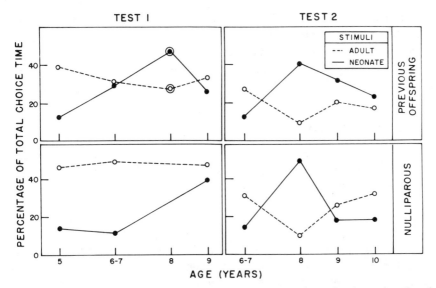

FIGURE 13. Preference for an adult female versus a neonate shown by rhesus females of different ages. The subjects had no offspring (nulliparous) or had had one or more babies, prior to testing. The circled data for 8-year-olds on Test 1 were not included in statistical analyses as none were available on that test who had not delivered an offspring.

On Test 1 nulliparous females of all three ages preferred the adult, with a statistically reliable preference occurring for the 5- and 6-to7-year-olds (both $p < .01$). Females that had prior offspring preferred the adult at age 5 ($p < .01$) and showed no reliable difference between the adult and neonate at ages 6 to 7 or 9. On Test 2, 6- to 7-year-old females preferred the adult regardless of their parity status (both $p < .05$). Eight-year-old females who had, or who did not have, previous infants both preferred the neonate (both $p < .001$). Nulliparous animals over 8 years old had a small but reliable adult preference (both $p < .05$), while multiparous females at these ages showed a small neonate preference (both $p < .05$). Thus, these data show that the preference for neonates shown by 8-year-old laboratory-raised rhesus monkey females is independent of experience with previous offspring.

This maturation effect, in which neonate attraction becomes markedly pronounced at an age well beyond the development of reproductive maturity, seems of major importance in understanding the influence of infants on potential monkey caregivers. It may be that some subtle but important change in female hormone function occurs at ages well beyond sexual maturity. Such changes may correlate with changes in irritability and emotionality, such that older females may be biologically more fit to raise infants than younger females. A fuller understanding of this phenomenon awaits replication and studies designed to identify the physiological-developmental source of this effect.

SUMMARY AND CONCLUSIONS

The data reviewed in this article suggest that attractiveness of neonates and infants to adult female macaques that live under laboratory conditions is determined by a relatively small set of critical factors.

1. *Maternal parity*: Past experience in rearing infants seems to be a major factor. Nulliparous females reared in free-ranging environments or reared without a mother or peer contact in a laboratory do not find neonates attractive. Wild-born females who have had previous offspring are attracted to infants, but laboratory-raised motherless females do not find infants attractive even after they have raised several of their own. However, an important exception occurs for 8-year-old laboratory-born females, which prefer neonates over adults whether they have or have not had prior offspring.

2. *Mother-infant separation*: After separation, females that have reared an infant for 2 to 8 months under confined cage conditions prefer their own to other infants, but they do not prefer infants to adult females. The exception to this occurs in females that have been separated from their infants 2 to 4 weeks after the baby's birth. These adult females do prefer infants to adults.

3. *Confinement*: Females that rear babies under confined cage conditions that provide little opportunity to interact with animals other than their babies do not exhibit high levels of attraction to infants. However, females that rear their babies in situations that provide physical access to other animals show much higher levels of attraction.

Infant attractiveness thus appears to be determined largely by three major sources. The first involves the adult female's past experience in raising infants. The second involves the type of mothering experiences that the female had when she was an infant. The third, and perhaps most important, involves the physiological-hormonal-maturational condition of the animal. One major conclusion from these preliminary studies is that an understanding of the influence of primate infants on primate caregivers should proceed by studying the differential effects that infants, as stimuli, can have upon the behavior of potential caregivers which vary in hormonal condition, and in as yet unknown developmental factors which mature years after reproductive stages of physical development are reached.

References

Arling, G. L., & Harlow, H. F. Effects of social deprivation on maternal behavior of rhesus monkeys. *Journal of Comparative and Physiological Psychology*, 1967, 64, 371–377

Bowlby, J. *Attachment and loss*. Vol. 1. London: Hogarth Press, 1969.

Castell, R., & Sackett, G. P. Motor behaviors of neonatal rhesus monkeys: Measurement techniques and early development. *Developmental Psychobiology*, 1973, 6, 191–202.

Griffin, G. A. The effects of multiple mothering on the infant-mother and mother-infant affectional systems. Unpublished doctoral dissertation, University of Wisconsin, 1966.

Harlow, H. F., & Harlow, M. K. Effects of various mother-infant relationships on rhesus monkey behaviors. In Foss, B. M. (Ed.), *Determinants of infant behavior*. Vol. 1. London: Methuen, 1969.

Hinde, R. A. Development of social behavior. In Schrier, A. M., & Stollnitz, F. (Eds.), *Behavior of nonhuman primates*. Vol. 3. New York: Academic Press, 1971.

Mitchell, G. D. Intercorrelations of maternal and infant behaviors in *Macaca mulatta*. *Primates*, 1968, 9, 85–92.

Mitchell, G. D. Sound motion pictures of the birth process in laboratory housed rhesus monkeys. Shown at the annual meeting of the American Psychological Association, Honolulu, September 1972.

Ruppenthal, G. A., & Sackett, G. P. Effects of separation age on maternal motivation of pigtail monkey (*Macaca nemestrina*) mothers. *In preparation, 1972.*

Sackett, G. P. Abnormal behavior in laboratory-reared rhesus monkeys. In Fox, M.W. (Ed.), *Abnormal behavior in animals*, Philadelphia: Saunders, 1968. Pp.293–331.

Sackett, G. P., Porter, M., & Holmes, H. Choice behavior in rhesus monkeys: Effects of stimulation during the first month of life. *Science*, 1965, 147, 304–306.

Sackett, G. P., Griffin, G. A., Pratt, C., Joslyn, W. D., & Ruppenthal, G. A. Mother-infant and adult female choice behavior in rhesus monkeys after various rearing experiences. *Journal of Comparative and Physiological Psychology*, 1967, 63, 376–381.

Sackett, G. P., Suomi, S. J., & Grady, S. Species preferences by macaque monkeys. Cited by Sackett, G. P. Unlearned responses, differential rearing experiences, and the development of social attachments by rhesus monkeys. In L. A. Rosenblum (Ed.), *Primate Behavior*, Vol. 1. New York: Academic Press, 1970. Pp. 111–140.

Suomi, S. J., Sackett, G. P. , & Harlow, H. F. Development of sex preference in rhesus monkeys. *Developmental Psychology*, 1970, **3**, 326–336.

CHAPTER 9

Mother and Infant at Play: The Dyadic Interaction Involving Facial, Vocal, and Gaze Behaviors[1]

DANIEL N. STERN

Columbia University and New York State Psychiatric Institute

The social interaction between mother and infant is a unique human interchange. Many of the social behaviors performed by mothers occur only in the presence of their infants and represent unusual variations of normal adult social behavior. Similarly, many of the infant's social behaviors are seen in their fullest form only during the interaction with a caregiver. Accordingly, the forms and functions of these social behaviors must be studied in the presence of the other partner, and in a natural setting which permits the behaviors of both members to be mutually elicited and maintained. An interactive model is thus adopted in which the interaction is viewed as a dyadic system in which influences flow in both directions between mother and infant.

In this chapter we describe behaviors that each partner brings to the interaction and behaviors that are elicited during the interaction. We examine how the mutually elicited behavior of each member in turn influences the behavior of the other member, and indicate the possible significance of these mutual influences for development. An attempt is made to relate findings and hypotheses generated under experimental conditions to interactive events found in natural social situations. To do this, data at different levels of objectivity are utilized, including objective measures, clinical descriptions and, at times, subjective impressions.

The clinical observations and quantitative data that form the nucleus of this

[1] The number of entries into a state does not always equal the number of exits. There are two reasons for this. The first state in any sequence has no entry, and the last state has no exit. Several sequences have been summed in this diagram. For example, most play sequences end but rarely begin in state $(I-, M-)$, therefore it is entered more often than exited. Second, double simultaneous transitions have been omitted, that is, when both mother and infant change state within 0.6 seconds, for example, $(I-, M-) \blacklozenge (I+, M+)$. These are relatively rare but contribute to the inequality between state entrances and exits.

The research has been supported by The Grant Foundation, and the Research Foundation for Mental Hygiene, New York State Psychiatric Institute.

187

chapter come from an ongoing study of mother-infant interaction. In this study we have adopted the strategy of closely examining the moment-by-moment events that occur during one of the most important naturally occurring interactions: spontaneous social play. The period of observation has been limited to the infant's third to fourth month of life. Finally, we have focused on social behaviors mediated by distance receptors, namely, visual attention to the partner, and the facial and vocal behaviors used to hold or "recapture" the partner's visual attention. The rationale for these choices is elaborated below.

DEVELOPMENTALLY UNIQUE ASPECTS OF GAZE AND SOME EARLY FUNCTIONS OF GAZE

Normally, the visual-motor system reaches functional maturity by the third month of life, a point in development when other motor behaviors are relatively less mature (White, Castle, & Held, 1964). Accordingly, the gazing patterns between a mother and her infant of this age constitute the first dyadic system in which both members have almost equal control over and facility with the same behavior.

The implications of the early development of this system are considerable. Control of the eyes gives some measure of control over perceptual input. The role of gaze in regulating perceptual input, however, cannot be separated from its role in regulating internal physiological state—particularly arousal and affect (Stechler & Carpenter, 1967; Stechler & Latz, 1966; Walters & Parke, 1965). The infant can reduce his state of arousal by turning away from a stimulus that is too intense, too complicated, or too discrepant from an internal model. Similarly, he can turn away from a redundant and boring stimulus to seek a new stimulus, thereby increasing his state of arousal (Fantz, 1964; Kagan & Lewis, 1965; McCall & Kagan, 1967). The early control of perception thus allows the infant to self-regulate his internal state within a given range.

Since the dual function of regulating perception and internal state also applies to social stimuli, the control of gaze allows the infant to regulate from instant to instant the amount of social visual contact (Robson, 1967). Accordingly, social gazing behavior bears an important relationship to the early operation of defensive and coping phenomena. The origin of such phenomena is certainly not to be found exclusively in the early operation of the visual-motor system, but rather in many or all perceptual and motor systems as they develop, as well as in shifts in state. What is important, however, is that control of the eyes is one of the few effective operations regulating perception and state that is fully available to the infant during this transient development period. The study of gaze behaviors thus permits the observation of some of the earliest operations related to the precursors of these defensive and coping maneuvers. For example, we have repeatedly seen in normal 3- to 4-month-old infants extreme head aversion function to terminate intrusive maternal behavior (Stern, 1971). It is relevant in this light that one of the most consistent features of infantile autism is an exaggerated and persistent form of gaze aversion (Hutt and Ounsted, 1966).

Gaze in early life appears to serve other related functions. Rheingold (1961), Robson (1967), and others have emphasized the importance of gaze as a cardinal attachment behavior. Gaze also serves a signal function in human interaction. The onset of visual gaze, as a signal, indicates a readiness and intention to engage in an interaction and has been considered a "releaser" of social behaviors (Chance 1962; Goffman, 1963). Similarly, gaze aversion is a signal of the termination of, or reduction in the intensity of an interaction and has been compared to social "cut off" behaviors in other animal species (Chance, 1962; Hutt & Ounsted, 1966). A final early function of gaze is that of providing experience with a form of "dialogic" exchange. Later in development gazing patterns become coordinated with speech, so as to facilitate the flow of dyadic communication (Kendon, 1967). Recent evidence suggests that mathematical regularities in the gross temporal pattern of mother-infant gaze are identical to those found in adult verbal conversations. This suggests that such regularities describe a property of human interaction that predates the onset of speech and is first seen in an attention-regulating behavior (Jaffe, Stern, & Peery, 1973).

Fraiberg's observations of blind infants presented in Chapter 10, and elsewhere (Fraiberg, 1971), give a perspective on the importance of vision for social development. Development can proceed fairly well in the congenitally blind, providing there is sufficient compensatory "dialogic experience" in other sense modalities. However, even in the more fortunate cases, social interaction with a blind infant or child is different. The child's face never becomes a primary emitter of social signals, and the effect of the muted blind face on an adult interactant is eloquently described by Fraiberg in Chapter 10. Valuable as the studies of blind children are, they cannot tell us what direct role vision plays in the normal development of the sighted.

PLAY ACTIVITY BETWEEN MOTHER AND INFANT

Play between mothers and infants has been chosen because it consists mainly of social interaction; there is no other "task" at hand except to interact. In addition, much evidence indicates that some of the early developmental differences between infants relate in part to differences in the amount and richness of social stimulation (Thompson & Grusec, 1970), much of which is provided during play. A more detailed knowledge of the interactive parameters of play may provide a fuller understanding of the specific behaviors and stimulus events that determine the relative "richness" or deprivation of this experience.

Social play at this developmental period is concerned mainly with the mutual regulation of stimulation in order to maintain some optimal level of arousal which is affectively positive. In other words, the issues are interest and delight in one another.

With these considerations in mind, we describe the behaviors and response biases brought to the play situation by the mother and by the infant, the dyadic patterns that emerge from the interaction of the two, and some of the consequences of the resultant patterns for development.

METHOD

Subjects

Eighteen infants, 12 twins and 6 singletons, have been observed from their third to fourth month of life. Many of the observations and clinical impressions come from this group. The dyadic gazing data are taken solely from the last 8 twin infants included in the study. Data scoring and reduction methods were available only for this last group. Methodological issues for this group alone are considered. The 8 normal twin infants consisted of two monozygous and two dizygous sets, 5 girls and 3 boys. For the purpose of this chapter, individual differences relating to zygosity and sex are not discussed. Three infants were premature by weight criteria (2132, 2118, and 2332 grams). All infants, however, evidenced a normal developmental course. The mothers were primiparous, white, middle socioeconomic class, with high school or college education.

Data Collection

All data were collected in the home with a portable television camera (Sony ½ in.). After an initial warm-up visit, home visits were made weekly (in some cases twice weekly) from the infants' third to fourth month of life. A full morning was set aside to record all play and feeding interactions as they normally unfolded on the mother's schedule. The experimenters interacted as little as possible with the mother and infant, and the mothers were directed simply to do whatever they normally did. Each interaction was initiated whenever the mother deemed appropriate and terminated whenever she felt it had run its natural course. Data were not scored if there were gross changes in infant state, for example, fussiness and crying, or if the mother used a visual target other than her face, for example, a rattle. Accordingly, interactions were of variable duration. For all the infants together, this resulted in 37 play sessions. Only interactions between a mother and one baby alone were used, that is, no triads were involved.

It is difficult to judge from a television tape exactly where a mother and infant are looking—in particular, when they are gazing at the other's face. To record this accurately along with the interaction, one observer was placed several yards behind the mother, and another behind the infant, but out of the television picture. They operated by pushbutton small lights which were placed in the camera's view but not seen by mother or infant. A recording of gaze direction was thus present in the television picture of the interaction. Two trained observers achieved .96 agreement as to the presence of a gaze-at the other's face, and .93 agreement as to its duration.

Data Scoring for Dyadic Gaze

To evaluate the mother-infant dyadic gazing pattern, television tapes were played back and observed by two trained observers who operated a two-channel magnetic tape event recorder. One observer scored whether the infant's gaze was "on" or "off" the mother's face; the other simultaneously scored whether the mother's gaze was "on" or "off" the infant's face. This resulted in four possible dyadic gazing states: (1) neither gazing at the other (I−, M−); (2) infant gazing at mother, mother gazing away (I+, M−); (3) infant gazing away, mother gazing at infant (I−, M+); and (4) both gazing at each other (I+, M+). Every 0.6 seconds a determination was made as to which dyadic state was occurring. If, for example, the mother and infant were in mutual gaze for 1.2 seconds and then the infant looked away, sampling at 0.6-second intervals, the record read: (I+, M+) ◗ (I+, M+) ◗ (I−, M+). There are two transitions in this sequence, state (I+, M+) proceeds during the next 0.6 seconds to state (I+, M+), that is, it follows itself, and then in the next 0.6 seconds proceeds to state (I−, M+). A transition matrix is accumulated showing the probability in the next 0.6 seconds of any dyadic state proceeding to any other dyadic state, including itself. The transition matrix can be converted into a state transition diagram, an example of which is shown in Figure 4 and is commented on below. In addition, the gazing behavior of each individual can be separately reconstructed from the four-state transition matrix. Portions of the television tapes of particular interest were kinescoped and studied frame by frame to aid in finer clinical descriptions.

RESULTS

This section is divided into three parts: (1) maternal behaviors; (2) infant behaviors; and (3) the dyadic patterns that result from the interaction of the two, and some of the consequences of the resultant patterns. Clinical descriptions are coordinated with quantitative data on gazing.

Maternal Behavior in the Play Interaction

We are so accustomed to maternal behavior that we tend to overlook how "deviant" a mother's communicative behaviors with her infant may be as compared to her normal behavior with adults. Many of her behaviors represent unusual variations of intra-adult interpersonal behavior. Talking "baby talk" is an obvious example. What is just as unusual as the words or syllables uttered is the exaggeration in other linguistic elements. The range of pitch is expanded, especially at the high end, and the speed of changing pitch is most often markedly slowed but sometimes unusually fast. Ferguson (1965), in an examination of baby talk by mothers in six languages, has commented on the altered range and contour of pitch in this "subsystem." Similarly, the range of loudness is altered, as is the speed of changes in loudness. Changes in rhythm and stress are also different from adult patterns. In general there appears to be an elongation of vowel duration. Imagine the ways a mother might say to her gazing infant, "Hi- swee-e-e-et-ee, Hi-i-i, Hi-i-iya, whatcha lookin' at?, Hu-u-uh? O-o-o-o-o-o. Yeah, it's mommy, ye-e-a-ah." Anderson and Jaffe (1972) measured vowel duration in adult and child speech and found that children's vowels are markedly longer than those of adults. It seems likely that during baby talk mothers slow down speech elements to more closely match the infant's perceptual capabilities and speech production abilities. Infant-elicited maternal paralinguistic behavior is an important area of speech research about which little is known at present.

The facial expressions made by mothers for their babies during play are also quite extraordinary, especially in their degree of exaggeration, slowed tempo of formation, and long duration. The often seen "mock surprise" expression of mothers is a good example. The eyebrows go way up, the eyes open very wide, the mouth opens and purses and usually emits a long "Ooooooooo," and the head comes up and forward sometimes to within inches of the baby's face. This expression may take many seconds to slowly come to a full bloom and then may be held for an unusually long time. Such an expression directed toward an adult would be experienced as quite bizarre. Mothers also violate adult cultural norms of interpersonal space utilized by frequently bringing their faces very close to the infants' during interaction.

The presence and extent of these maternal variations of behavior in the presence of an infant are certainly determined by many factors: maternal attitude, personality, sociocultural factors, and so on. It is relevant in this light that Moss, Robson, and Pedersen (1969) found a correlation between maternal educational level and the quality of the mother's speech with respect to its animation.

Nonetheless, aspects of these maternal variations may prove to be species-specific behaviors which adults bring to the interaction, ready to be elicited by the infant. These exaggerations of expressive behavior appear to be fairly ubiquitous. Furthermore, this suggestion is made attractive by the testable probability that the slowed tempo and grossness of the exaggerations in performance closely match the range of infant preferences and tolerances of rate and degree of stimulus change. The slowing of the tempo, along with the full extent of the exaggeration, may enable the infant to maintain the identity of the mother's face across its various physical transformations and thus facilitate the acquisition of a stable face schema. "Normal" adult facial expressions flash very rapidly and conceivably could present the infant with a discontinuous sequence of faces.

These striking maternal facial and vocal behaviors are elicited not simply by the presence of the infant, but specifically by his gaze at her. If the infant then smiles, coos, or otherwise is facially expressive while gazing at her, the likelihood of elicitation of the maternal behavior will be increased, or if already in action, heightened. Wolff (1963) and others have commented on the dramatic effect of eye-to-eye contact on increasing maternal responsiveness.

The mother's gaze behavior is also "deviant." Gazes are extraordinarily long, compared to average adult gaze exchanges (Argyle & Kendon 1967; Exline, Gray, & Schuette, 1965; Kendon, 1967). Mutual gaze between mother and infant often lasts over 30 seconds. Such long mutual gazes rarely occur between adults in this culture, except between lovers and people about to fight (Scheflen, personal communication).

Infant gaze-at mother has the effect of reducing the likelihood of her gazing away. A comparison of the probability that the mother will terminate a gaze when the infant is gazing at her, and when the infant is not gazing at her, demonstrates the effect of infant gaze on maintaining maternal gaze. This is accomplished by comparing the probability of the following dyadic state transitions: $(I+, M+) \blacktriangleright (I+, M-)$ and $(I-, M+) \blacktriangleright (I-, M-)$. Table 1 shows the number of opportunities for each of these transitions and their observed probability of occurrence. The two probabilities are compared for each infant separately by the Cochran method of strengthening the common x^2 for all play sessions of each infant (Cockran, 1954). A Yates correction for the discreteness of the data is utilized (Fleiss, 1972). In all eight cases the probability of the transition $(I-, M+) \blacktriangleright (I-, M-)$ is greater than the probability of the transition $(I+, M+) \blacktriangleright (I+, M-)$: Twin A1, $x^2 = 14.59$, $p \le .001$; Twin A2, $x^2 = 15.53$, $p \le .001$; Twin B1, $x^2 = 4.34$, $p \le .05$; Twin B2, $x^2 = 7.62$, $p \le .01$; Twin C1, $x^2 = 9.81$, $p \le .01$; Twin C2, $x^2 = 9.42$, $p \le .01$; Twin D1, $x^2 = 20.80$; $p \le .001$; Twin D2, $x^2 = 5.25$, $p \le .05$. The effect of the infant's gaze on inhibiting maternal gaze aversion is strong, and reaches significance for all mothers with both of their infants.

These variations in normal adult social gazing behavior constitute an important effect of the infant on the mother. In adult-adult conversational dialogue, the listener generally gazes at the speaker most of the time. The speaker usually gazes at the listener at the beginning of his utterance and then gazes away, glancing back periodically, until near the end of his utterance when he returns his gaze to the listener. This return of gaze acts as a signal to the listener to prepare to exchange roles (Kendon, 1967). The mother deviates from the adult cultural pattern by assuming the role of an almost continuously gazing "listener," and acts as if the infant were talking. In fact, it is the mother who talks, often for both of them; that is, she makes up the infant's "speaking" part as well as her own, and it is the infant who listens and rarely vocalizes.

All three maternal variations of normal adult interpersonal behavior, gaze, facial expression, and vocalizations, are generally elicited together,. The

TABLE 1 The Effect of Infant Gaze on the Probability of Maternal Gaze Aversion

| | | Maternal Gaze Aversion When Infant is Gazing at Mother | | Maternal Gaze Aversion When Infant is Gazing Away | |
| | | State Transition: $(I+, M+) \blacktriangleright (I+, M-)$ to $t+0.6$ second | | State Transition: $(I-, M+) \blacktriangleright (I-, M-)$ to $t+0.6$ second | |
Twin	Session No.	p of Observed Transitions	Number of Opportunities	p of Observed Transitions	Number of Opportunities
A1	1	.005	387	.018	386
	2	.004	227	.025	198
	3	.012	252	.014	143
	4	.000	249	.011	792
	5	.015	545	.054	56
	6	.000	135	.024	337
	7	.005	192	.012	609
A2	1	.013	473	.039	285
	2	.006	354	.026	76
	3	.001	301	.030	134
	4	.004	465	.008	632
	5	.017	1144	.017	241
	6	.008	370	.037	81
	7	.004	524	.015	963
B1	1	.008	364	.053	19
	2	.016	129	.031	990
	3	.000	29	.010	579
	4	.000	74	.031	985
B2	1	.018	228	.037	81
	2	.014	145	.038	814
	3	.000	60	.032	340
	4	.000	92	.031	908
C1	1	.042	96	.125	16
	2	.010	209	.000	18
	3	.000	92	.059	17
	4	.006	338	.036	169
C2	1	.035	86	.045	222
	2	.000	406	.023	217
	3	.011	460	.034	355
	4	.000	57	.072	180
	5	.008	626	.009	215
D1	1	.011	539	.065	184
	2	.006	171	.035	143
	3	.007	294	.009	320
	4	.014	70	.091	88
D2	1	.008	248	.023	1077
	2	.008	375	.032	124

integration of these behaviors was made clinically evident through a series of attempts to manipulate experimentally maternal behavior—all of which failed. When we asked mothers to gaze "normally" but not speak or move their faces, it invariably resulted in upset mothers, or infants, or experimenters. When we asked mothers to make their usual "faces at baby" but direct them away from the baby or execute them when the infant was not looking at her, it made the mothers feel ridiculous and usually ended up with everyone laughing. When we asked mothers to talk to the baby as if she were looking at him, but without actually looking at him, it resulted in a difficult and stilted acting performance. All manipulations were abandoned. In short, these behavioral variations belong together, with the partial exception of speech which can function more independently.

The mother then, in the presence of an infant, alters her normal adult interpersonal behaviors and performs what can be called infant-elicited maternal facial, vocal, and gaze behaviors. These "unusual" behaviors make up a major part of the infant's world of social stimuli during play and may best be considered supernormal human stimuli. Mothers who can not perform these behaviors, or who have a restricted range of such behaviors elicit less "play" from their infants.

Infant Behavior in the Play Interaction

The infant may also perform an array of facial, vocal, and gaze behaviors. Each of the separate infant behaviors seen during the interaction can also be seen, although often only in a partial form, in the presence of stimuli other than a human face and even "*in vacuo.*" However, the exact form of the behaviors seen during an interaction, as well as the combinations of behaviors and their sequencing, appear to be relatively specific to the stimulus conditions provided by an interacting human caregiver. Much is now known about the separate developmental history of several of these infant behaviors. For example, the changes in the form and function of the smile as it proceeds from a spontaneous reflex to a social response are described (Ambrose, 1961; Emde & Harmon, 1972; Freedman, 1964; Gewirtz, 1965; Spitz & Wolf, 1946; Wolff, 1963). However, we still have little systematic descriptive data on the clustering and sequencing of the many different infant expressive behaviors, including gaze behaviors, as they occur under the eliciting conditions of a natural interaction. As a step toward this goal we focus alsmost exclusively on the continuously operating "on" and "off" of infant visual attention, which provides the regulatory background in which other expressive behaviors are largely prepared for, occur, and terminate.

Gaze Alternation as an Intrinsic Behavior · Gaze behavior with someone is so clearly a social phenomenon that we tend not to consider that the eye and head movements that constitute gaze shifting in a social situation may also be the manifestation of underlying biological events which are only partially related to the behavior of a partner or even his presence. The alternate shifting of the eyes from side to side or up and down is a regular feature of central nervous system activity during states of relative arousal. It is seen during the active phase of sleep, dreaming sleep, as rapid eye movement (REM), when there is no external visual stimulus. This is true for newborns as well as adults (Roffwarg, Muzio, & Dement 1966). Alternating eye movements are also observed in infants during "quiet wakefulness" (alert inactivity), when no particular visual target is presented or identified (Prechtl & Lennard, 1967).

Through observation of play, the possibility was raised that the first intrinsic

TABLE 2   Percent of Session Time Infant Gazes at Mother's Face, the Median Gaze-to-Gaze Interval, and the Median Duration of Gaze-at and Gaze-away from Mother, for Each Play Session

Twin	Session	Percent of Session Time Infant Gazes at Mother	Median Gaze-to-Gaze Interval (Seconds)	Median Infant Gaze at Mother (Seconds)	Median Infant Gaze away from Mother (Seconds)
A1	1	47	10.2	2.2	0.8
	2	52	4.2	3.0	0.6
	3	63	4.5	2.5	1.3
	4	24	13.8	1.9	5.0
	5	87	7.5	7.2	0.5
	6	27	9.6	2.1	3.3
	7	24	4.2	1.3	1.8
Mean		46	7.7	2.9	1.9
A2	1	61	5.4	2.6	1.5
	2	80	6.6	5.7	0.6
	3	69	9.0	3.3	3.3
	4	42	5.4	1.9	2.7
	5	82	7.5	3.8	0.9
	6	82	5.1	4.5	1.1
	7	35	5.4	2.4	1.8
Mean		64	6.3	3.5	1.7
B1	1	90	9.0	3.0	3.3
	2	11	6.6	0.9	4.8
	3	5	7.8	1.0	7.8
	4	7	9.9	0.9	9.6
Mean		28	8.3	1.5	6.4
B2	1	72	6.2	2.1	2.7
	2	14	9.6	0.9	5.4
	3	16	7.8	1.1	6.9
	4	9	6.0	0.8	3.6
Mean		28	7.4	1.2	4.7

Table 2 (continued)

Twin	Session	Percent of Session Time Infant Gazes at Mother	Median Gaze-to-Gaze Interval (Seconds)	Median Infant Gaze at Mother (Seconds)	Median Infant Gaze away from Mother (Seconds)
C1	1	67	5.6	2.7	0.7
	2	88	7.3	6.9	0.6
	3	74	5.1	4.2	0.7
	4	65	5.9	2.4	1.7
Mean		73	6.0	4.1	0.9
C2	1	28	9.0	2.7	3.9
	2	64	7.2	2.7	1.0
	3	54	5.7	1.7	1.9
	4	25	4.8	0.8	1.9
	5	74	6.6	5.7	1.0
Mean		49	6.7	2.7	1.9
D1	1	56	6.0	3.8	0.9
	2	52	5.4	2.2	1.5
	3	47	5.1	2.9	2.0
	4	39	5.6	2.3	4.5
Mean		49	5.5	2.8	2.2
D2	1	16	4.8	0.9	2.8
	2	70	7.8	6.9	2.6
Mean		43	6.3	3.9	2.7
For all sessions:					
Mean		49	6.8	2.8	2.6
S.D.		26	2.0	1.8	2.1

behavioral process the alert infant brings to the social situation is some process of gaze alternation, which is a manifestation of the biology of the central nervous system as well as the product of interactive events. During play there is wide variability in the infant's interest in gazing at the mother from day to day or even within the same day. The percentage of total session time the infant spends gazing at the mother offers a convenient measure of overall interest. As can be seen in Table 2, the variability in this measure is almost as great for the same infant on different days as it is across infants, with a range of 5 to 90%. Mothers are well aware of these fluctuations which are not always attributable to gross shifts in infant state, for example, fussiness. However, when the infant is "interested" in gazing at the mother he does not gaze back at her steadily. Likewise, when he tries to avoid contact he does not maintain gaze aversion throughout. In spite of whether he appears to seek or avoid contact with mother, the alternation between gazing-at mother and gazing-away continues. What appears different, depending upon his interest, is the duration of the gazes-at or gazes-away.

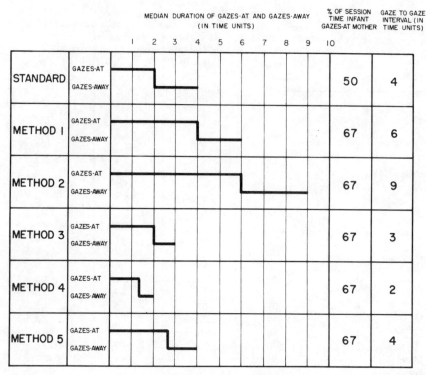

FIGURE 1. A schematic representation of five different relationships between the parameters of gazing-at and gazing-away, which permit an increase in the percentage of total gazing time from 50 to 67%.

In most studies in which visual attention is the crucial variable, different measures of attention have been reported: mean gaze duration, number of visual fixations, and percentage of stimulus presentation time the infant spends gazing at the stimulus. Rarely are all three reported together. In addition, less attention has been given to the parameters of gazing away from the stimulus, and almost none to the relationships between the parameters of gazing-at and gazing-away. An examination of these relationships is essential in the consideration of gaze alternation as a biological event. This is best done with an example. Figure 1 shows schematically five possible methods by which an infant can increase from 50 to 67% the percentage of total session time spent gazing-at the mother.

In Method 1, the median gaze-at duration is doubled, while the median gaze-away duration is unchanged. The median duration of a complete gaze alternation cycle, that is, from gaze onset to the next gaze onset has to become longer. This is the median gaze-to-gaze interval.

In Method 2 both the median duration of gazes-at and gazes-away are increased, but the increase in gazes-at is relatively greater. The median gaze-to-gaze interval becomes markedly longer. In this case greater visual interest is accompanied by decreased gaze alternations.

In Method 3 the median gaze-at duration is unchanged, while the median gaze-away duration is halved. The median gaze-to-gaze interval becomes shorter.

In Method 4 both the median durations of gazes-at and gazes-away are decreased, but the decrease in gazes-away is relatively greater. The median gaze-to-gaze interval becomes markedly shorter. In this case greater visual interest is accompanied by increased gaze alternations.

In Method 5 the median duration of gazes-at is increased by one-third, while the median duration of gazes-away is simultaneously decreased by one-third. The median gaze-to-gaze interval thus remains unchanged.

To examine these relationships all play sessions were divided into three groups: low interest in gazing at mother's face (0 to 33% of session time spent gazing at mother's face); middle interest (34 to 66%); and high interest (67 to 100%). Figure 2 shows the frequency distribution of the duration of gazes-at and gazes-away for the three different interest groups. It is evident that an increase in the median duration of gazes-at is compensated for by a decrease in the median duration of gazes-away, and vice versa. The two distributions change reciprocally. This is the relationship predicted by Method 5 which also postulates that if the distributions of durations of gazes-at and gazes-away change reciprocally the median gaze-to-gaze interval need not change as a function of changes in overall interest in gazing at mother.

To further test whether infants utilize Method 5, correlations were performed between the crucial variables across all play sessions. Table 2 shows for each play session the percentage of session time the infant spends gazing at the mother, the median gaze-to-gaze interval, the median gaze-at duration, and the median gaze-away duration. As predicted by Method 5, across all play sessions for all infants the median gaze-to-gaze interval shows no significant correlation with the percentage of infant gazing time at mother ($r = -.17$). The median duration of gazes at mother correlates positively with the percentage of infant gazing time ($r = .87$, $p < .001$). The median duration of gazes away from mother correlates negatively with the percentage of infant gazing time ($r = -.71$, $p < .001$), and the median gaze-at and gaze-away durations correlate negatively with each other ($r = -.54$, $p < .001$). These correlations, which are compatible only with Method 5, also obtain when the changes across the sessions of each individual infant are considered separately.

These findings suggest that the distribution of gaze-to-gaze intervals is the manifestation of a process not influenced by the reinforcing or aversive value of the mother's face which changes greatly from session to session. The distribution

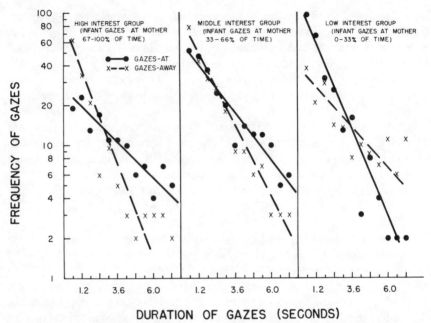

FIGURE 2. The frequency distributions of durations of gazes-at mother and gazes-away, for three different interest groups. (The high-interest group consists of six infants contributing 11 play sessions, the middle-interest group consists of six infants contributing 14 sessions, and the low-interest group consists of five infants contributing 12 sessions.)

of gaze-to-gaze intervals is also independent of other variables related to maternal behavior. Across all play sessions it shows no significant correlation with the mother's median gaze-to-gaze interval ($r = .11$), or with the percentage of time the mother spends gazing-at the infant ($r = .08$), or with the mutually determined percentage of time spent in mutual gaze ($r = .11$).

These findings indicate that while the separate distributions of gazes-at and gazes-away shift reciprocally depending on the infant's interest in gazing at the mother, the distribution of gaze-to-gaze intervals remains relatively more stable and does not reflect changes in the infant's visual interest. The infant, then, while in the physiological state associated with play, appears to be "given" by his underlying biology a relatively stable distribution of gaze-to-gaze intervals. These intervals, however, can be differentially divided into gazes-at or gazes-away, depending on the level of visual interest.

It is noteworthy that the frequency distribution of both gazes-at and gazes-away in all groups approximates a negative exponential function; that is, there are many short gazes, and progressively fewer ones as their duration increases. When the logs of the frequencies of gazes-at for each infant in each session are summed, and the same procedure followed for gazes-away, the frequency distributions shown in Figure 3 are obtained. The maximum number of gazes, whether -at or -away, are extremely short, about 0.6 seconds. As gaze duration increases, there is a monotonic decline in the frequency which approximates a negative exponential. In addition, there is a variable proportion of gazes shorter than 0.6 seconds.

These results are of particular interest because the distribution of the duration of intervals between successive side-to-side alternating eye movements in other physiological states is similar in form. During REM sleep in infants, the intervals between each eye shift show a roughly negative exponential distribution with a

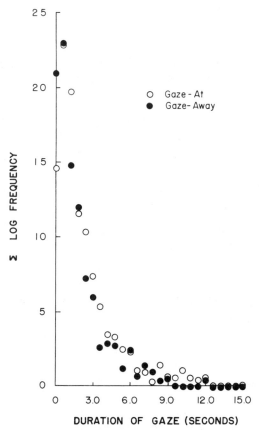

FIGURE 3. The log frequency distribution of duration of gazes-at and gazes-away for all infants in all sessions. The logs of the gaze-at distribution for each session have been summed, and the gaze-away distributions treated similarly. $n = 1199$ gazes-at, 1182 gazes-away.

maximum of about 0.3 seconds (Prechtl & Lennard, 1967). This distribution appears to change little with maturation after the newborn period (De Lee & Petre-Quadens, 1968; Jacobs, Feldman, & Bender, 1971). Similarly, during quiet wakefulness, when no particular visual target is presented or identified, alternating eye movements show a similar pattern which is also distributed as a negative exponential function but with a steeper slope (Prechtl & Lennard, 1967). The distribution we find for gazes also describes a roughly negative exponential function but has a shallower slope than either of the above distributions.

We are not suggesting that the alternating eye movements seen in REM sleep are simply transformed into gazes-at and gazes-away in a waking social situation. The evidence does not support such a conclusion. The REM and the gaze are different behavioral units, of different duration, collected differently, and occur during different physiological states and with different slopes. It can only be conjectured whether the same or related biological events that produce a given distribution of REMs when the infant is in the physiological state of REM sleep produce a given distribution of gazes when the infant is in the physiological state of alertness associated with an arousing visual stimulus. Prechtl concludes that the REM phenomenon results from random processes related to the organization of the brain. The distribution of gaze durations during play may be a similar random phenomenon. Nonetheless, an adaptive task can utilize a random process.

It is important to emphasize that we have been talking about distributions and not rhythms or rates; that is, knowing the duration of any one particular gaze-at need not predict the duration of its subsequent gaze-away. If it did, the constraint in social gazing would be immense, and the flexibility required for the social task would not be available. To examine if there are constraints within each individual gaze-at and gaze-away pair, a product moment correlation between the duration of each gaze-at and its subsequent gaze-away was performed. There exists a tendency for a long gaze-at to be followed by a short gaze-away and vice versa, but in no session did the negative correlation between successive gaze durations reach significance.

To summarize, the evidence suggests that neurophysiological processes produce a fairly stable distribution of gaze-to-gaze intervals, which is available to the organism to be pressed into the service of different adaptive functions—one of which is social gazing. For this distribution to be utilized for social gazing, we expect at least two requirements to be fulfilled. First, the direction of side-to-side alternation of gaze will become fixed to an external reference point, namely, the face as a visual target, so that the gaze alternations become relative to the target's position, that is, toward or away from the face. Second, we expect that the timing of any given gaze initiation or termination will be a function of both the ongoing interactive events, and the infant's internal state. This requirement is considered in the next section on the stimulus effects of maternal facial, vocal, and gaze behavior on the timing of the infant's gaze initiations and terminations.

Infant Responsivity to the Mother's Gaze Behaviors

Through the work of Fantz and Nevis (1967), Haaf and Bell (1967), and others, it is clear that the human face has unique stimulus value for the human infant. The differential effect on visual attention of the human face compared to control stimuli has been repeatedly demonstrated under experimental conditions in the laboratory. In a naturally occuring play situation, these experiments cannot be replicated without disrupting the activity. However, a related issue can be addressed, namely, whether the infant responds differently when the mother is gazing at him as compared to when she is not. Actually, this is the more germain question for a study of social interaction. The problem with this question is that it cannot determine if differences in the infants' responses are related to the presence of her gaze alone, or the fuller face presentation that almost always accompanies it, or the presence of speech and facial expressions of widely different stimulus value which may also accompany her gaze.

Accordingly, the first crucial question we asked of the naturally occurring interaction was whether the presence of maternal gaze, with or without its other attendant stimulus phenomena, affects the infants' gazing behavior. We hereafter refer simply to the effect of maternal gaze as if it were the single effective stimulus and make finer distinctions where possible.

There are two different possible effects of maternal gaze on infant gaze behavior. Does maternal gaze alter the probability of the infant initiating a gaze at her, and does it alter the probability of his terminating a gaze at her? The salient stimuli for attention-getting need not be the same for attention holding. This has recently been demonstrated for a checkerboard pattern (Cohen, 1972). Indeed, many of the attention-getting behaviors of mothers are rarely used to hold the infant's attention. We begin with the first question. The probability that the infant will initiate a gaze at the mother when she is not looking at him is compared with the probability that he will initiate a gaze at her when she is looking at him. This is accomplished by comparing the probability of the dyadic state transitions $(I-, M-) \blacktriangleright (I+, M-)$ and $(I-, M+) \blacktriangleright (I+, M+)$. In all eight cases the probability of the transition $(I-, M+) \blacktriangleright (I+, M+)$ is greater than the probability of the transition $(I-, M-) \blacktriangleright (I+, M-)$: Twin A1, $x^2 = 15.88$, $p < .001$; Twin A2, $x^2 = 12.64$, $p < .001$; Twin B1, $x^2 = 4.98$, $p < .05$; Twin B2, $x^2 = 13.65$, $p < .001$; Twin C1, $x^2 = 8.94$, $p < .01$; Twin C2, $x^2 < 3.80$, N.S.; Twin D1, $x^2 = 34.52$, $p < .001$; Twin D2, $x^2 = 0.31$, N.S. In all infants mother's gaze at him increases the probability of his initiating a gaze at her. This effect reaches significance in six of eight infants. Preliminary findings indicate that the likelihood of infant gaze initiation is increased by maternal speech without gaze, as well as by maternal gaze without speech. Gaze and speech together produce the greatest effect. It is evident that the infant can discriminate gross changes in maternal gaze direction through his peripheral vision.

The effect of maternal gaze on infant gaze terminations is examined by a similar procedure. In all eight cases the probability of the transition $(I+, M-) \blacktriangleright$ $(I-, M-)$ is greater than the probability of the transition $(I+, M+) \blacktriangleright (I-, M+)$: Twin A1, $x^2 = 49.71$, $p < .001$; Twin A2, $x^2 = 15.47$, $p < .001$; Twin B1, $x^2 = 23.40$, $p < .001$; Twin B2, $x^2 = 0.01$, N.S.; Twin C1, $x^2 = 29.10$, $p < .001$; Twin C2, $x^2 = 12.90$, $p < .001$; Twin D1, $x^2 = 10.11$, $p < .01$; Twin D2, $x^2 = 16.11$, $p < .001$. During play all infants are less likely to avert gaze and look away if the mother is looking at them. This effect is significant in seven of eight cases.

In summary, maternal gaze and the constellation of vocal and facial behaviors that may accompany it exert a strong effect on both eliciting and holding infant gaze. These findings are quite expected, yet difficult to demonstrate in a naturally occurring interaction. (The effects of maternal gaze described for a play interaction do not obtain during bottle feeding. During bottle feeding we usually observe gaze alone, which is less often accompanied by speech and rarely by exaggerated facial expression—if it is, feeding is likely to be interrupted and play begins. This suggests that it is not maternal gaze alone that affects the probability of infant gaze initiation and termination, but the entire configuration of gaze with vocal and facial expressions. The different infant responsivity during bottle feedings, however, cannot be attributed solely to the difference in maternal behavior. The infant while sucking is in a different physiological state. We do not know which of these differences is more crucial, but the ultimate result is a different gazing pattern.)

The timing of the infant's gaze initiations and termination thus becomes dependent on interactive events—the mother's behavior. In this way the infant's responsivity to maternal stimuli organizes his gaze alternations to serve a social function. The likelihood of infant gaze initiation is increased in the presence of maternal gaze and decreased in the absence of maternal gaze; likewise, the probability of infant gaze aversion is decreased in the presence of maternal gaze and increased in its absence. The result is that the occurrence of mutual gaze is maximized.

Dyadic Patterns Resulting from the Interaction of Mother and Infant Behaviors and Some Consequences of These Patterns

When mother and infant behaviors and responsivities are brought together in an interaction, the following typical dyadic gazing pattern emerges. Figure 4 is a state transition diagram for the mother and Twin A1. It shows for all their play sessions the number of dyadic state transitions, and their probability of occurrence. A determination of dyadic state is made every 0.6 seconds. As a fairly typical example, this diagram is used to describe the role of gaze in regulating social contact and stimulation.

Beginning with neither member looking at the other, the mother is more likely than the infant to initiate gazing (.281 versus .023). Once the mother is looking at the infant, she holds her gaze a relatively long time, usually until he responds by gazing at her; that is, the probability of her terminating gaze is less than the probability of his joining her in gazing (.016 versus .083). Accordingly, mutual gaze is the most likely outcome of her gaze initiation. If, however, the infant looks first, the mother will respond relatively quickly by gazing back at him before he gazes away, and mutual gaze is again the most likely outcome (.519 versus .370). The significance of this finding, which may seem intuitively obvious, is that it documents the way in which mutual gaze is the probable consequence of each member's responsivity to the other.

Once mutual gaze has occurred, most of the time is spent shifting back and forth between states (I+, M+) and I−, M+), that is, the mother holds gaze at the infant while he looks at her, then looks away, then back again, and so on. This, in fact, is the most striking feature of the dyadic gazing pattern.

A consequence of this resultant pattern is that it is the infant and not the mother

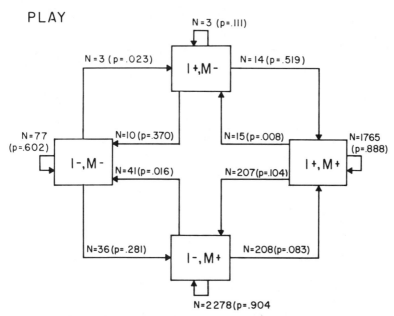

FIGURE 4. A dyadic state transition diagram for all play sessions between Twin A1 and her mother. Sampling every 0.6 seconds, the number and probability of transition from each dyadic state to any other dyadic state including itself is shown.

who "makes" and "breaks" mutual gaze. Figure 4 shows the number of infant initiations and terminations of mutual gaze. The infant initiates and terminates 94% of all mutual gazes. Of the two modes of regulating the degree of social contact and stimulation, the infant relies mainly on control of his visual attention, and the mother more on the modulation of her facial and vocal behaviors. This division is appropriate to the infant's developmental stage, since his control of vision surpasses his use of vocal and facial behaviors to recapture and hold maternal visual attention. Later in development each uses both modes more equally.

DISCUSSION

The fact that much of the gazing interaction consists of the infant turning toward and away from the mother's almost constantly gazing face makes the play situation analogous to most laboratory experiments in which a stimulus is presented uninterruptedly for about ½ minute while the infant gazes at it for a few seconds, then away for several seconds, and then back again, many times over. In both cases each infant gaze can be considered a learning trial. The analogy of course breaks down because the mother's face, as stimulus, changes continually in an experimentally uncontrolled fashion. Nonetheless, many of the findings and theories emerging from laboratory experimentation are relevant to and ultimately testable in a natural interaction.

We briefly review some of these experimental findings as they relate to play interactions. One of the crucial issues in both the experimental and natural situation boils down to the question: Why does the infant terminate a gaze-at the moment he does, and why does he initiate a gaze-at the moment he does?

The answer is not known, but the nature of the interaction between perceptual input, schema formation, and internal state is becoming clearer and points to tentative answers. Through the work of many investigators, several hypotheses have emerged (Berlyne, 1960; Fantz, 1964; Haith, Kessen, & Collins, 1969; Kagan & Lewis, 1965; McCall & Kagan, 1967; Sokolov, 1960; Stechler & Carpenter, 1967). The essential dimensions of a stimulus event are: the distribution of the salient stimulus elements in time and space, and the schema of the expected distribution of salient stimulus elements in time and space. The "discrepancy principle" postulates that a distribution of stimulus elements that is moderately different from the one predicted by the schema elicits more attention than a distribution that is identical or totally novel compared to the schema. It is further suggested that, as the degree of discrepancy increases from no discrepancy to greater discrepancy, there is a corresponding increase in the level of arousal and affect, from lower levels of arousal or boredom and neutral affect at degrees of discrepancy less than optimal, to levels of moderate arousal and positive affect, which correspond to some optimal degree of discrepancy.

Beyond the optimal range of discrepancy, the arousal level is higher and the affect reverses and becomes negative. The infant then turns away from the stimulus (Stechler & Carpenter, 1967).

The phenomenon of visual habituation, or response decrement in the infant's visual attention to presentation of the same stimulus, involves many of the same principles. Most workers assume that, during visual fixations of the stimulus, an internal model of it begins to form. As the internal model forms, the stimulus, or at least some of its salient elements, become progressively less discrepant relative to the internal model, and visual interest decreases (Lewis, Goldberg, & Campbell, 1969).

We explore the usefulness and limitations of these concepts as they apply to a play interaction. For this purpose we rely mainly on clinical impressions and frame-by-frame film analysis of kinescoped portions of television tapes. Current research in our laboratory is directed at more systematic examination of these observations.

In natural interaction all the essential variables accounted for in these hypotheses of discrepancy and habituation are seen to be operating. The presence of the infant's gaze, especially in combination with other expressive behavior, tends to elicit unique maternal facial and vocal behaviors and tends to hold the mother's gaze on the infant. The mother then modulates the stimulus configuration of her facial and vocal performance, using as cues the infant's state of arousal and affect and the quality of his visual attention. At some point in the course of her behavior, the infant gazes away, shutting off the stimulus and accordingly readjusting his level of arousal and affect. During his gaze aversion, while his internal state is changing, the mother's facial and vocal performance is altered and often stopped. After a short while the infant looks back again for the next "round" of mutual gaze. However, this time the mother has, as may the infant, a memory of the previous mutual gaze episode to help modify her behavior for the current gazing episode during which she tries to find, in a sense, the infant's current optimal range. The immediate "past history" of the previous gaze includes the way the infant averted gaze, the duration of his aversion, and a memory of the mother's behavior at the instant the infant averted gaze. A history of sequential events with possible trends is accumulated. For instance, over several successive gazing episodes, the infant's duration of gaze at mother may become progressively shorter. If she discriminates the trend, she can modify her behavior to increase his interest. This is analogous to the experiments on visual habituation in which a "new stimulus" (S_2) is presented after the response decrement to the repeated presentation of S_1 (Lewis, et al., 1969). When an entire play session is analyzed to show overall response decrement to the mother's face, however, none is found. This does not mean that the phenomenon does not occur for short runs within the interaction. Our impression is that such runs do occur but are "washed out" by the mother rapidly responding to any response decrement by recorrecting the stimulus level of her behavior. In fact, that is one of her "tasks" during play.

It is assumed that by 3 months the infant has a forming schema of the mother's face (Kagan, 1967; Lewis, 1969). However, a face schema at this age, in a real interaction cannot mean simply the static arrangement of features as in a photograph, or an unmoving face. The face schema must include a range of change in the salient features both with regard to the extent of change (in space), that is, the degree of exaggeration of feature arrangement, and the rate of change (in time). What is most interesting about infant-elicited maternal facial and vocal behaviors is exactly the exaggerations in space and time of the stimulus events she provides. It has been suggested that the distribution of an infant's visual attention is a function of schema formation. We are suggesting that in a play interaction many different schemata are beginning to form and integrate: namely, schemata of different rates and spatial configurations of feature change—that is, schemata of human facial expressions. The infant, after all, is learning to live in a social world where it is the changes in the face and voice that tell the story. This is especially true until speech is understood. In the course of an average human life, probably as much time is spent looking at human faces as any other class of visual stimuli. The immense subtlety of changes in facial behavior that adults discriminate is not surprising in this light. However, early in development the exaggerated maternal facial expressions provide the infant with an array of nonsubtle stimulus events from which the earliest schemata form.

In the course of viewing mother-infant interactions, we frequently recieve the impression that, in an attempt to maintain the infant's interest, the mother often progressively escalates the degree of exageration in the extent or timing of facial and vocal behaviors, up to some point of extraordinary exaggeration at which the infant rapidly averts gaze. Possibly some optimal point of discrepancy from a forming schema of a human expression has been exceeded. Even more frequently we receive the impression that some mothers, either all the time, or on some days (when they feel less "playful"), have a restricted or "unimaginative" repertoire of facial and vocal variations, and on such occasions have more difficulty keeping their infant's attention; that is, their behavior, as a stimulus event, constantly falls below an optimal range of discrepancy for human expressiveness.

There is another interactive sequence in which these formulations seem to apply. During play a sequence is often observed between mother and infant. In our laboratory we call it the "pre-peek-a-boo game," with no certainty of its relationship to later peek-a-boo. It consists of the infant looking at the mother, smiling , vocalizing, and showing other signs of mounting arousal and positive affect, including increasing motor activity. As the intensity of his state increases, he begins to show signs of displeasure, momentary sobering, and a fleeting grimace, interspersed with the smiling. The intensity of arousal continues to build until he suddenly averts gaze sharply with a quick but not extensive head turn which keeps the mother's face in good peripheral view, while his level of "excitement" clearly declines. He then returns gaze, bursting into a smile, and the level of arousal and affect build again. He again averts gaze, and so on. The infant gives the clear impression of modulating his states of arousal and affect within certain limits by regulating the amount of perceptual input. Stechler and Carpenter (1967) have described a similar regulation of the "dose" of perceptual input in the presence of an aversive experimental stimulus.

If we assume that the infant does in fact "turn the stimulus off and on" to bring both his state of arousal and the intensity and direction of affect back and forth across some upper threshold, additional questions arise. Any self-correcting feedback system such as this is set to operate within a given tolerance range. One of the striking features of the pre-peck-a-boo game is that the infant appears to hover within a very narrow range about his upper level of tolerance. Furthermore, the entire experience seems to be one of pleasurable excitement. Such behavior, whatever its origin, repeated over and over, most probably has the effect of facilitating the progressive extension of the infant's optimal range of pleasurable arousal. These behaviors are certainly relevant to the development of the capacity for joy or glee, which begins to be much in evidence during this life phase.

We now turn to the several phenomena occuring during play that are difficult to explain by these hypotheses and findings. The most frequent such event is simply the large number of infant gaze aversions and initiations which appear to bear no noticeable relationship to ongoing stimulus events, or manifest shifts in internal state. Some of these may be attributable to the process of gaze alternation disassociated from interactive events.

The most qualitatively important event that is difficult to explain in these terms is the occurrence of a special type of mutual gaze: the long "loving" mutual looks between mother and infant during which little else occurs in the way of facial or vocal behavior on either side. It often has the aura of a very quiet magic moment. However, one of its hallmarks is the apparent stimulus monotony which at other times would make the infant look elsewhere.

Given our current state of knowledge, what is now required is the utilization of physiological measures along with a larger, more precise descriptive body of kinesics to be coordinated with the measurments described here and applied to natural interactions. Until that time, some tentative conclusions can be suggested.

An essential feature of a natural interaction such as play is that its very nature involves an almost continuous change in stimuli and periodic shifting in the forming subsets of schemata of the mother's face in change. There is also an almost continual, although often small, change in the infant's state of arousal and affect. Given this unstable system, even in the hands of the most ideally sensitive and repsonsive mother, the array of stimuli the mother provides and the infant's level of arousal and affect repeatedly fall below some optimal level where interest is lost, and repeatedly climb above some optimal level where active aversion is executed. In either case both mother and infant can readjust their behavior to bring the infant's state temporarily back into an optimal range, where it fluctuates until the boundaries are again exceeded. Much of play is spent crossing and recrossing the upper and lower boundaries, as well as within the optimal range. If appropriate readjustments cannot be made after repeated attempts, the interaction is terminated and play stops.

The clinical import of this situation is that the infant acquires experience with the regulation of his state of arousal and affect on the basis of another person's interpersonal behavior. He learns when in the course of the mother's behavior to initiate and maintain interactive contact and when to disengage, depending on the effect of her behavior on him. When it is considered that the stimulus events are interpersonal behaviors, this is no less than the execution of early coping and defensive operations, and it is a necessary consequence of the nature of play activity.

Summary

A view of mother-infant play has been presented. The goal of play activity is the mutual regulation of stimulation so as to maintain an optimal level of arousal which is affectively positive. The mother contributes to the regulation by almost constantly altering her behavior, using as cues, changes in the infant's visual attention and state. The maternal behaviors that are the stimulus events for the infant are a special subset of human behaviors. They are infant-elicited variations of normal adult interpersonal behaviors which differ in their degree of exaggeration and slowed tempo of performance. It is suggested that these infant-elicited variations in adult behavior are particularly adapted to the infant's stage of neurological development and enhance the infant's acquisition of schemata of human behavior.

The infant contributes to the regulation largely through the control of gaze, which allows him to titrate perceptual input of the stimulus events provided by the mother, so as to maintain his internal state within an optimal range. The infant's gaze initiations and terminations which accomplish this regulation appear to be a functional adaptation of an intrinsic biological process of gaze alternation.

During the play activity both members are almost constantly making readjustments in their behavior so as to achieve the goal of the activity. The infant, in so doing, acquires experience with the precursors of interpersonal coping and defensive operations.

Acknowledgments

The author wishes to thank Dr. Joseph Jaffe for his assistance with many theoretical and methodological issues, and Dr. Joseph Fleiss for statistical consultation. In addition, the assistance of J. Craig Peery and Edward Lorick is acknowledged.

References

Ambrose, J. A. The development of the smiling response in early infancy. In B. M. Foss (Ed.), *Determinants of infant behavior.* Vol. 1. New York: Wiley, 1961. Pp. 179–195.

Anderson, S. W., & Jaffe, J. The definition, detection and timing of vocalic syllables in speech signals. Department of Communication Sciences, New York State Psychiatric Institute. Scientific Report No. 12, 1972.

Argyle, M., & Kendon, A. The experimental analysis of social performance. In L. Berkowitz (Ed.), *Advances in Experimental Social Psychology.* Vol. 3. New York: Academic Press, 1967. Pp. 55–99.

Berlyne, D. E. *Conflict, arousal, and curiosity. New York: McGraw-Hill, 1960.*

Chance, M. An interpretation of some agonistic postures. *Symposium of the Zoological Society of London,* 1962, **8:** 71–89.

Cochran, W. G. Some methods for strengthening the common chi square test. *Biometrics,* 1954, **10,** 417–451.

Cohen, L. B. Attention-getting and attention-holding processes of infant visual preferences. *Child Development,* 1972, **43,** 869–879.

DeLee, C., & Petre-Quadens, O. Les Mouvements oculaires du sommeil. *Acta Neurologica Belgica,* 1968, **68,** 327–331.

Emde, R. N., & Harmon, R. J. Endogenous and exogenous smiling systems in early infancy. *Journal of the American Academy of Child Psychiatry,* 1972, **11:** 177–200.

Exline, R., Gray, D., & Schuette, D. Visual behavior as affected by interview content and sex of respondent. *Journal of Personality and Social Psychology,* 1965, **1,** 201–209.

Fantz, R. L. Visual experience in infants: Decreased attention to familiar patterns relative to novel ones. *Science,* 1964, **146,** 668–670.

Fantz, R. L., & Nevis, S. Pattern preference and perceptual-cognitive development in early infancy. *Merrill-Palmer Quarterly,* 1967, **13,** 77–108.

Ferguson, C. A. Baby talk in six languages. In J. Gumperz and D. Hymes (Eds.), *The Ethnography of communication: American Anthropologist.* 1964, **66**(2), 103–114.

Fleiss, J. L. *Statistical methods for rates and proportions.* New York: Wiley, 1973. Section 22.

Fraiberg, S. Intervention in infancy: A program for blind infants. *Journal of American Academy of Child Psychiatry,* 1971, **10,** 381–405.

Freedman, D. Smiling in blind infants and the issue of innate vs. acquired. *Journal of Child Psychology and Psychiatry*, 1964, **5**, 171–184.

Gewirtz, J. L. The course of infant smiling in four child-rearing environments in Israel. In B. M. Foss (Ed.), *Determinants of infant behavior*. Vol. 3. New York: Wiley, 1965. Pp. 205–248.

Goffman, E. *Behavior in public places*. New York: Free Press of Glencoe, 1963.

Haaf, R. A., & Bell, R. Q. A facial dimension in visual discrimination by human infants. *Child Development*, 1967, **38**, 893–899.

Haith, M. M., Kessen, W., & Collins, D. Response of the human infant to level of complexity of intermittent visual movement. *Journal of Experimental Child Psychology*, 1969, **7**, 52–69.

Hutt, C., & Ounsted, C. The biological significance of gaze aversion with particular reference to the syndrome of infantile autism. *Behavioral Science*, 1966, **11**, 346–356.

Jacobs, L., Feldman, M., & Bender, M. B. Eye movements during sleep. I. The pattern in the normal human. *Archives of Neurology*, 1971, **25**, 151–159.

Jaffe, J., Stern, D. N., & Peery, J. C. "Conversational" coupling of gaze behavior in pre-linguistic human development. *Journal of Psycho-linguistic Research*, 1973, **2**(2).

Kagan, J. The growth of the face schema: Theoretical significance and methodological issues. In J. Hellmuth (Ed.), *The exceptional infant*. Vol. 1. Seattle: Special Child Publications, 1967. Pp. 335–348.

Kagan, J., & Lewis, M. Studies on attention in the human infant. *Merrill-Palmer Quarterly*, 1965, **11**, 95–127.

Kendon, A. Some functions of gaze-direction in social interaction. *Acta Psychologica*, 1967, **26**, 22–63.

Lewis, M. Infant's responses to facial stimuli during the first year of life. *Developmental Psychology*, 1969, **1**, 75–86.

Lewis, M., Goldberg, S., & Campbell, H. A developmental study of learning within the first three years of life: Response decrement to a redundant signal. *Society for Research in Child Development Monographs*, 1969, **34**(9), No. 133).
133. R. B., & Kagan, J. Stimulus-schema discrepancy and attention in the infant. *Journal of Experimental Child Psychology*, 1967, **5**, 381–390.

Moss, H. A., Robson, K. S., & Pedersen, F. Determinants of maternal stimulation and consequences of treatment for later reaction to strangers. *Developmental Psychology*, 1969, **1**, 239–247.

Prechtl, H. F. R., & Lenard, H. G. A study of eye movements in sleeping newborn infants. *Brain Research*, 1967, **5**, 477–493.

Rheingold, H. L. The effect of environmental stimulation upon social and exploratory behavior in the human infant. B. M. Foss (Ed.), *Determinants of infant behavior*. Vol. 1. New York: Wiley, 1961. Pp. 143–177.

Robson, K. S. The role of eye-to-eye contact in maternal-infant attachment. *Journal of Child Psychology and Psychiatry*, 1967, **8**, 13–25.

Roffwarg, H. P., Muzio, J. N., & Dement, W. C. Ontogenetic development of the human sleep-dream cycle. *Science*, 1966, **152:** 604–619.

Sokolov, E. N. *Perception and the conditioned reflex.* New York: MacMillan, 1960.

Spitz, R., & Wolf, K. The smiling response. *Genetic Psychology Monographs*, 1946, **34,** 57–125.

Stechler, G., & Carpenter, G. A viewpoint on early affective development. In J. Hellmuth (Ed.), *The exceptional infant.* Vol. 1. Seattle: Special Child Publications, 1967. Pp. 163–189.

Stechler, G., & Latz, E. Some observations on attention and arousal in the human infant. *Journal of the American Academy of Child Psychiatry*, 1966, **5,** 517–525.

Stern, D. N. A micro-analysis of mother-infant interaction: Behavior regulating social contact between a mother and her 3½ month-old twins. *Journal of the American Academy of Child Psychiatry*, 1971, **10,** 501–517.

Thompson, W. R., & Grusec, J. Studies of early experience. In P. H. Mussen (Ed.), *Carmichael's handbook of child psychology.* New York: Wiley, 1970. Pp. 565–656.

Walters, R. H., & Parke, R. D. The role of distance receptors in the development of social responsiveness. *Advances in Child Development and Behavior*, 1965, **2,** 56–96.

White, B. L., Castle, P., & Held, R. Observations on the development of visually-directed reaching. *Child Development*, 1964, **35,** 349–364.

Wolff, P. H. Observations on the early development of smiling. In B. M. Foss (Ed.), *Determinants of infant behavior.* Vol. 2. New York: Wiley, 1963. Pp. 113–138.

CHAPTER 10

Blind Infants and Their Mothers: An Examination of the Sign System [1]

SELMA FRAIBERG

University of Michigan Medical School

In this chapter I bring together observations from our longitudinal studies of infants blind from birth, which describe the elements of communication between baby and mother that must be derived from a nonvisual vocabulary of signs and signals.

Before describing our sample, our methods, and our observations of mothers and their blind infants, I propose to introduce the problems under consideration by first choosing a neutral frame of reference: observations of myself, self-observations of our research staff, and observations of visitors to our project in response to blind babies.

Understandably, there will be questions as we introduce our findings. A mother who has just delivered a blind baby, or who has just learned that her baby is blind, must cope with immeasurable grief and despondency. When we describe the extraordinary problems of a blind baby and his mother in finding a sign vocabulary, how can we know what belongs to the obliteration of a visual sign system and what belongs to psychological pain as a deterrent to the mother's reading of signs? The self-observations of the researcher and observations of visitors to our project may offer some measure of the meaning of blindness to an adult where blindness is not a personal tragedy.

SELF-OBSERVATIONS

I began the developmental study of blind infants 12 years ago. I gradually became aware of many differences in my behavior toward blind infants when I watched myself with sighted infants. Many of these feelings are still with me, and catch me by surprise. Yet, I think I am reasonably without prejudice toward

[1] This research has been supported since 1966 by Grant No. HD01-444 from the National Institutes of Child Health and Human Development and funds from the Department of Psychiatry of the University of Michigan Medical School and since 1969 by Grant No. OEG-0-9-322108-2469 (032) from the Office of Education.

the blind and, as far as I can judge, my feelings have not been an impediment in my work.

The first self-discoveries came to me in New Orleans when David Freedman and I began our study of a 5-month-old blind baby, Toni. We had been visiting Toni for 6 months when we were asked by a social agency to evaluate another blind baby, Lennie, then 9 months old. We arranged for a home visit.

Somebody had made a mistake. Lennie was not blind. We found a neglected baby lying in a filthy crib. If we exerted ourselves in testing, we elicited brief regard of our faces and tracking. It was the absence of sustained fixation that had led someone to believe that Lennie was blind when he was 3 months of age. Since that time he had been reared as a blind child and as the unwanted fourteenth child in an impoverished family.

After concluding our testing and a long discussion with the mother, I began to write up notes for a social agency referral. As I put the observations in sequence, I made notations on the conditions that elicited visual regard. I was describing Lennie's responses to my voice when something struck me as strange. It was my monolog. But I always talk to babies I told myself. No. I don't always talk to babies. I don't talk to Toni in the same way.

I searched my memory. It was true. I did very little talking when I was with Toni. This troubled me. Toni was a responsive and endearing child. Lennie depressed me. I enjoyed holding Toni. I had to overcome some feelings of revulsion when I held Lennie. But I talked to Lennie. What was the reward? When I searched my memory again, I came up with two pictures. When I talked to Lennie long enough, I elicited brief moments of visual fixation of my face and a meeting of eyes. When I sustained his fixation long enough, I elicited a ghost of a smile.

Later, I could make use of this self-observation when I was with Toni. I talked to her more frequently, but always I had the sense of something missing, something that should be coming back to me from Toni. There was of course no fixation of my face. And something else was missing. Although Toni smiled frequently in response to her mother's voice, she rarely smiled to our voices as observers. Later, in the course of years, I was to learn much more about the stimuli that evoke smiling in the blind infant. The voice, even the voice of the mother, does not automatically evoke smiling in blind infants. I missed that in Toni. I still miss it in blind infants, and my team members share this feeling with me.

Twelve years later there are still surprises for me. A few months ago 5-year-old Karen, who is blind, was visiting our office. I saw Karen playing in one of the offices and stopped to talk with her. Her back was turned to me. When she heard me speak to her she stopped her play for a moment and listened. She did not turn around immediately. Then as I continued to talk, Karen slowly turned around and met me full face. I had a moment's shock. The words came into my mind, "She's blind!" But I had known for nearly 5 years that Karen was blind.

Sometimes when we have professional visitors at the project to look at films or videotapes, I steal glances at their faces when the child is seen on the screen. With sighted children it is always interesting to see the resonance of mood on the viewer's face. We smile when the baby on the film smiles; we are sober when the baby is distressed. We laugh sympathetically when the baby looks indignant at the examiner's sneakiness. We frown in concentration as the baby frowns when the toy disappears. When he drops a toy, we look below the movie screen to help him find it.

But the blind baby on the screen does not elicit these spontaneous moods in the visitor. Typically, the visitor's face remains solemn. This is partly a reaction to blindness itself. But it is also something else. There is a large vocabulary of expressive behavior that one does not see in a blind baby at all. The absence of differentiated signs on the baby's face is mirrored in the face of the observer.

One afternoon recently our staff devoted a session to the discussion of self-observations in relation to blind infants. Our consensus, as a team of researchers and clinicians who have worked with blind children for several years, was that we have never overcome this sense of something vital missing in the social exchange. And yet our rewards from blind children have been very great. All the staff members have strong attachments to children we have known since the first year of life. With rare exceptions the babies have grown into preschool children who are healthy, active, freely mobile, talkative and mischievous, surely a group of highly personable and attractive youngsters. Among ourselves we talk about them the way proud parents do. We are never aware that something is missing in our response until a sighted child comes to visit.

When a sighted child comes to visit, there is spontaneous rapport and we trot out our repertoire of antics with babies. We are back in the tribal system where the baby plays his social game and we play ours. If one has worked very largely with blind babies for many years, as we have, the encounter with a sighted baby is absurdly like the experience of meeting a compatriot abroad after a long stay in a country where the language and customs are alien. The compatriot, who can be a perfect stranger asking for directions, is greeted like a friend, his regional accent and idiom are endearing, and with nothing more in common than a continent two strangers can embark upon a social exchange in which nearly all the tribal signs are understood and correctly interpreted.

What we miss in the blind baby, apart from the eyes that do not see, is the vocabulary of signs and signals that provides the most elementary and vital sense of discourse long before words have meaning.

In this chapter, I describe through our observations some of the unique problems of a blind infant and his mother in finding a vocabulary of signs.

THE SAMPLE

The data summarized in this report are derived from a longitudinal study of 10 babies, 5 boys and 5 girls. So far as possible we have brought babies into the study soon after birth, but the actual age at the point of first observation has ranged from 23 days to 7 months for eight children, and two children were first seen at 9 and 11 months. Within the range of medical certainty, we have selected babies who have been totally blind from birth or who have light perception only and no other defects.

Our sample, then, is highly selective, and our findings cannot be generalized for the total blind infant population. (A typical blind population includes children with a range of useful vision, who are still legally classified as "blind," and children who have other sensory and motor handicaps and neurological damage.) Our babies, then, are advantaged in a blind child population by the intactness of other systems and are disadvantaged as a group by having no pattern vision. (These restrictive criteria have given us a very small population, even though we called upon the referral network of a major medical center.)

It is important to note that we have provided a concurrent educational and guidance service for all babies in the research program. We know that the early development of blind babies is perilous. In the general blind child population there is a very high incidence of deviant and nondifferentiated personalities and arrested ego development (even when we exclude cases of brain damage and multiple handicaps which are also common to this population). As our own research progressed, we were able to link certain developmental road blocks with a clinical picture seen in the older blind child (Fraiberg, 1968; Fraiberg & Freedman, 1964). As these findings became available to us, they were readily translatable into a program of prevention and education. We felt that no benefits to the research could justify withholding this knowledge and began to provide a home-based educational program which has been highly effective in promoting the development of our blind babies (Fraiberg, 1971; Fraiberg, Smith, & Adelson, 1969).

We can say then that the observations in this report are derived from a group of healthy, otherwise intact infants; their families represent a good range of socioeconomic conditions; their mothers are at least adequate and, in four cases, are rated as superior. The development of these babies has probably been favored by our intervention. See Table 1 for sample characteristics.

OBSERVATIONAL PROCEDURES

Observers

Each baby is assigned to a team of two observers. The primary responsibility for observation is given to the senior staff member who is present at each visit.

TABLE 1   Sample Characteristics

Criteria
  Total blindness from birth or only minimal light perception
  No other known handicaps of neurological damage
  Less than 1-year-old
  Within 50 miles of our office
Description

Sex:	5 boys, 5 girls
Age at referral:	1 to 11 months
Age last seen:	2 to 6 years
Ordinal position in family	
only	(5)
First of two	(1); of three (1)
Second of two	(1)
Fifth of five	(1)
Sixth of six	(1)
Diagnosis	
Hypoplasia of optic nerve	(3)
Retrolental fibroplasia (3 months premature birth)	(3)
Infantile glaucoma	(2)
Ophthalmia neonatorum	(1)
Resorption of vitreous humor	(1)
Social class by father's occupation[a]	
Managerial	(1)
College student	(2)
Skilled	(2)
Semiskilled	(3)
Unskilled	(2)

[a]Based on Edwards Occupational Index.

Methods

The baby is visited in his home at twice monthly intervals for a 1½-hour session. (We travel within a radius of 100 miles to cover our home visits.) We try to time our visits to coincide with a morning or afternoon waking period, and to fit our observations into the normal routine of that period. Nearly all the data required for our study can be obtained through observing a feeding, a bath, a playtime with mother, a diapering or clothes changing, and a period of self-occupation with or without toys. A small amount of time in each session may be employed for testing procedures by the examiner in the areas of prehension and object concept.

The observers record a continuous narrative with descriptive detail. Once monthly we record a 15-minute, 16-mm film or video sample covering mother-child interaction, prehension, and gross motor development, which is employed for close analysis by the staff.

Since the areas we are studying have not been previously researched, our data collection procedures had to insure coverage of hundreds of items for comparative study, yet needed to be open, flexible, and rich in detail for qualitative study.

Our study of human attachment was of course one of the central areas of this study. Since nothing was known regarding the characteristics of human attachments in the blind infant, we had to design a study that permitted the blind baby to teach us what kinds of sense information he uses when he makes selective responses to his mother, his father, and other familiar persons, how he differentiates mother and stranger, how he reacts to separation from his mother, and how he demonstrates affection, joy, need, grief, anger, and the range of human emotion that normally tell us about the quality of human bonds during the first 18 months.

Our observations, then, covered differential responses (smiling, vocalizing, motor responses) to the human voice, to touch, to holding, and to lap games, with familiar and unfamiliar persons, with mother present and, when appropriate for testing, with mother absent. The data covering the first 18 months of life were classified, yielding 25 categories which were employed for analysis of differential responses.

THE ABSENCE OF AN EYE LANGUAGE

I have described some of the reactions of professional observers in social exchanges with blind babies. The blind eyes that do not engage our eyes, that do not regard our faces, have an effect upon the observer which is never completely overcome. When the eyes do not meet ours in acknowledgment of our presence, it feels curiously like a rebuff. Certainly, mothers attribute "knowing" and "recognition" to a baby's sustained regard of the face long before he can actually discriminate and recognize faces, and this is only because the engagement of the eyes is part of the universal code of the human fraternity, which is read as a greeting and an acknowledgment of "the other" long before it can have meaning to the infant.

It is a potent sign. Robson (1968) describes the role of eye-to-eye contact in eliciting maternal responses to the infant. In his report mothers speak of the first feelings of love in response to the infant's fixation of the face, of the sense of the baby "becoming a person." Roskies (1972), in her work with the mothers of thalidomide babies, describes two mothers who were considering institutionalization of their deformed babies soon after birth. The baby's eyes "looking back," the eyes "talking" to the mother, were moments recalled by both mothers as compelling. The decision to keep the baby was remembered by both mothers within the context of this engagement of the eyes.

"How will he know me?" This question, sometimes explicit, sometimes implicit, may come to us from the mother soon after she has learned of her child's blindness. And while we know that under all favorable circumstances the blind baby will come to know his mother and that the course of human attachments will closely parallel that of a sighted child, the imagination of the mother may be strained to encompass a "knowing" without vision. Discrimination, recognition, preference, and valuation are signs that the mother normally reads through visual responses of the infant. And while a mother can acknowledge that there can be recognition, "knowing" through tactile, kinesthetic, and auditory experience, the registration of this "knowing" is normally interpreted through differentiated facial signs. Eye contact connotes greeting and acknowledgement. Eye contact elicits the smile. Visual discrimination leads to preferential smiling. In the case of the blind infant, a large vocabulary of signs is either obliterated or distorted for the mother, as I describe in the sections that follow.

Vision affords the sighted child an elementary form of initiative in human partnership long before there can be intention. From the responses of the mother of a baby under 2 months of age, we can say that the baby woos his mother with his eyes. He elicits social exchange through the automatic smile in response to the human face gestalt. At 5 months of age, the sighted child extends or uplifts his arms in the gesture, "Hold me," "Pick me up," which most mothers find irresistible, even an imperative.

But the blind baby has a meager repertoire of behaviors that can initiate social exchange and, beyond the vocal utterances of need and distress, he has virtually no sign vocabulary that elicits an automatic response from his mother. Instead, the absence of eye contact gives the negative sign of "no interest." The absence of a smile in response to the presentation of the human face has the negative value of "not friendly." The smile to mother's voice, which is in the repertoire of the blind baby, is not an automatic smile and is not employed to initiate a social exchange. The gesture, "Hold me," "Pick me up" does not appear, even among our most adequate blind babies, until the end of the first year, at which time the voice of the mother can elicit a directional reach and the reach becomes a meaningful gesture to the mother.

Our records document the extraordinary problems for a mother in reading the nonvisual sign language of the blind baby. Only 2 mothers among our group of 10 found their way unaided by us. Both were extraordinary mothers, and both had had extensive experience with babies. Other mothers in our group, including those who had older children, showed us at the time of our first meeting that they found their blind babies perplexing and "unresponsive," that it was hard to know what the baby "wanted." No criticism is implied here. A sighted baby does not need an extraordinary mother in order to make the vital human connections and to find the developmental routes in infancy. We provided much help to all the parents of our blind infants. As we ourselves became experienced in understanding the nonvisual vocabulary of the blind baby and the developmental road blocks, we were able to become the translators for the blind baby and his perplexed parents. When the mother learned the language, the rewards for the baby and his parents were very great.

THE SMILE LANGUAGE

Our observations on smiling in blind infants were reported in an earlier article (Fraiberg, 1971). The material that follows is a summary.

As early as the fourth week, we have observations in which a blind baby responds to his mother's and his father's voice with a smile. Our findings show close correspondence with those of Wolff (1963), who demonstrated that the sighted baby shows a selective smile to the sound of his mother's voice as early as 4 weeks of age.

At this age, as Emde and Koenig (1969) point out, the familiar voice, as well as several other stimuli, can irregularly elicit a smile in the sighted child. And while it is impressive to see how the blind baby can respond selectively to the voices of his mother and father, we should note that this is not an automatic or a regular response. As the number of babies in our sample increased, differences between the characteristics of smiling in blind and sighted infants appeared in a clear pattern.

At 2 to 2½ months, when for the sighted child the visual stimulus of the human face evokes an automatic smile with a high degree of regularity, there is no equivalence in the blind baby's experience. Thus the blind baby's smile becomes more frequent, and although the pattern of selective smiling becomes increasingly demonstrated in favor of the mother, even the mother's voice does not regularly elicit a smile. There is no stimulus in the third month or later that has true equivalence for the human face gestalt in the experience of the sighted child.

For the mother of the blind baby, the selective response smile to her voice signified "knowing" and "preference" and, the first fears of "How will he know me?" were diminished by appearance of the universal sign. When observers tried experimentally to elicit a smile through their voices, they were only rarely rewarded, and we used our failures to help the mother to see the smile for her as being "special" and the beginning of "knowing" the mother.

But the smile was not automatic. In our records and on film we see the mother coaxing a smile. Sometimes several repetitions of her voice were needed before the smile appeared. Clearly, something was needed that was not automatically given.

Then, in our records of this period, we begin to see that the most reliable stimulus for evoking a smile or laughter in the blind baby is gross tactile or kinesthetic stimulation. As observers we were initially puzzled and concerned by the amount of bouncing, jiggling, tickling, and nuzzling that all of our parents, without exception, engaged in with the babies. In several cases we judged the amount of such stimulation as excessive by any standards. We had rarely seen among parents of sighted babies, in such a range of homes, so much dependence upon gross body stimulation. Then we began to understand; these games provided an almost certain stimulus for a smile, while the parents' voices alone provided at best an irregular stimulus. The parents' own need for the response smile, which is normally guaranteed with the sighted child at this age, led them to these alternative routes in which a smile could be evoked with a high degree of reliability.

When we exclude vision as a factor in the socialization of the smile, other differences in smiling emerge. Once a familiar voice is heard, the blind child may respond by smiling, but he does not initiate contact through a smile. The smile to initiate, the automatic greeting, is largely mediated through visual signs and is normally reinforced through visual rewards (the return or exchange smile of the partner).

This leads us to the observation that our blind babies do not smile as frequently as sighted babies do (the consensus of our staff and a very large number of independent observers who have reviewed films with us over the years.) And even when we have all the criteria for a mutually satisfying mother-child relationship, the smile of the blind infant strikes us as a muted smile. The joyful, even ecstatic smile that we see in a healthy sighted baby is a comparatively rare occurrence among blind babies. This suggests that the smile on the face of "the other" is a potent reinforcer—even in infancy—of one's own smile.

The effects upon the human partner of a baby who does not greet with a smile, who smiles infrequently and without predictability to the social stimuli presented to him, are best seen in the judgments made upon the blind baby's personality and his state both by clinicians and laymen who have not had experience with blind babies.

"She looks depressed," says a visitor watching one of our blind babies on film. "No affect! The face is so bland. No expression." The visitor wonders if the mother is giving the baby enough stimulation.

The baby in question is a perfectly adequate blind girl (17 months) who has given a demonstration on film of her attachment to and preference for her mother, of locomotor achievements close to sighted norms, and a rapt exploration of a new toy with her sensitive fingertips. The amount of "stimulation" provided by the mother must be judged as adequate to produce this kind of investment in persons and things in a blind baby of this age.

Yet, we understand what the visitor is experiencing. The visitor misses the signs of affectivity, of investment, of social response which register on the face of a sighted baby and are automatically translated by us. Only when we see a blind baby do we fully appreciate that most of these signs are differentiated through vision.

THE ABSENCE OF DIFFERENTIATED FACIAL SIGNS

In the range pleasure-displeasure, we can read the signs at both ends of the arc for a blind baby. A blind baby who smiles "looks happy." A blind baby who is crying for a delayed dinner "looks unhappy." But between the contrasting states, which everyone can read, there is a tremendous range of modulated affect and attitudes which is normally discerned by human partners through expressive facial signs. By any reasoning the modulations must exist for blind babies as states of feeling, but we cannot easily read these states by scrutinizing the face.

If we make a brief inventory of expressive facial signs in the sighted child, at 6 months of age, we can immediately see how the child's own eyes lead the way and give us the signs we read as "affect," "investment," and "attention."

1. "He looks attentive" (attention inferred from sustained visual regard).
2. "A look of longing" (can be read through the baby's prolonged visual fixation, visually oriented postures).
3. "He looks quizzical" (visual inspection of an unfamiliar phenomenon).
4. "He looks doubtful" (visual inspection with mixed positive and negative emotion).
5. "A coy look" (a visual peek-a-boo game: now you're here; now you're not).
6. "She is bored" (restless or unfocused searching or scanning with the. eyes).

The list can be compounded for the sighted child before he has reached 6 months of age. In the third and fourth quarters, imitative signs begin to enter the repertoire for the sighted child (Piaget, 1962), giving personal style to the face and extending the differentiated vocabulary of facial expression. All this is closed out in blindness.

The blind baby, by contrast, has an impoverished repertoire of facial signs. The blind baby does not "look attentively," "look quizzically," "look doubtfully," "look coyly." He has no object of visual fixation that can elicit these differentiated signs. This leads the uninitiated mother or observer to feel as our visitors do, "He looks depressed," "Nothing interests him."

The absence of signs is misleading. We have no reason to believe that the affective state of longing, for example, does not exist for the healthy blind baby, but the motor expression of longing which is read by us through sustained visual fixation (and visually oriented postures) is not available to him. Since we normally read affective states through expressive facial signs, the absence of the differentiated sign on the blind baby's face is misread as "no affect."

(There are of course blind babies who are, properly speaking, depressed, withdrawn, and apathetic. But to make the clinically valid diagnosis, we need much more than a reading of the face.)

For the healthy, adequately stimulated blind baby, there are registrations of affective states with motor expression. But we have to turn our eyes away from the face to discover them. To do this is so alien to normal human discourse, that we might not have discovered the other signs if we had not been looking for something else.

THE HAND LANGUAGE

Our developmental observations included the study of prehension in blind infants. Very early in our work we saw that adaptive hand behavior followed another route in blind babies. There was no adaptive substitution of the ear for the eye in reaching and attaining an object at 5 months of age. Our question was, "How does the blind baby achieve the coordination of ear and hand which leads him to localize a sound object in space, to reach directionally for the object and attain it?" We were to find that "reach on sound" was not achieved by any baby in our group until the last quarter of the first year (Fraiberg, 1968; Fraiberg, Siegel, & Gibson, 1966).

We became "hand watchers" as a staff. To examine the sequential patterns in adaptive hand behavior, we analyzed many thousands of feet of film on a variable-speed projector, viewing at one-third speed. Our prehension film samples were always photographed under circumstances in which the full range of the baby's experience with human partners as well as inanimate objects could be included.

As we watched the baby's hands, we found what we were looking for, and we also found a large number of things that we were not looking for.

We began to see the expressive motor signs in the hands themselves. We began to read "I want" and intentionality through fleeting, barely visible motor signs in the hands. Our staff film reviews took on a curious aspect. When we examined mother-child reciprocity, we looked at the mother's face and the baby's hands. (The baby's face told us very little.) When we studied investment in a toy or toy preference, we looked at the baby's hands. When we examined emotional reactions to momentary separation from the mother, or toy loss, we looked at the hands. It was—and still is—a bizarre experience for us to read hands instead of faces in order to read meaning into emotional experience. (As a clinician with sighted children, I normally read faces for signs of emotionality. I picked up cues from the hands either peripherally or as an alternative when the face masked emotionality.)

As we ourselves became sensitive to the motor expressions in the hands themselves, we began to read them as signs and responded to them as signs.

What we saw we could easily help the mother to see too, and some of our mothers became as adept as the observers in reading and translating the baby's hand language.

Since it took us a considerable time as professional observers to "read hands," we should now fairly consider the dilemma of the mother of a blind baby without professional guidance. In the absence of a repertoire of expressive facial signs, the mother of the blind baby had no differentiated sign vocabulary in which modulated affective states or wants were registered, and from which an appropriate response from the mother was elicited. And since many of the baby's signs could not be "read" by his mother, his own experience in eliciting specific responses to need was largely restricted to elemental need states. "Hunger," "contentment," "fussiness," "rage," and "sleepiness" could be read by the mother, but the full range of affective expression which becomes socialized in the first year could not be exploited until the signs could be read by the mother.

Let me give a few examples of the problem:

Toni is 10 months old. Her mother (a very experienced mother with five older children) tells us, "She's not really interested in her toys."

We assemble a group of Toni's crib toys, stuffed animals and dolls, and invite the mother to present them to Toni, one by one. As each of the toys is placed in her hands, Toni's face is immobile. She gives the impression of "staring off into remote space." Naturally, the totally blind child does not orient his face toward the toy in his hands. Since visual inspection is the sign that we read as "interest," and averted eyes and staring are read as the sign of "disinterest," Toni "looks bored."

Now we watch Toni's hands. While her face "looks bored," her fingers scan each of the toys. One stuffed doll is dropped after brief manual scanning. A second doll is scanned, brought to the mouth, tongued, mouthed, removed, scanned again. Now we remove doll No. 2 and place doll No. 1 in Toni's hand. A quick scanning of fingers and she drops it again. She makes fretful sounds, eyes staring off into space. We return doll No. 2 to her hands. She quiets instantly, clutches it, brings it to her mouth and explores its contours.

In short, there is no message from the face which Toni's mother can read as "interest" or "preference." But the behavior of the hands showed clear discrimination and sustained exploration of one toy and not another.

Examples such as this multiply throughout our records. The immobile face, the vacant eyes, "no interest," but the fingers explore the tiny crevices of the rattle, the clapper of the bell, the bumps on the soap dish, the bristles of the pastry brush.

The problem is compounded when the mother needs to read "wanting" or intention in her blind baby. No mother of a sighted baby at 6 months is at a loss in reading "I want" from a very large number of visually directed behaviors. At this age the sighted child is very good at getting what he wants within range. He also reaches for things out of range, with eyes fixed determinedly on their target, hands and torso extended, and urgent vocalizations just in case somebody cannot read sign language. He has in fact a differentiated vocabulary of motor signs in orientation of the head, and extended arms and hands, which we read instantly as "I want," "Gimme," "Pick me up," "No, not that," "Oh, please." All these signs are mediated by vision (e.g., eye and hand) and depend upon visual fixation of the target and a motor expression of want or supplication for a quick reading of intention by the adult partner. If, for example, we had the implausible situation in which a 6-month-old sighted baby produced the motor sign of "Gimme" and the eyes did not fixate a target, we would not be able to read intention.

This means of course that, even when the blind baby reveals his wants or his intentions through the motor expression of his hands, the sign not only requires fine reading by us or by the parents, but there are many wants that cannot be expressed through the hands without orientation and gesture to identify the target. It is only at the close of the first year, when the sound object is localized and the blind baby begins to make a directional reach for the object, that we begin to see the sign of "I want" through the extended hand, and the sign of "Pick me up" through extended arms.

A toy drops from his hand and the blind baby at 6 months may make no sound of complaint, no gesture of retrieval. The face registers nothing that we can read as disappointment. In the blind baby's world of evanescent objects, the manifestation of a toy, its comings and goings, are subjected to a capricious fate. Things materialize out of a void, manifest themselves when grasped, heard, mouthed, or smelled, and then are lost, swallowed in a void. The sighted child of this age can follow the trajectory of a falling toy, and the registrations of "I want" on the face and in the hands are sustained through visual contact with the toy that has left his hand.

The blind baby "looks bored," "not interested," as we read his face when the toy drops from his hand. But if we watch his hands, another story emerges.

The toy drops to the floor. Robbie "looks bored." But now Robbie's open hand can be seen sweeping across the table surface, and then sweeps back. The "hand watchers" read this instantly as a search. The play table surface is the place where toys are usually found; a toy "belongs to" this space, as it were; it materializes from this space. The exploratory sweep of the hand is the sign of "I want" for the blind baby.

At 8 months of age, if we bring Robbie's musical dog within easy reach of his hands and play its familiar music, he will not reach for the toy. Does he want it? His face does not register yearning or wanting. But now as the music plays we see his hands in an anticipatory posture of holding, grasping, and ungrasping.

At 9 months of age, we ring our test bell within easy reach of Robbie's hands. The bell is a favorite toy for Robbie. He does not reach for the bell. Does he want it? We watch his hands, and then we see the hands execute a pantomime of bell ringing as he hears the bell "out there."

This leads us to consider the more central problems for the blind baby and his mother in establishing the vital human connections. The alien sign language of the blind baby is not only an impediment to the reading of want and intention in the baby. The baby's sign vocabulary of selective interest, preference, and valuation of his human partners, which constitute the earliest language of love, is distorted for the mother of the blind baby. The blind baby's face does not reveal signs of discrimination, preference, and recognition.

Yet once again, if we shift our attention from the face of the blind baby to his hands, we can read an eloquent sign language of seeking, wooing, preference, and recognition, which becomes increasingly differentiated during the first 6 months.

We have observations and film records of 3 of our 10 babies during the first quarter. In the early weeks the behavior of the hands does not yet differentiate, for my eyes, a blind baby and a sighted baby. During feeding, while being held in the mother's arms, we see the blind baby's hands on film, making chance contact with the mother's face, or hands, grasping or lightly fingering. In the second month we see the beginnings of active seeking of contact with the mother, the hand, for example, returning to a point of prior contact after interruption. This behavior corresponds to Piaget's protocols for Laurent at the same age. (Piaget, 1952). The number of examples of manual tactile seeking begins to proliferate for two of the children between 2 and 5 months of age. The hands, not engaged, seek engagement with the mother's hand or her body. The hands linger, lightly finger or grasp, withdraw, and return. Sometimes we catch on film a kind of ballet in which the baby's hands seek and find the mother's hand, and the mother's hand sustains or responds to the signal.

I am sure we can see an identical hand language in watching sighted babies and their mothers. But the sighted child, even at 2 months, sustains an eloquent dialogue of eyes, smiles, and motor responses to invite and sustain contact with his mother. To a very large extent the blind baby is dependent upon his hands to woo, to maintain contact, and to affirm the presence of the mother. During the period 2 to 6 months, we can follow the blind baby's adaptive exploitation of the hand in establishing human connections.

Between 5 and 8 months of age (as reported for eight children in the sample), we have examples for all the children in which the blind baby's hands explore the mother's or father's face, the fingers tracing features with familiarity and giving the sense to the viewer of anticipation of what he will find. The film record gives strong evidence that these exploring hands are discriminating, and that the information from the fingers brings recognition as well as nonrecognition.

In one example on film, I hold Toni at age 7 months, 2 days, to test her reactions to me as a stranger. She begins to strain away from me and to whimper. Then her hands seek my face, finger my nose and mouth in a quick scanning of this unfamiliar map; she cries louder, and clutches my arm in frozen terror. When I return her to her mother's arms, she settles , still crying, then scans and rescans her mother's face with her fingers, and finally is comforted.

This tactile language can speak eloquently to the mother who "knows" it. The two mothers who found their way unaided by us in intuiting their blind baby's needs were mothers whose own tactile sensibilities were large, and who not only provided abundant tactile experience for their babies but responded with spontaneity to the baby's tactile sign language. Other mothers needed our help both in understanding the blind baby's need for tactile intimacy and manual tactile experience, and in interpreting the tactile sign language of the blind child.

What we ourselves learned from hand language we brought to the mothers of our blind babies. It was most welcome help. When the baby's expressive signs could be read, the dialogue between mother and baby was facilitated with predictable rewards. The mother who felt out of contact, uncertain, not competent, found her way as a mother who could minister to her child's needs. Even grief could be managed when the baby brought his own rewards in response, in diversity of social exchange, and in becoming an active partner in the love relationship—a partnership that is really possible only when the language of need and intention can be understood.

THE VOCAL DIALOGUE

The vocal dialogue that is available to the blind baby and his parents is, finally, the one channel that remains open and available as a relatively undistorted language system between mother and child. Even in this area we see some qualitative differences (and, we think, some differences in quantity too), but our data do not suggest that blindness is an impediment to the acquisition of language in the first and second years. Here, again, we are speaking of our highly selective and advantaged group of blind infants. Scales available for the larger blind population show marked delays by sighted child standards.

Within our own sample the expressive vocalizations, the emergence of vowel-consonant syllables, and imitative sounds, "mama," "baba," "dada," and so on, appear within the Bayley ranges for sighted children. Two of our children used the words "mama," "dada," and "bopple" (bottle) as correct referents between the ages of 8 months and 12 months (Bayley median 14 months). In the second year, which is not under consideration in this article, naming, expression of wants, and simple sentences appeared within the range for sighted children. A linguistic study of one of our children conducted by Eric Lenneberg showed that her language competence at 2 years of age compared favorably with that of sighted children (reported in Fraiberg & Adelson, 1972).

Yet, throughout the first year, it seemed to us that the spontaneous vocalizations of our blind babies were sparse. In the absence of quantitative measures for sighted children of comparable age, we can only offer our impression and that of several independent observers that our babies seemed "very quiet" in comparison with sighted babies, that vocalization for self-entertainment was infrequent and scant (even among the high vocalizers of our group), that vocalizations to greet were rarely recorded, and that the initiation of a "dialogue" with mother or other partners was rarely observed. However, response vocalizations in "dialogue" with the mother are recorded for all the children in our group.

These differences, which we can only support impressionistically, may reflect the poverty of eliciting stimuli in a blind child's world. Where visual stimuli afforded by people, food, toys, a colorful object, and a moving object, can produce a volley of utterances from the sighted child, even under 4 months of age—and these stimuli are omnipresent from the moment the child opens his eyes—there is no equivalence among the exogenous stimuli in the blind child's world. Sound, voices, and tactile-kinesthetic stimulation are not "at the disposal of" the blind child in the way that visual stimuli are available from the moment the eyes open. The sound-touch stimuli of the blind child are actually at the disposal of someone outside the infant self, the human partners whose voice and touch are not constant components of the waking hours. (Only a nonstop talking and touching mother could provide equivalence in quantity of stimuli.)

There may be other factors not explored in our study that have bearing on the seeming poverty of spontaneous vocalization in our blind babies. We do not know, for example, if blindness is an impediment for the mother in her vocalizing to the infant. Does the absence of eye contact and of the automatic smile reduce the spontaneity of utterances on the part of the mother (as I reported in my self-observations at the beginning of this chapter)? Is this a reciprocal effect of blindness on discourse between the two partners in which a reduced level of utterances from the mother has correspondence in a reduction of vocalizations in the baby?

During the 4-to-8-month period, our blind infant observations show that the mother's or father's voice is the prime elicitor of vocalizations. We have a large number of examples of "dialogues" between parent and baby which do not distinguish our blind babies from sighted babies under circumstances in which the adult himself initiates the dialogue.

Vocalizations to initiate contact appear later (in the second year) for our blind children. It is not easy to understand why. In families in which the rewards for vocalizations are very large, with much parental "talking to" the baby and echoing of his sounds, we are still struck by the absence of initiative in the baby. We can only guess that vision is a potent elicitor of vocalizations and that what appear as "greeting vocalizations" in sighted babies are stimulated by and reinforced by visual signs (e.g., the human face gestalt). But why, in the circular causality available to the blind infant at 6 to 8 months doesn't he vocalize with the magical expectation that his sound making will produce sounds from his partners?

I realize that in the area of vocalizations and language in the first year I am raising more questions than I can answer.

When we consider how many social signs are obliterated by blindness, and how resourceful and inventive the mother of the blind baby must be to read her baby's alien sign language, no comment is needed from me on the significance of the early vocalizations and the blind baby's discovery of the spoken language in the partnership of mother and baby. With the first words there is, for the first time, a common language.

THE ACHIEVEMENT OF HUMAN BONDS

From this discussion we can see that the mother of a blind baby faces extraordinary problems in learning the alien language of her child. Grief and self-recriminations which come with the first shock of blindness are compounded by the sense of estrangement from a baby who cannot communicate in the universal code. The perils to the baby are very large. In the general blind population, there is a significant number of blind children, otherwise intact, who show grave impairment in their human-object relationships. In our consultation service (a separate program not reported in this chapter), we see blind children in the second, third, and fourth years who appear to have no investment in persons or things. These are children of families for whom no guidance was available in the crucial sensorimotor period.

Our research sample can tell us more fairly about the capacities for human attachments in blind infants when the nonvisual vocabulary of the infant "speaks to" the mother and the mother responds and is rewarded by her baby.

For those mothers (the majority) who could not find their way unaided into the alien experience of the blind baby, we shared our own understanding. The benefits to the baby and the mother were demonstrable in all developmental areas. In the area of human attachments, I briefly summarize our findings:

In the course of the first year, the characteristics of human attachments in the blind infants of our research group closely paralleled those of sighted children. Discrimination, preference for, and valuation of the mother were seen in differential smiling, differential vocalization, manual tactile seeking, embracing, spontaneous gestures of affection, and comfort seeking. In the period 7 to 15 months, negative reactions to a stranger (avoidance, manifest distress) are recorded for 9 of the 10 babies. During the same period the unfamiliar person was refused as a substitute in feeding, in comforting, as a game partner, and in vocal exchanges. As with the sighted child, the stranger was an intruder into the magic circle.

In the second year anxiety at separation from the mother and comfort at reunion spoke for the blind baby's valuation of the mother as the indispensable human partner. With mobility in creeping and walking, we saw tracking (on sound cue) of the mother from room to room, independent exploration, and return to the mother as a secure base.

As milestones in human attachment during the first 2 years of life, these achievements compare favorably with those of sighted children.

References

Emde, R. N., & Harom, R. J. Endogenous and Exogenous Smiling Systems in Early Infancy, *Journal of the American Academy of Child Psychiatry*, 1972, **11** (2), Pp. 177–200.

Emde, R. N., & Koenig, K. L., Neonatal smiling, frowning and rapid eye movement states. II. Sleep-cycle study, *Journal of the American Academy of Child Psychiatry*, 1969, **8** (4). Pp. 637–656.

Fraiberg, S. Parallel and divergent patterns in blind and sighted infants. *Psychoanalytic Study of the Child. Vol. XXIII*. New York: International Universities Press, 1968. Pp. 264–300.

Fraiberg, S. "Smiling and Stranger Reaction in Blind Infants." In J. Hellmuth (Ed.), *The Exceptional Infant*. New York: Brunner/Mazel, 1971. Pp. 110–127.

Fraiberg, S. Intervention in infancy, *Journal of the American Academy of Child Psychiatry*, 1971, **10** (3). Pp. 381–405.

Fraiberg, S. & Adelson, E. Self Representation in language and play: Observations of blind children, 1973, in press.

Fraiberg, S. & Freedman, D. Studies in the ego development of the congenitally blind child. In *Psychoanalytic Study of the Child. Vol. XIX*. New York: International Universities Press, 1964. Pp. 113–169.

Fraiberg, S., Siegal, B., & Gibson, R., The role of sound in the search behavior of a blind infant. In *Psychoanalytic Study of the Child. Vol. XXI*. New York: International Universities Press, 1966. Pp. 327–357.

Fraiberg, S. Smith, M., & Adelson, E. An Educational program for blind infants, *Journal of special education* , 1969, **3** (2). Pp. 121–139.

Piaget, J. *Play, dreams and imitation in childhood*, New York: Norton, 1962.

Piaget, J. *Origins of intelligence*. New York: International Universities Press, 1952.

Robson, K., The role of eye to eye contact in maternal infant attachment. In S. Chess & A. Thomas (Eds.), *Annual progress in child psychiatry and child development*. New York: Brunner/Mazel, 1968. Pp. 92–108.

Roskies, E. *Abnormality and normality: The mothering of thalidomide children*, Ithaca: Cornell University Press, 1972.

Wolff, P. H. Observations on the early development of smiling. In B. M. Foss (Ed.), *Determinants of infant behavior*, London: Methuen, 1963. Pp. 113–134.

CHAPTER 11

Social Responses of Animals to Infants with Defects

GERSHON BERKSON

Illinois State Pediatric Institute

That animals sometimes are far from feeling sympathy is too certain; for they will expel a wounded animal from the herd, or gore or worry it to death. This is almost the blackest fact in natural history, unless, indeed, the explanation which has been suggested is true, that their instinct or reason leads them to expel an injured companion, lest beasts of prey, including man, should be tempted to follow the troop. . . . Many animals, however, sympathize with each other's distress or danger. This is the case even with birds. Captain Stanbury found on a salt lake in Utah an old and completely blind pelican which was very fat, and must have been well fed for a long time by his companions. Mr. Blyth, as he informs me, saw Indian crows feeding two or three of their companions which were blind. . . . [Charles Darwin, *The Descent of Man*, 1871]

A simplistic view of the "struggle for existence" sees animal populations living in well-defined environments to which their structure and behavior are closely adapted. Individuals with defects tend to be excluded from these ecological niches by intraspecific territorial mechanisms, and, as a consequence both of their defects and exclusion, have less access to food and are more than normally vulnerable to predation (Errington, 1967; Lack, 1954). The result of course is that defective animals tend not to reproduce, and in the main only genes of those that are well adapted are transmitted to succeeding generations.

However, modern evolutionary theory recognizes that survival of many animal species has depended on the development of complex societies in which individuals cooperate with one another to acquire food, rear young, and defend against predation (Allee, 1958; Hamilton, 1964; Trivers, 1971). The major proposition of this chapter is that these kinds of cooperation promote survival of abnormal individuals and that the presence of abnormal animals provides a way of analyzing the physical and social ecology of animal groups.

[1] The studies reported here were supported by funds from the Illinois Department of Mental Health, University of Illinois Research Board, Delta Regional Primate Research Center, and the Carribean Primate Research Center.

ABNORMAL ANIMALS IN NATURAL POPULATIONS

In 1937 members of the Asiatic Primate Expedition collected an extensive sample of gibbon skeletons. Schultz (1956), who was responsible for the anatomical analyses, noted with some surprise that a large proportion of the specimens had evidence of healed or partially healed bone fractures. In a review of naturally occurring bone abnormalities in a wide range of nonhuman primate species, he remarked that

"anyone who has observed monkeys in the treetops as they leap without hesitation for incredible distances is not surprised that sooner or later many do meet with accidents which fracture their bones. What is surprising is the fact that wild monkeys can survive even severe and numerous fractures which become repaired with widely varying success. . . ." (p. 975)

Washburn, Jay, and Lancaster (1965), in summarizing field studies of monkeys and apes, indicate that the field worker sees instances of sick and practically disabled animals making great efforts to stay with their groups and that wounded rhesus monkeys have been observed to enter langur groups after leaving their own. Schaller (1963) reported that gorillas can survive and maintain high social status despite injuries as severe as loss of an arm above the elbow. Carpenter (1964) showed that senile animals are tolerated in gibbon groups. In fact, most field studies of primates indicate that a defective individual was part of the group. In other mammals seals with corneal opacities have been noted (Newby, Hart, & Arnold, 1970), and wild dogs have been seen to feed wounded animals in their group (Schaller & Lowther, 1969).

These reports confirm the principle that certain environments permit rather dramatic variability in structure and behavior. An important implication is that one method of analyzing the ecology of an animal group might be to describe the extent to which various environments select for particular defects. As an instance, Sunquist, Montgomery, and Storm (1969) reported the case of a blind raccoon surviving for an extended period in nature and having a relatively normal pattern of movement throughout his home range. This suggests that the environment at the moment obviously was not selecting raccoons for visual ability. However, Errington's account (1967) of the high predation of diseased muskrats by minks indicates that the environment was selecting with respect to that disease.

The cases of the blind raccoon and the muskrats also dramatize a complementary principle of the use of defects for ecological analysis. Defects can help in describing those characteristics of the individual that are or are not necessary for survival at any particular time and place. The raccoon's fairly normal movement throughout his range apparently did not depend on normal vision. However, Errington felt that the vocalizations of diseased muskrats might have increased the probability of predation by minks.

The presence of defects in natural populations therefore can help to define the selecting properties of a specific environment and to describe those characteristics of an animal that are or are not important for its survival in that environment. This is especially important to mention, since it is not necessarily true that because a species possesses a particular characteristic this characteristic is important for survival and reproduction at all times and places.

Recognition of the importance of defects in ecological analysis opens the way for their use in experimental investigation of environment-species relationships. Kling and his co-workers (Dicks, Myers, & Kling, 1969; Kling, Lancaster, & Benitone, 1970) have used such an experimental method in their studies of the effects of brain lesions on survival of monkeys in free-ranging groups. Their results suggest that amygdalectomy in adult animals affects survival by interfering with normal intraspecific social mechanisms, but that this does not apply to amygdalectomized juvenile animals.

SOCIAL RESPONSES TO DEFECTIVE INDIVIDUALS

That this brain lesion affects viability by interfering with normal social mechanisms emphasizes that any ecological analysis employing defective animals must include a detailed consideration of social responses to them. This is consistent with a general intellectual tradition represented by Kropotkin (1955) and Allee (1958), and more recently by expansion of the study of animal social behavior (Wynne-Edwards, 1962). Intraspecific social behavior results in the exclusion of grossly deviant animals from the reproductive group (e.g., through sexual selection and territorial mechanisms), but survival of the species also depends on intricate group adjustments which protect individuals.

How this protection is accomplished can be observed through analyzing ways in which social factors influence survival of defective individuals. One instance has been reported by Southwick and Siddiqi (1967), who showed that a dominant male rhesus monkey was able to maintain his social status despite suffering extensive disabling wounds, apparently because he had been dominant for a long period prior to being wounded. Another instance is Berkson's (1970) finding that mother monkeys gave compensatory care to blind infants by retrieving and carrying them at an age when control infants stayed with their group by themselves. In that sense, the mothers responded to the blind infants as they would have to younger animals.

The point then is that responses to abnormal individuals are not uniquely different from those to normals; they represent instances of social behavior ordinarily evoked by normal animals, but which also are expressed toward abnormal individuals. This means that the approach in studying social responses to a defective individual regards him as similar to a general class of social stimuli, with the defect being a modification of that class. Any specific alteration from the normal social stimulus situation the defective animal presents to his group may or may not produce a change in the behavior of the group toward him, depending on whether the alteration is relevant to normal social interaction at the time.[2]

Considering a defective individual as presenting social stimuli that are more-or-less deviant from a normal stimulus class is similar to an emphasis on the importance of stimuli that young infants present in normal parent-infant interaction (Bell, 1971; Harper, 1971). Exemplified by this approach are studies by Beach and Jaynes (1956) and Noirot (1964), who studied stimulus factors of the young controlling rodent maternal behavior. They showed that normal rodent pups were retrieved to the nest more readily than pups that did not vocalize or move. Equally significant, however, is the fact that dead infants or even small pieces of meat were often returned to the nest and cared for as normal infants. This means that infant stimulus factors determining differential maternal responses to deviant individuals may be quite subtle, and that their effect may be overwhelmed by stronger maternal care tendencies. It further suggests that there are limits to the generally held view that animal mothers destroy abnormal young and thereby act as agents of natural selection.

The existence of defective animals in natural groups is prima facie evidence that social factors are not necessarily highly efficient in eliminating defective individuals. First, normal social protective mechanisms compete with influences tending to select out abnormal animals (Trivers, 1971). Second, social factors that eliminate or protect defective individuals may be time-limited. Not only are young animals treated differently from older ones, but differential treatment of defective and normal individuals may vary over days during the developmental period. Thus Smith and Berkson (1973) showed that mother rats retrieved control pups more quickly than sedated ones when they were 5 days of age, but that there was no difference at 2, 10, and 15 days.

Furthermore, the degree to which social factors are influential in natural selection depends on the social and physical context in which the defective animal lives. Free-ranging Japanese monkey groups living in environments where there is a plentiful food supply and no predators contain many animals who survive and reproduce despite gross congenital bone abnormalities (Furuya, 1966). Undoubtedly, the general level of aggression within the group, interspecific differences in tolerance of deviation, familiarity of the defective individual, and also the character and severity of his defect are other factors important in his status.

An especially important aspect of the social ecology of defects is the probable

---

[2] Latané, Joy, Meltzer, Lubell, and Cappell (1972) were the most recent to state that stimulus combinations and those involved in reciprocal interactions, rather than static stimuli to one sense modality, are most effective in controlling social responsiveness.

effect of population concentration. Many social factors are sensitive to population levels, and one major issue of interest is whether density-dependent social factors select differentially for abnormal individuals. There has been substantial interest during the last 20 years in identifying social factors controlling population levels, and it is clear that their influence is most manifest in situations in which predation and disease are negligible, food is unlimited, and emigration from an area impossible (Archer, 1970). In such situations populations grow to asymptotic levels, and a variety of species-typical limitations on the number of animals (e.g., increased fighting, decreased sexual activity, breakdown in parental care, and infanticide) take effect. Although one might expect that such limitations might work more heavily on defective individuals than on normals, there is as yet little evidence that this is so. One way of studying this dimension would be to compare the behavior of expanding and asymptotic populations in their responsiveness to abnormal conspecifics.

It is likely that comparisons of expanding and asymptotic populations would reveal a complex situation. In some instances differential selection of normal and defective individuals would occur only if the defect were related to a specific social mechanism becoming operative only at high densities. Thus if nest destruction controlling the number of infants reaching maturity were the main factor limiting numbers, a wound sustained in adulthood might not specially affect an animal's status at high densities. However, it may be that social selection for certain defects is characteristic at any population level, and then the issue is whether those factors limiting population and those selecting for defects are additive or whether they interact. There are as yet few data available to differentiate these possibilities for mammals, since population concentration studies have not been concerned with the analysis of defects. However, the simplest initial hypothesis is that they make independent contributions.

RESPONSES OF MONKEYS TO INFANTS WITH VISUAL DEFECTS

With these general considerations in mind, I turn now to a description of some studies we have done recently on primate group responses to infants with defects. Primates have been used in these studies because of their close phylogenetic relationship to man, and because it is in primate societies where enduring social relationships based on mutual recognition of individuals are most highly developed. Primates are also characterized by a low female to infant ratio; single individuals are born at intervals of 1 to 3 years and the period of infant dependency is prolonged.[3] In this context of low reproductive efficiency, one might expect that it would be adaptive for the group to carry its members over

---

[3] The factors considered here probably also apply to other mammals (e.g., elephants, cetaceans) that have similar social organization characteristics.

temporary periods of weakness. That this is possible has been verified by Rumbaugh (1965) and by Rosenblum (Chapter 7), who have shown that mothers retrieve and carry temporarily immobilized infants. Rumbaugh's study is especially interesting because it suggested that the responses of the mother included some behaviors not ordinarily seen in the maternal behavior repertoire of the species he studied. This was not the case in Rosenblum's experiments or in the ones I describe.

Although care of temporarily disabled infants has therefore been demonstrated in primates, the issue still was whether individuals with chronic disabilities would also be nurtured. Lindburg (1969) studied the first year of social development of infant rhesus monkeys that had phocomelia produced by thalidomide. In this study of mother-infant pairs in the laboratory, the mothers held the experimental infants somewhat more than controls and thereby compensated for their inability to cling and groom. Otherwise, however, social development was quite normal, and the infants survived until 31 weeks of age when the experiment was terminated.

Our studies have pursued this line of investigation further, by looking at determinants of survival of monkey infants with visual disabilities. Ocular defects were used because the macaque monkeys we worked with are primarily diurnal animals and much of their interaction with the social and physical environment is dependent on vision. A visual defect is therefore expected to have dramatic consequences on the infant's behavior, and represents a valid test of the social consequences of a severe disability. Another feature of the program is that it looks at social development in a variety of environments ranging from small laboratory cages to a severely selecting natural habitat. Furthermore, it assesses social responses of members of the group other than the mother, and it is also concerned with the period beyond the first year of the infant's life.

The general design of our studies, then, involves imposing a visual defect on infant monkeys soon after birth and determining for a variety of habitats whether they live and how various members of their group respond to them. The infant is removed from the mother and anesthetized with a short-acting anesthesia. An incision is made across the pupil of each eye and, since recovery from anesthesia is rapid, the infant is returned to the mother fully awake within an hour of its removal from her. This surgery is fairly simple to accomplish, and no animal has died as a direct result of it. In a few days a scar forms over the pupil and often involves the lens (Figure 1). The lesion results in markedly reduced visual acuity (Berkson and Karrer, 1968). Figure 2 gives a general impression of the extent of the deficit as measured by a discrimination learning task. In a complex environment the infant's locomotion is clumsy, and it almost never jumps. It shows a searching optical nystagmus and gropes for food on the ground. It is apparently normally responsive to stimuli to other sense modalities (Adland & Berkson, unpublished).

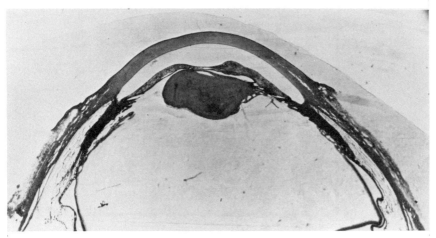

FIGURE 1. An instance of the lesion producing partial blindness.

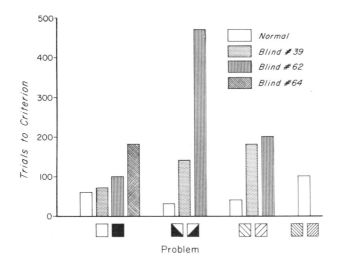

FIGURE 2. Number of trials to criterion (80% correct on three successive days). Not shown are graphs for individuals not learning in 500 trials when testing was terminated.

In a first study with crab-eating monkeys (*Macaca fascicularis*), the social development of blind and sighted infants with their mothers was compared during the first 6 months in a small laboratory cage (Berkson & Karrer, 1968). In this simple situation locomotion of the blind infants was normal, and no differences in social development between them and controls were seen (Figure 3), although the visual defect was apparent in a novel situation.

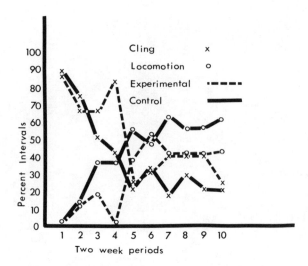

FIGURE 3. Levels of infant clinging and independent locomotion during the first 20 weeks of life.

The first study therefore demonstrated that an infant with an acuity deficit can survive for at least 6 months, and that its mother tends to respond to it as to a normal infant. This was not particularly surprising since, in the simple context of the laboratory cage, the infant's behavior was quite normal despite the acuity deficit. The experiment made us wonder whether in a more complex environment, where the deficit would affect the infant's behavior, more dramatic social effects might not be seen. At this time I had an opportunity to study a natural group of crab-eating monkeys living on a 60-acre island in Thailand (Berkson, 1970). Not only was the forest environment of the island more complex than the cage we had studied, but the habitat was potentially selecting for the visual defect. A large monitor lizard lived there, and there were long arid periods during which no fresh water was available. We trapped four mother-infant pairs, imposed the visual defect on two infants, left the other two as controls, and released all the animals. Wild forest monkeys are difficult to observe, and our goals for the experiment were therefore restricted primarily to determining for how long the infants remained with the group. However, some behavioral observations were made possible by observing the group from a blind in an area baited with bananas to attract them there.

As normal infant monkeys grow, their mothers increasingly tend to leave them in the forest close by when they forage. The infants vocalize and thereby presumably inform their mothers of their location as both animals move around. Normal infants return to their mothers when they wish. The disabled infants were also left in the forest and vocalized, but they did not move far from the tree in which they had been left and did not return to their mothers. In this sense they behaved like younger normal infants. In this context there were a number of occasions when I came upon the group unexpectedly or made a noise from the blind. If the blind infant was within 10 ft. of its mother, she would pick it up and the group would move away from me into the forest. However, sometimes the infant was further away, and its defect prevented it from following the group. Then the group would remain about 30 ft. from me, threatening and uttering alarm calls. If I withdrew and hid myself, the mother returned and retrieved the infant, and the group continued on its way. Thus the effects of the visual defect were apparent, and the group altered its behavior to compensate for the infant's inability to stay with it.

When they were about 7 months old, the blind infants disappeared, but the circumstances were ambiguous. The disappearance occurred during a period when no natural freshwater sources were available. However, the thickness of the secondary forest of the island prevented a determination of whether the infants had died of thirst or were wandering by themselves. Moreover, the adult females were breeding, and it was not clear whether or not this resulted in reduced maternal care, with consequent increased susceptibility to predation by the lizard.

In an attempt to clarify these ambiguities, James Loy and I are performing a modified repetition of the experiment in a free-ranging rhesus monkey (*Macaca mulatta*) colony at La Cueva, an island near La Parguera, southwest Puerto Rico (Berkson, 1972). The island comprises 80 acres, half of which is mangrove forest, and houses about 280 monkeys which live in four main groups. Aside from the species difference and the fact that the population concentration is heavy, there are three factors that differentiate this experiment from the one done in Thailand. At La Cueva there are no predators. Food and water are available *ad libitum* from feed stations at four places on the island, and observation conditions are excellent. These differences permit a somewhat more detailed look at the behavior of the groups than was possible in Thailand. Moreover, a rough assessment is possible of conditions determining viability of defective infants in a situation in which nonsocial selecting factors are minimal and in which the population is crowded but still expanding.

In June 1971, seven mother-infant pairs were trapped from three of the four groups on the island. All infants were less than 40 days old as determined from their tooth development (Hurme, 1960). Four experimentals and three controls were prepared, and the animals released the next day.

In the ensuing 12 months, the groups were searched by the staff of the island every day to determine if the infants were still with the group. On August 24, 1971, one of the blind infants died after a short period in which it was judged to be weakening (Lee Drikamer, personal communication). Its mother carried it during this time and for 2 days after its death. No wounds were found on the carcass, so that death could not be attributed to maternal neglect or group aggression directed at the infant.

During September, December, March, and June, I visited La Cueva and spent about 40 hours during each trip observing the groups. On each occasion 100 momentary observations were made to determine average distance between each mother and her infant and the proportion of time one was visible without the other. The proximity data are shown in Figure 4.

In September, when the infants were about 4 months old, the effects of the visual defect were apparent. The experimental animals made their way slowly in the mangrove, groping for roots as they went. In open terrain they proceeded more quickly, but their mothers had to stop and wait for them, as do mothers of younger normal infants. The blind animals ate and drank at the feeders but only when the mothers took them there. However, they foraged on leaves, flowers, and residue among the roots in the mangrove. They played by themselves and with other infants. In social play they were clumsy and tended not to initiate play bouts. They frequently put their muzzles close to another animal's face, and this once evoked one of the numerous instances in which they were harassed by juvenile and adult animals. Ordinarily, these attacks were short, but even in an instance in which it was more prolonged, their mothers who were generally close by ignored the interaction. However, when the infant was well-separated from the mother, she generally retrieved it when there was a commotion.

In September, the blind animals stayed closer to their mothers than the controls. However, in December the situation had changed so that the average differences between the groups was negligible. December is the height of the breeding season at La Parguera. At this time one control and two experimental mothers were repeatedly seen consorting with adult males. When they withdrew from the main group with the males, they sometimes took their blind babies with them but often left them in the mangrove. Sighted babies might follow their mothers but the blind ones could not do so and stayed in the forest or on open ground, often calling hoarsely. The blind babies were never left completely alone, however. It is remarkable that there was always another animal of the group near them. In addition, two individuals regularly stayed with the blind infants during this time, retrieved them when they were in trouble, and carried them if the group moved. One of these animals was a 2-year old male, another an ovariectomized adult female. Neither was related to the mothers of the blind infants.

The breeding season is characterized by a high degree of intragroup aggression. In this context one may ask how the blind infants fared. On one occasion an adult male grabbed at a blind infant, and on another an adult female attacked one. However, these attacks were short, and the infants were not harmed. Ordinarily, the blinded infant climbed over adult females and sat with adult males with impunity.

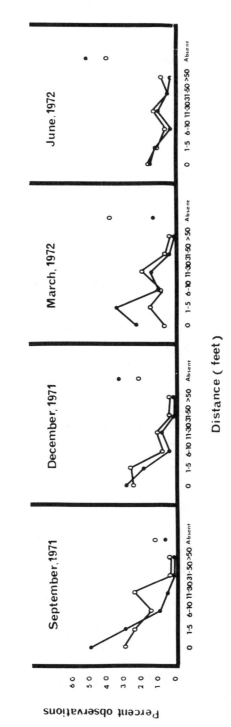

FIGURE 4. Distance from the mother at at four age levels.

243

Observations in December therefore showed that the blind infants survived despite high intragroup aggression. When the mothers left them, care that compensated for their defect was given by other group members. In no case, however, was this care qualitatively different from that given to younger normal animals.

By March the breeding season was over, and the blind babies again stayed closer to their mothers than did the controls. The animals who had previously cared for the infants in the mothers' absence continued to do so, and instances of compensatory care were seen. In June, a year after initiation of the experiment, social distance from the mother had declined in both groups, and there was no difference between them.

At this time two females in the experimental group and one in the control group had new babies. The birth of the new babies allowed us to ask whether the blind yearlings would now receive reduced care. The answer was ambiguous. One reason for this was that the ovariectomized female who had previously cared for the blind infants stole the new baby of one of the experimental mothers the day after it was born. During that day the blind yearling became separated from its mother, and the one instance of an attack by several males on a blind infant was noted (Lee Drikamer, personal communication). The blind yearling sustained a minor facial wound. After her infant had been stolen, the mother continued to care for her blind yearling as before. The other experimental female continued to care for both her new baby and her blind yearling, carrying the blind one on her back and the normal one on her chest when necessary. All blind infants were more independent than before, and in this period two were repeatedly seen interacting with closely related animals when their mothers were absent.

In September 1973, the blind infants were still alive and living in their group. The La Cueva study has thus far shown that infants with an acuity deficit can survive even in crowded populations until at least 28 months of age, as long as food and water are available and predators are absent. Their deficit partially disables them in moving around and in initiating social behavior, but various members of the group compensate for their disabilities. Other individuals tolerate them even under conditions promoting high aggression.

The evidence thus points to the view that primates do protect and do not eliminate infants with defects from the group. It is conceivable, however, that this generalization does not apply to older individuals. The group organization of the primate species we have been studying is characterized by a complex dominance hierarchy. It is likely that individuals with gross defects will fall to the bottom of this hierarchy as they become older and could be driven from the group, since dominance is partially mediated by aggression.

We are following the La Cueva animals to determine if this happens, and are also pursuing a series of studies in standard laboratory groups of crab-eating monkeys. The new laboratory studies involve observation of partially and totally blind monkeys from birth through adulthood to determine in greater detail than has been possible before how the group responds to them. The first group we worked with was established 4 years ago, and two partially blind infants who are approaching 4 years of age are still alive despite the fact that the caging conditions are crowded. Their visual defect is apparent in that they tend not to initiate social responses and do not jump. However, they are otherwise quite normal, and the group tolerates their awkward behavior.

We have preliminary data on the social development of six partially blind and one totally blind (enucleated) individual during the first 20 weeks of development (Figure 5). Employing the crude proximity measure we have used before, it looks as if development of independence of the partially blind infants is once again normal despite their awkwardness in this relatively complex laboratory situation. However, the totally blind animal is retarded in its social development.

We plan to continue following these animals through reproductive maturity and expect that they will survive. Since they will probably be low in the dominance hierarchy, they may not reproduce as readily as normal animals, but this prediction probably will be more true of blind males than blind females.

We also wish to look at other factors that could affect the status of disabled animals. Our studies so far have been concerned with defective individuals that have been part of the group from birth. Intraindividual tolerance of members of a primate group is not as readily seen toward conspecifics outside the group, although this may vary with age. It is probable that an abnormal animal that is not part of the group may be even more vigorously excluded than a normal one if it cannot demonstrate the gestures appropriate to reducing aggression from other animals.

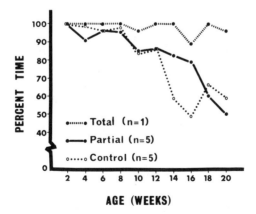

FIGURE 5. Time in contact with the mother during the first 20 weeks of life.

Related to the factor of an animal new to the group is the age of imposition of the defect. An animal that is disabled when older may change its behavior so suddenly as a consequence that the ability of the group to adapt quickly to the change might be severely challenged. The result could be a dramatic reduction of its dominance and exclusion from the group, while abnormal individuals of the same age are tolerated.

CONCLUSIONS

These findings suggest that survival of disabled animals of certain species in nature is a product of several factors whose relative influence is changing. External selecting agents (predation, disease, and food supply) are traditionally regarded as major controls of population level. Whether they select differentially for normal and abnormal individuals is one of the major questions presented here. Certainly, the answer must be a complex one bearing on analyses of the relationship between specific selecting agents and the character of the abnormality. However, I speculate that predation and food supply are becoming less important in controlling wild monkey populations. Large carnivores are generally believed to prey on monkeys, and there is some evidence that this is true (Schaller, 1967). However, man is eliminating large carnivores rapidly, and it is man himself who is becoming the main predator of monkeys. To the extent that conservation practices take force in the next century, it may be expected that this influence will also be reduced and there is some question whether man's hunting selects differentially for normal and abnormal animals. With respect to food supply, it is true that within broad limits primate populations are dependent on the food and water available to them. However, their food habits are also very adaptable, and it is probable that, as long as the disability does not interfere with the actual act of eating or digestion, food is of negligible importance in differentiating survival of normal and abnormal animals.

This leaves primarily disease and social factors as important agents. Rather little is known about disease in natural populations. The studies reported here, however, provide the beginning of a picture of the influence of social factors. They suggest that compensatory care for disabilities is found in animal groups with low reproductive rates, which have complex permanent societies characterized by social learning of individual characteristics, a long developmental period of the young, social behaviors bringing the group to feeding areas, and protection of the group from predators. Intragroup aggression is prominent in these societies, but it seems clear that aggression serves to control individual relationships and does not appear to kill abnormal animals.

In keeping with the theme of this volume, the basis of compensatory care of defective infants may be sought in analyses of stimulus characteristics of the infants and how they interact with the physiological and social characteristics of the other animals in the group. Looked at from this perspective, one might expect that to the extent that the defect produces a retardation of some aspect of behavior, the group will treat the infant as younger than he actually is because he behaves like a younger animal. However, if at the same time his physical growth is normal, care patterns evoked by such factors as body size or hair color might no longer be evident, and the effect of the behavioral retardation might be attenuated. This type of analysis points to the notion that compensatory care is most reasonably seen as normal care evoked by infantile characteristics.

Although such care may continue well beyond the infant period, it is improbable that it would continue indefinitely. Hormonal and social organizational characteristics are partial determinants of the development of independence. To the extent that maternal care is dependent on hormonal status of females in the group, and to the degree that this changes, maternal behavior will also be modified. Since some aspects of social organization are adapted to care of dependent individuals, compensatory care is expected. However, limits on compensatory care should be evident to the degree that other group functions (e.g., foraging, defense against predators) are expressed.

The implications of these findings for man are of course tentative. Our species has already reached the point where predation is negligible. Food production and disease control are rapidly making these factors less important in determining human welfare, and social factors are becoming more important.

In considering the implications of our animal studies for man, it is well to note that defective individuals have been members of human society since Neanderthal times (Stewart, 1958; Straus & Cave, 1957). Human societies are capable of responses ranging from protection to exclusion. Exposure or euthanasia has existed (Dentan, 1967; Freeman, 1971; Neel, 1970). However, it is rare and is as often associated with population and sex ratio control as with elimination of abnormal individuals.

The far more frequent pattern is for the society to provide for the disabled individual but to give him a special status, with attitudes ranging from derisive tolerance to worship (Edgerton, 1970). No doubt these various attitudes are related to ideological and social organizational differences. However, Edgerton (1970) states that, "We are discovering more and more ways in which men everywhere, and sociocultural systems everywhere, are more alike than they are different," (p. 555) and it is conceivable that certain general features of human society are a reflection of biologically based behavioral patterns which are common to man and the higher mammals (Campbell, 1965). For example, certain universal characteristics such as provision for care of young through a long period of development, tendencies to create permanent differentiated social roles, and social responses to fluctuating population levels might be related to responses to defective individuals in most groups of higher mammals including man.

Whatever determines differential treatment of individuals with defects across cultures, it seems clear that in evolution there has been a development of social behaviors which maintain rather than exclude individuals from society. It remains to be seen whether the general similarity of all higher primate societies makes subhuman primate social behavior a useful model for analyzing responses to handicapped individuals.

References

Allee, W. C. *The social life of animals*. Boston: Beacon, 1958.

Archer, J. Effects of population density on behaviour in rodents. In J. H. Crook (Ed.), *Social behaviour in birds and mammals*. London: Academic Press, 1970.

Beach, F. A., & Jaynes, J. Studies of maternal retrieving in rats. III. Sensory cues involved in the lactating female's response to her young. *Behaviour*, 1956, **10**, 104–125.

Bell, R. Q. Stimulus control of parent or caretaker behavior by offspring. *Developmental Psychology*, 1971, **4**, 63–72.

Berkson, G. Defective infants in a feral monkey group. *Folia Primatalogica*, 1970, **12**, 284–289.

Berkson, G. Social responses to abnormal infant monkeys. Paper presented at the meeting of the International Primatological Society, Portland, Oregon, 1972.

Berkson G., & Karrer, R. Travel vision in infant monkeys: Maturation rate and abnormal stereotyped movements. *Developmental Psychobiology*, 1968, **1**, 170–174.

Campbell, D. T. Ethnocentric and other altruistic motives. In D. Levine (Ed.) *Nebraska Symposium on Motivation*. Lincoln: University of Nebraska Press, 1965, 283–311.

Carpenter, C. R. A field study in Siam of the behavior and social relations of the gibbon. In C. R. Carpenter (Ed.) *Naturalistic Behavior of Nonhuman Primates*. University Park: Pennsylvania State University, 1964, 145–271.

Dentan, R. K. The response to intellectual impairment among the Semai. *American Journal of Mental Deficiency*, 1967, **71**, 764–766.

Dicks, D., Myers, R. E., & Kling, A. Uncus and amygdala lesions: Effects on social behavior in the free-ranging rhesus monkey. *Science*, 1969, **165**, 69–71.

Edgerton, R. B. Mental retardation in non-Western societies: Toward a cross cultural perspective on incompetence. In H. C. Haywood (Ed.), *Sociocultural aspects of mental retardation*. New York: Appleton, Century, Crofts, 1970, 523–559.

Errington, P. L. *Of predation and life*. Ames: Iowa State University, 1967.

Freeman, M. M. R. A social and ecologic analysis of systematic female infanticide among the Netsilik Eskimo. *American Anthropologist*, 1971, **73**, 1011–1018.

Furuya, Y. On the malformation occurred in the Gagyusan troop of wild Japanese monkeys. *Primates*, 1966, **7**, 488–492.

Hamilton, W. The genetical evolution of social behavior. II. *Journal of Theoretical Biology*, 1964, **7**, 17–52.

Harper, L. V. The young as a source of stimuli controlling caretaker behavior. *Developmental psychology*, 1971, **4**, 73–88.

Hurme, V. O. Estimation of monkey age by dental formula. *Annals of the New York Academy of Science*, 1960, **85**, 795–799.

Kropotkin, P. *Mutual aid.* Boston: Extending Horizons, 1955.

Kling, A., Lancaster, J. & Benitone, J. Amygdalectomy in the free-ranging vervet *(Cercopithecus aethiops). Journal of Psychiatric Research*, 1970, **7**, 191–199.

Lack, D. *The natural regulation of animal numbers.* Oxford: Clarendon Press, 1954.

Latané, B., Joy, V., Meltzer, J., Lubell, B., & Cappell, H. Stimulus determinants of social attraction in rats. *Journal of Comparative and Physiological Psychology*, 1972, **79**, 13–21.

Lindburg, D. G. Behavior of infant rhesus monkeys with thalidomide-induced malformations. *Psychonomic Science*, 1969, **15**, 55–56.

Neel, I. V. Lessons from a "primitive" people. *Science*, 1970, **170**, 815–822.

Newby, T. C., Hart, F. M., & Arnold, R. A. Weight and blindness of harbor seals. *Journal of Mammalogy*, 1970, **51**, 152.

Noirot, E. Changes in responsiveness to young in the adult mouse. IV. The effect of an initial contact with a strong stimulus. *Animal Behavior*, 1964, **12**, 442–445.

Rumbaugh, D. M. Maternal care in relation to infant behavior in the squirrel monkey. *Psychological Reports*, 1965, **16**, 171.

Schaller, G. B. *The mountain gorilla.* Chicago: University of Chicago Press, 1963.

Schaller, G. B. *The deer and the tiger.* Chicago: University of Chicago Press, 1967.

Schaller, G. B., & Lowther, G. R. The relevance of carnivore behavior to the study of the early hominids. *Southwestern Journal of Anthropology*, 1969, **25**, 307–341.

Schultz, A. H. The occurrence and frequency of pathological and teratological conditions and twinning among non-human primates. *Primatologia*, 1956, **1**, 965–1014.

Smith, L. & Berkson, G. Litter stimulus factors in maternal retrieval. *Animal Behavior*, 1973, in press.

Southwick, C. H. & Siddiqi, M. R. The role of social tradition in the maintenance of dominance in a wild rhesus group. *Primates*, 1967, **8**, 341–353.

Stewart, T. D. Restoration and study of the Shanidar I Neanderthal skeleton in Baghdad, Iraq. *Yearbook of the American Philosophical Society*, 1958, 274–278.

Straus, W. L., Jr., & Cave, A. J. E. Pathology and posture of Neanderthal man. *Quarterly Review of Biology*, 1957, **32**, 348–363.

Sunquist, M. E., Montgomery, G. G., & Storm, G. L. Movements of a blind raccoon. *Journal of Mammalogy*, 1969, **50**, 145–147.

Trivers, R. L. The evolution of reciprocal altruism. *Quarterly Review of Biology*, 1971, **46**, 35–57.

Washburn, S. L., Jay, P. C., & Lancaster, J. B. Field studies Old World monkeys and apes. *Science*, 1965, **150**, 1541–1547.

Wynne-Edwards, V. C. *Animal dispersion in relation to social behavior.* Edinburgh: Oliver and Boyd, 1962.

Author Index

Numbers in *italics* indicate the pages on which the full references appear.

Aaronson, E., 70, *75*
Adamo, G., *75*
Adams, M. S., 89, *99*
Adelson, E., 218, 229, *232*
Ainsworth, M. D., 4, 5, *17*
Akiyama, Y., 123, 124, 128, 130, 132, 135, *137, 139*
Alberman, E. D., 89, *100*
Allee, W. C., 233, 235, *248*
Amatruda, C. J., 123, *138*
Ambrose, J. A., 195, *211*
Amiel-Tison, C., 91, *99*
Anders, T. F., 124, 135, *137*
Anderson, S. W., 192, *211*
Archer, J., 237, *248*
Argyle, M., 193, *211*
Arling, G. L., 163, 172, *185*
Arnold, R. A., 234, *249*
Ashton, R., 125, *137*

Bach, L. M., 133, *139*
Baer, D. M., 12, *16*
Balint, M., 112, *118*
Ban, P., 12, *18*, 28, *47*
Banik, N. D. D., 81, *99*
Barbey, P., 134, *140*
Barten, S., 107, *118*
Beach, F. A., 236, *248*
Beason, L. M., 107, *120*
Beavin, H. J., *76*
Beckwith, L., 13, *16*
Beintema, O., *76*
Bell, R. Q., 1, 13, 14, *16*, 108, 111, 113, 118, *118*, 131, *137*, 203, *212*, 236, *248*
Bell, S. M., 4, 5, *17*
Bender, M. B., 202, *212*
Benirschke, K., 79, *101*
Benitone, J., 235, *249*

Benjamin, J., 116, *118*
Benson, R. C., 92, 93, *100*
Berberich, J. P., 1, *17*
Berges, J., *137*
Berkson, G., 235, 236, 238, 239, 240, 241, *248, 249*
Berlyne, D. E., 206, *211*
Bernal, J., 4, *17*
Bertini, M., 133, *137*
Beuntema, D., 92, *102*
Bhagwanani, S. G., 97, *99*
Billewicz, W. Z., 81, 86, *103*
Birch, H. E., 11, *17*
Birdwhistell, R. L., 68, *75*
Birns, B., 8, *17*, 107, 108, *118*, 132, *140*
Blank, M., 108, *118*
Blom, S., 95, *100*
Bobbitt, R. A., 145, *160*
Boisselier, F., *137*
Bower, T. G., 53, *75*
Bowlby, J., 9, *17*, 73, *75*, 163, *185*
Brackbill, Y., 11, *17*
Brackbill, Y. A., 55, 60, *75*
Brazelton, T., 8, *17*
Brazelton, T. B., 50, *75*, 109, *119*
Bridger, W., 8, *17*
Bridger, W. H., 108, 113, *119*
Brook, C. G. D., 98, *100*
Brooks, V., 3, *17*
Brown, B. H., 95, *100*
Brownfeld, E. D., 113, *119*
Bruck, K., 123, 129, 130, *139*
Bruck, M., 123, 129, 130, *139*
Bruner, J. S., 9, *17*, 53, 74, *75*
Burns, P., 130, *140*
Butler, N., 89, *100*
Butler, N. R., *100*

Subject Index